Listening to Hanna Segal

Jean-Michel Quinodoz provides the reader with a comprehensive overview of Segal's life, her clinical and theoretical work, and her contribution to psychoanalysis over the past sixty years by combining actual biographical and conceptual interviews with Hanna Segal herself or with colleagues who have listened to Segal in various contexts.

Listening to Hanna Segal explores both Segal's personal and professional histories, and the interaction between the two. The book opens with an autobiographical account of Segal's life, from her birth in Poland to her analysis with Melanie Klein in London where she became the youngest member of the British Psychoanalytical Society. Quinodoz goes on to explain Segal's contributions in various fields of psychoanalysis including:

- the psychoanalytic treatment of psychotic patients
- the introduction of the "symbolic equation"
- aesthetics and the creative impulse
- the analysis of elderly patients
- introducing the work of Melanie Klein.

Quinodoz concludes by examining Segal's most recent contribution to psychoanalysis – exploring nuclear terror, psychotic anxieties, and group phenomena.

Throughout the interviews Segal speaks of her close relationships with prominent colleagues such as Klein, Rosenfeld, and Bion, making this book both a valuable contribution to the history of psychoanalysis and an indication of the evolution of psychoanalytic ideas over the past six decades. This clear summary of Hanna Segal's life and her contribution to psychoanalysis will be an essential guide to anyone studying Segal and her contemporaries.

Jean-Michel Quinodoz is a Psychoanalyst in private practice in Geneva. He is a member of the Swiss Psychoanalytical Society and Honorary Member of the British Psychoanalytical Society. Jean-Michel Quinodoz is author of *The Taming of Solitude, Dreams That Turn Over a Page* and *Reading Freud*.

THE NEW LIBRARY OF PSYCHOANALYSIS

General Editor   Dana Birksted-Breen

The New Library of Psychoanalysis was launched in 1987 in association with the Institute of Psychoanalysis, London. It took over from the International Psychoanalytical Library, which published many of the early translations of the works of Freud and the writings of most of the leading British and Continental psychoanalysts.

The purpose of the New Library of Psychoanalysis is to facilitate a greater and more widespread appreciation of psychoanalysis and to provide a forum for increasing mutual understanding between psychoanalysts and those working in other disciplines such as the social sciences, medicine, philosophy, history, linguistics, literature and the arts. It aims to represent different trends both in British psychoanalysis and in psychoanalysis generally. The New Library of Psychoanalysis is well placed to make available to the English-speaking world psychoanalytic writings from other European countries and to increase the interchange of ideas between British and American psychoanalysts.

The Institute, together with the British Psychoanalytical Society, runs a low-fee psychoanalytic clinic, organizes lectures and scientific events concerned with psychoanalysis and publishes the *International Journal of Psychoanalysis*. It also runs the only UK training course in psychoanalysis that leads to membership of the International Psychoanalytical Association – the body which preserves internationally agreed standards of training, of professional entry, and of professional ethics and practice for psychoanalysis as initiated and developed by Sigmund Freud. Distinguished members of the Institute have included Michael Balint, Wilfred Bion, Ronald Fairbairn, Anna Freud, Ernest Jones, Melanie Klein, John Rickman and Donald Winnicott.

Previous General Editors include David Tuckett, Elizabeth Spillius and Susan Budd. Previous and current Members of the Advisory Board include Christopher Bollas, Ronald Britton, Catalina Bronstein, Donald Campbell, Sara Flanders, Stephen Grosz, John Keene, Eglé Laufer, Juliet Mitchell, Michael Parsons, Rosine Jozef Perelberg, Richard Rusbridger, David Taylor and Mary Target.

ALSO IN THIS SERIES

In Pursuit of Psychic Change: The Betty Joseph Workshop Edited by Edith Hargreaves and Arturo
  Varchevker
The Quiet Revolution in American Psychoanalysis: Selected Papers of Arnold M. Cooper Arnold M.
  Cooper. Edited and introduced by Elizabeth L. Auchincloss
Seeds of Illness, Seeds of Recovery: The Genesis of Suffering and the Role of Psychoanalysis
  Antonino Ferro
The Work of Psychic Figurability: Mental States Without Representation César Botella and Sára
  Botella
Key Ideas for a Contemporary Psychoanalysis: Misrecognition and Recognition of the Unconscious
  André Green
The Telescoping of Generations: Listening to the Narcissistic Links Between Generations Haydée
  Faimberg
Glacial Times: A Journey Through the World of Madness Salomon Resnik
This Art of Psychoanalysis: Dreaming Undreamt Dreams and Interrupted Cries Thomas H. Ogden
Psychoanalysis as Therapy and Storytelling Antonino Ferro
Psychoanalysis in the 21st Century: Competitors or Collaborators? Edited by David M. Black
Recovery of the Lost Good Object Eric Brenman
The Many Voices of Psychoanalysis Roger Kennedy

TITLES IN THE NEW LIBRARY OF PSYCHOANALYSIS TEACHING SERIES

Reading Freud: A Chronological Exploration of Freud's Writings Jean-Michel Quinodoz
Listening to Hanna Segal: Her Contribution to Psychoanalysis Jean-Michel Quinodoz

THE NEW LIBRARY OF PSYCHOANALYSIS:
TEACHING SERIES

2

General Editor: Dana Birksted-Breen

Listening to Hanna Segal

Her Contribution to Psychoanalysis

Jean-Michel Quinodoz

Translated by David Alcorn

Routledge
Taylor & Francis Group

LONDON AND NEW YORK

First published 2008
by Routledge
27 Church Road, Hove, East Sussex BN3 2FA

Simultaneously published in the USA and Canada
by Routledge
270 Madison Avenue, New York, NY 10016

Routledge is an imprint of the Taylor & Francis Group, an informa business

Copyright © 2008 Jean-Michel Quinodoz
Translation (selected material) © David Alcorn

Typeset in Times by RefineCatch Limited, Bungay, Suffolk
Printed and bound in Great Britain by
TJ International Ltd, Padstow, Cornwall
Paperback cover design by Sandra Heath
Paperback cover photograph by Michael Feldman

This publication has been produced with paper manufactured to strict
environmental standards and with pulp derived from sustainable forests.

British Library Cataloguing in Publication Data
A catalogue record for this book is available from the British Library

Library of Congress Cataloging in Publication Data
Quinodoz, Jean-Michel.
  Listening to Hanna Segal : her contribution to psychoanalysis /
Jean-Michel Quinodoz ; translated by David Alcorn.
     p. ; cm. – (New Library of psychoanalysis teaching series)
  Includes bibliographical references and indexes.
  ISBN 978-0-415-44493-4 (hbk) – ISBN 978-0-415-44085-1 (pbk)   1. Segal,
Hanna.   2. Psychoanalysis.   I. Segal, Hanna.   II. Title.   III. Series.
  [DNLM: 1. Segal, Hanna.   2. Psychoanalysis.   3. Psychoanalysis—
Interview. WM 460 Q7L 2008]
  RC438.6.S44Q56 2008
  616.89′17–dc22

                                                                2007020597

ISBN 978-0-415-44493-4 (hbk)
ISBN 978-0-415-44085-1 (pbk)

CONTENTS

INTRODUCTION

Hanna Segal: The Teacher and Her Teaching

In the seminars and supervisions that Hanna Segal conducted in Geneva from 1979 until 1989, I was able to appreciate the perspicacity of her clinical approach, as well as the clarity and concision with which she communicates her thinking. How could that invaluable teaching be conveyed to the reader in a sufficiently lively manner? I had the idea that a series of live interviews with Hanna Segal in which she would discuss her creativeness as a psychoanalyst and the part she has played in the history of psychoanalysis – she herself, after all, has been one of its outstanding representatives for some sixty years now – could perhaps go some way to doing just that.

She welcomed the project all the more enthusiastically, she told me, because it corresponded exactly to one of her dearest wishes: to bear witness to the decisive influence that certain events in her own early childhood had had on her vocation to be a psychoanalyst. Although such factors are readily acknowledged as being decisive for understanding how someone's personality has developed, she added, they are hardly ever mentioned in biographies – almost never, indeed, in those of psychoanalysts.

On several occasions between 2004 and 2006, I travelled to London to interview Hanna Segal. Our discussions were mainly in English, with some sequences in French, a language that Hanna Segal speaks fluently. The interviews were recorded on cassette tapes, which were subsequently transcribed by Mary Block, her private secretary, and later supplemented in a few brief telephone conversations.

Here, then, verbatim, is almost the entire series of interviews. Some editorial changes have been made, without, of course, altering the original text to any significant degree. I have, for example, brought together certain ideas relating to topics discussed in various chapters; a few minor stylistic corrections make the text easier to follow; and I decided on my own initiative to eliminate some material of a more personal nature that did not add anything to the overall content of the interviews. Any such cuts in the transcribed text are shown in the usual manner, *viz..*: [. . .]. Hanna Segal authorized me in writing to publish the transcripts *in extenso*; in addition, she asked me to deposit the original tapes and transcripts with the *Melanie Klein Archives* once I no longer needed them. They can be consulted there, under certain conditions. At the end of each transcribed section I have indicated on which tape the relevant extract can be found.

My original plan was to publish these interviews as they stand, with no accompanying editorial comment. It soon became obvious, however, that some presentation of Segal's main contributions to psychoanalysis would have to be added to the interviews themselves so as to shed a little more light on what she says. I realized that those readers who were not particularly familiar with Hanna Segal's work might well feel frustrated if they did not have some guidelines to help them on their way. I was thinking particularly of readers from outside the English-speaking world, to whom Hanna Segal is known more perhaps for her role as an ambassador of Melanie Klein's work, rather than in her own right, in spite of the fact that her own work amounts to a highly original contribution.

In order to have a contemporary perspective on Hanna Segal's ideas, I contacted a number of psychoanalysts in various parts of the world, asking them what relevance Segal's ideas have to present-day psychoanalysis, what criticisms have been levelled at them, and what, if any, new developments they have encouraged. It is true, of course, that several British psychoanalysts who have known Hanna Segal for many years have already put what they think into writing, in a book under the general editorship of David Bell (1997). I wanted, all the same, to have the opinion of psychoanalysts who are not native English speakers; in addition, this would give the reader some indication of the influence she has had outside the English-speaking world. The diversity of their points of view is really quite impressive, as are their stylistic differences. Their comments go to show also that Hanna Segal, no doubt too modest to have founded a "school of thought" of her own, has nonetheless had an enormous impact on contemporary psychoanalysis.

With the idea of sketching out a vivid and lively portrait of Hanna Segal and her work, I have chosen a multifocal approach in order to illustrate not only the content of her teaching but also the personality of the teacher. Some may be surprised by this choice, with its seemingly non-academic perspective that goes beyond traditional textbook material. I would argue, however, that the standpoint I have adopted enables the reader to know more about Hanna Segal as a teacher and invites him or her to discover the papers and books she has written, while at the same time preserving the mystery of Hanna Segal as a person. With that in mind, I have quite deliberately left unfinished this portrait of Hanna Segal.

Hanna Segal is famous for the outspoken way in which she asserts her beliefs and says what she thinks, whether in her lectures or in her written papers. That is why, in this book, I have chosen a mixture of oral discussions and written work, with the hope that the reader will be able to "read" Hanna Segal more easily after having "listened" to her. I trust that the way in which I approach the person and her work will make some contribution to highlighting the originality of Segal's thinking in the midst of the many voices that characterize contemporary psychoanalysis. In my view, a constructive dialogue can be built up if we all start to listen to one another with the aim of acknowledging our similarities and clarifying our differences. From that perspective, the contro-versies that arose within the British Psychoanalytical Society, far from being simply a source of discord, have demonstrated their potentiality for mutual enrichment – an example, indeed, for us all.

Jean-Michel Quinodoz
Geneva
February 2007

ACKNOWLEDGEMENTS

My thanks go firstly to Hanna Segal herself for giving me the opportunity of carrying out this series of interviews with her (and granting copyright to me) and for her support all through the preparation and completion of the initial project; those colleagues who agreed to be interviewed must also be thanked. I am grateful too to Dana Birksted-Breen, editor of the *Teaching Series* of the *New Library of Psychoanalysis*, for the warm welcome she and her husband Jan gave me each time I visited London to work on this book. Special thanks must go to Mary Block, Hanna Segal's private secretary, for her work in transcribing the text of the interviews and for her help in researching the bibliography. The advice offered by the readers of the initial manuscript of this book proved invaluable – first of all my wife Danielle, who is usually indeed the first person to read my work; Augustin Jeanneau, Juan Manzano and Francisco Palacio-Espasa, together with Marie Bridge, Christoph Hering and the three anonymous readers of the British Psychoanalytical Society whose suggestions helped me shape this final version. I am grateful also to David Alcorn for his admirable translation into English of the sections of this book which were originally in French and for his work on the text of the Hanna Segal interviews. This research was partly funded by a grant from the Research Advisory Board of the International Psychoanalytical Association chaired by Robert S. Wallerstein. I am grateful also to all those at Routledge, and in particular to Kate Hawes, Nicola Ravenscroft and Jane Harris, for their support and for the care which they brought to preparing this volume for publication.

Jean-Michel Quinodoz

Chapter 1

HANNA SEGAL: A PSYCHOANALYTIC AUTOBIOGRAPHY

FROM BIRTH IN POLAND TO PSYCHOANALYTIC TRAINING IN LONDON (1918–1947)

Hanna Segal has always emphasized the dominant influence of early childhood experiences on the individual's subsequent development. In this, she follows the example of Melanie Klein; Hanna Segal is, indeed, one of the most noteworthy representatives of Klein's thinking. However, she does not content herself simply with applying these ideas to her work with her patients and in supervision, she applies them also to herself and to her own past history. That is why she insisted on beginning this series of interviews by narrating the experiences which, from a psychoanalytic point of view, had a significant impact on her as a child, as an adolescent and as an adult. More than a mere biographical account, these ideas make up a true psychoanalytic autobiography in which Segal shares with us not only the new perspectives she was able to construct in the 1940s thanks to her analysis with Melanie Klein, but also the links she made afterwards during her uninterrupted and ongoing self-analysis.

Here, I have briefly noted the main biographical landmarks in Hanna Segal's life, starting with her birth in 1918, until her marriage and her accreditation as a member of the British Psychoanalytical Society in 1947. The reader will find in the chapters that follow the autobiographical details she shared with me as regards later stages in her life and in her work up to the present day.

Some landmark dates

Hanna Segal was born on 20 August 1918 in Lodz, Poland. Her parents, Czeslaw Poznanski and Isabelle Weintraub, both came from well-assimilated Jewish families and lived for the most part in Warsaw, where her father was a practising lawyer.

1918:   When she was 3 months old, Hanna was abruptly weaned and separated from her mother, who had fallen ill during the epidemic of Spanish flu. Although her mother survived the epidemic, Hanna rarely saw her parents throughout her early childhood in Warsaw – most of the time she was looked after by nannies or maids.

1921:   Death of Wanda, Hanna's sister, at 4 years of age from scarlet fever. Hanna was approximately 2 years old when her sister died. It was a deeply traumatic event. Hanna can remember a dream she had just after her sister's death – an exceptionally early childhood memory. Hanna would henceforth remain her parents' only child.

1925:   At 6 years of age, Hanna rebelled after having been left on her own for much of the summer. She asked her parents to take her with them in future and not leave her behind. The first family holiday she had was spent in Biarritz – where she discovered the sea. That was to be the beginning of a love story between Hanna and the sea, one that would last all her life.

1925–1930:   Hanna's parents began to show more interest in their daughter. Her father, who had a vast humanistic culture, encouraged her to read and introduced her to literature and to art. Hanna discovered school life and made friends of her own age.

1930:   Her father tried to kill himself. This was a terrible disillusion, especially for Hanna, who admired him so much. Completely bankrupt and about to be prosecuted for gambling away his clients' money, he left Poland with his family to settle in Switzerland.

1931:   The family settled in Geneva, where Hanna's father found work as editor of the League of Nations *Journal*. Hanna began attending the International School. She became interested in French literature, and particularly in Proust. One of her parents' friends was Eugenie Sokolnicka, a Polish psychoanalyst who was a pupil of Freud's. That was the first time that Hanna heard her father mention psychoanalysis.

1934:   When she was 16, Hanna, feeling nostalgic about her native Poland, asked to be allowed to return to Warsaw to finish her schooling there. While in Poland, she became aware of how dramatic the social and economic problems were; she became an activist in the Student Section of the Polish Socialist Party and had Trotskyist leanings. After her Baccalaureate, Hanna decided to study medicine as a first step to becoming a psychoanalyst.

1938:   The League of Nations *Journal*, considered to be too anti-fascist, was shut down. Hanna's father thus lost his job and found himself stateless, the Polish authorities having withdrawn his passport. He therefore had to leave Switzerland. He and his wife settled in Paris.

1939:   When Hitler invaded Poland in September 1939, Hanna happened to be in Paris, holidaying at her parents' home. Unable to return to Warsaw, she continued her medical studies in France. In Paris she met once again Paul Segal, her future husband, whom she had known when they were children.

1940–1943:   Fleeing the invading German army, Hanna and her parents embarked on the very last Polish ship to leave for Great Britain. The family settled in London. Hanna sat the examinations required for admission to medical school first in Manchester, then in Edinburgh. While still a student, Hanna continued to explore psychoanalysis. In Edinburgh, she met Ronald Fairbairn, who spoke to her about Melanie Klein and Anna Freud. Hanna spent one year in analysis with David Matthew, one of Klein's pupils. She graduated as a doctor in 1943 and returned to London; Fairbairn wrote for her a letter of recommendation addressed to Winnicott.

1943–1946:   Hanna began her formal psychoanalytic training at the Institute of Psychoanalysis in London. After making it clear that she wanted Melanie Klein to be her analyst, Hanna thereupon began analysis with her. She worked as a surgeon in Paddington Green hospital. Six months later, she began working as a psychiatrist in Long Grove psychiatric hospital, Epsom; she worked there until the war ended. At the same time, she continued her psychoanalytic training in London, where her supervisors were Joan Riviere and Paula Heimann. Hanna's mother died of cancer at 54 years of age, shortly before the end of the war.

1946–1947:   Hanna completed her training as a psychoanalyst and married Paul Segal. While she was pregnant with their first child, she presented her first paper, "A psycho-analytical approach to aesthetics". At the age of 29, she became the youngest member of the British Psychoanalytical Society.

"I think I had a very traumatic childhood"

"I think if I had turned out to be schizophrenic, people would have said: 'No wonder, with *that* childhood!' "

Hanna Segal: I like talking about my early childhood, not only because old people like to reminisce but also because I find that in the biography of great analysts (and other people as well) information about their early childhood is always missing. We know a few things about Freud – that he was his mother's favourite and how he, I think out of jealousy, threw shoes out of the window, things like that, but nothing consistent. I am rather lucky in that way in that I have very clear memories of my childhood and of a number of things, thanks to Mrs Klein's approach, linked with it. What I can tell you is partly memory, partly what I discovered in analysis – certain links – and partly, let's say, my speculations about it. A good memory for one's childhood usually means more integration. Well, I consider my childhood decisive in the formation of my character and eventually in what took me to analysis. I think I had a very traumatic childhood. I think that if I had turned out to be schizophrenic, people would have said: "No wonder, with *that* childhood – mother not containing and so on", but things are not quite as simple as that. A trauma can make a good analyst out of you, but so can good experiences.

Weaned and separated from mother at 3 months

I know that I had a bad start because – that's not memory, it's what's been told to me – until the age of 3 months I screamed incessantly. I don't know what it was – perhaps my mother didn't have enough milk, or maybe it was what they call the three months' colic. And then suddenly I was weaned, because my mother had Spanish flu. But apparently I thrived on the bottle. I immediately put on weight. So, it was either three months' colic or something wrong with the feeding, but I know that I didn't see my mother. The loss of the breast was combined with the loss of the person because my mother disappeared, I think. She survived [the epidemic], but she had a very severe flu.

Death of her sister when Hanna was 2 years old

I remember very little of my parents from my early childhood, but my older sister died when she was 4 years old and I was a little over 2. I have very clear memories of my sister, so I must have been even younger than 18 months when she first fell ill. And I remember the dream I had soon after her death – it was a very amusing dream and it was important to me because ours was a sort of rich bourgeois household where children were in the hands of nannies.

I hardly ever saw my parents, I think, and basically my sister was my good object. I have a photograph of her holding my hand and I remember the occasion it was taken. The mythology is that she loved me very much – I'm sure that's true – but the amusing thing is that one day she stuffed my mouth with chocolate and I nearly choked, so it must have been ambivalent. I remember a blue carpet on which she was pretending to teach me to swim. She died of scarlet fever, and I remember her standing by my cot with my father feeding her. I remember the place I went to when the diagnosis was made – I was sent away immediately, of course.

Then the rest is very much what I reconstructed in analysis. I have a memory of my mother all in black and looking terribly detached and me running to her and getting no response. But what I worked out – certain things clicked – is that my mother's way of dealing with depression was always to travel, so she must have left me and travelled and that was her return. [. . .] So I was left with a very depressed father and a lot of stories from maids about what a pity it was that my sister had died rather than me, because she was the favourite and prettier and cleverer and so on. I think some of the comments must have been true, because she *was* a very bright and pretty child. Of course my parents didn't know that I was being fed all those stories. So that was the big trauma of my childhood.

Jean-Michel Quinodoz: Those are very early memories.

Yes, very early memories. I'll tell you the dream.

Memory of a dream at 2 years of age

The dream was that the window flew open and angel "thieves" (that's what I called them in the dream) rushed into the room and I woke up afraid. Now, I must have been told by some silly maid that the angels took my sister to heaven, but to my mind that wasn't such a good thing – so it was angel "thieves" that rushed into the room. I don't know if it was to take her or to take me.

Now, I think the trace that this left for me was very much a great attachment and protectiveness to sister figures, particularly younger sister figures because, although my sister was 4 when she died and therefore older than I was, to me she was always a younger sister. I was very taken up in analysis with being very inhibited in my ambition whenever I found myself in a situation of competition with sister figures. I can remember running in races, getting towards the head of the file and then just falling back as soon as I got nearer the finishing line. So I was always a very good team-player because for me it was brothers and sisters against the others. And I think there was a lot of survivor guilt.

Early years: feeling abandoned

Hanna's parents: "Jews who lived in Poland" or "Poles who happened to be Jewish"?

Now, with my parents. I was born, I always say, by mistake in Lodz because – it was the beginning of Polish independence – my father, who was an adviser to Pilsudski, was asked to go to Lodz to take over for the new Polish government the municipal organization of gas, electricity and so forth from the Germans. I always say that I was born there by mistake because I detested Lodz – which is an industrial town, a sort of Polish Manchester – whereas I adored Warsaw. My birth was actually registered in a church in Warsaw. At that time, there was no Public Records Office in Poland. My mother, whose maiden name was Weintraub, became a Christian in order to have their marriage registered. As for my father, whose name was Czeslaw Poznanski, he had converted to Catholicism in 1905 more in order to manifest his attachment to Poland than out of any real religious fervour.

My mother came from a Jewish family. I know very little about her parents. I met them a few times, but they lived in Wiesbaden and there were nine sisters, all of renowned beauty, particularly my mother. They were the sort of nine muses around that area, particularly in Lodz. My father also came from a Jewish family, one hundred per cent Jewish but very assimilated, very patriotic. His great-great-grandfather was a tailor during the first Polish insurrection against the occupation; his name was Rotblatt, and the Poles decided he was too good a patriot to have such a German name, so they called him Poznanski, someone who comes from Poznan. My father came from a line of jurists: his father was an eminent lawyer. His uncle was such a famous gynaecologist that when the wife of one of the French Presidents was pregnant she called on him to come from Warsaw to assist her. So my father came from this kind of assimilated family.

In 1905 there was a strike (you may remember that in 1905 there was a sort of miners' revolution). Nearly all the Jews broke the strike so my father, to identify with his Polish friends, converted to Catholicism. He was an atheist – he didn't care two hoots about religion, but he wanted to emphasize the distinction between a Jewish Pole and a Polish Jew. My mother's parents were Polish Jews in the sense that they felt they were above all Jewish. When they were in Russia they were Russian Jews, when they were in Poland they were Polish Jews. That kind of Jew would not take part in any strike against the Russian government. On the other hand, Jewish Poles are Poles, and Poles can be Jewish or Christian or Muslim – religion is secondary to national adherence. Of course, it had very much to do with the advent of Hitler and the rise of anti-Semitism. But nominally I'm Catholic: since in Poland there were no secular schools and no secular registration, you had to be born a little Muslim, or Protestant, or Jew or Catholic and the simplest was to register with the dominant religion, especially since it is the minority groups that are always fanatic.

JMQ: What memories do you have of your parents at that time?

Bad ones. Before I was analysed, I didn't realize just how much I hated both of them for having neglected me in my early years. I remember my father playing with me a little, but my mother hardly at all. We lived in a town apartment so I had no other children to play with and I was all day with maids. [. . .] I was always left in that flat unending Polish landscape, you know, that long valley which starts in the Ukraine and runs down to Germany. There was nothing.

"Take me with you, always!"

At the age of 6 I had a particularly bad holiday when I fell ill and had actually a lot of boils on my behind – my parents were away. That was when I told them that I didn't want to be left behind and I remember that I promised to be good if they'd take me with them.

JMQ: You already had quite a strong character!

No, I think that if I had protested at 3 or 4 – they were quite kind people, it was just that they didn't understand small children at all. So once I put my foot down and said "you're not to leave me any more", they didn't. And also by then of course I could talk, I could express myself and my father particularly was very verbal. So from then on they took me on holiday, and that was wonderful because that's when I discovered the sea – even to this day, swimming in the Mediterranean is the aim of my life, so to speak. I made friends and so on and also, soon after, I went to school – which I adored because I was very lonely. I had a few little cousins – I had a lot of cousins of course on my mother's side – but the main ones were little cousins of about my age; one was a girl whom I didn't like very much but she was older than me and lived in Warsaw. The other two, Johnnie and George, lived in Lodz but then they came to Warsaw – I don't know what age I was then – and we played games, usually very sexual games. For me, Freud's discovery about infantile sexuality was no discovery at all. I knew it very well indeed! And no associated guilt, actually. All part of exploration or fun. But apart from meeting my cousins I was a very lonely child until I went to school. So school was paradise for me.

From 13 to 16: Hanna's family live in Geneva

Her father's attempted suicide

JMQ: In 1931 your parents left Poland and moved to Geneva. What brought that about?

Things were complicated with my father and my mother. Up until adolescence, I very much idealized my father because he played with me more. When I was older I remember him teaching me art history and showing me things when we were travelling. He was the one who chose books for me when I was a child. He took much more interest in me and he was a real sort of Renaissance man with a lot of knowledge and interests. So I idealized him and I had a tendency to look down on my mother as not being a very intellectual person, and also I found her rather unapproachable. She didn't relate much to children. It was very much better after I was 7; she became very close to me.

Well, my father was a gambler and he gambled away his clients' money. He attempted suicide and that brought about a big sort of breakdown in the family. By the way, I don't know if telepathy exists or if it's just some kind of belief, but he suddenly disappeared and we had a friend called Osowiecki who was what he himself called a clairvoyant – but I am sure that it was telepathic communication mind to mind, because he told us that my father was in a hospital in a province somewhere after attempting suicide. We rang the hospital and, sure enough, we found him. So all this meant a tremendous collapse of my idealization, particularly the suicide attempt because I was very contemptuous of that. My mother, however, showed extraordinary resourcefulness and courage, she who had been so completely spoiled – she never even used to make so much as a cup of tea at home. When we went to Geneva, we were penniless – nowadays, it's quite common but in those days it wasn't common at all. She learned to cook, she learned to sew, she learned to run the house. She arranged for the gradual repayment of my father's debts. And it was the same during the Second World War – she had tremendous resources whenever there was a major change in our circumstances.

Opening up to the world at large

So I went to Geneva and I got very fat and depressed – I used to be such a skinny child. . . .

JMQ: It was very difficult to adapt – a change of language, a change of country.

Very difficult. French I knew a little because some of my bloody governesses were French (they were the worst – can you imagine what kind of girl would want to go to Poland to be a nanny!). So I had some French and the language therefore was not a problem. The problem was being separated from my friends. We were in a small flat and we missed Warsaw terribly. I never missed Poland as such, but all my life I have missed Warsaw. It was a wonderful city. Ugly as hell, but a beautiful city in every other way. And also being for the first time in a co-educational school – boys and girls. Being fat was quite an impediment.

On the other hand, I learned to love school because it was a real eye-opener for me. I think it's been taken over by Americans now, but in those days the International School was run by the daughter of a former professor of an *Ecole Normale Supérieure* in France; she was the headmistress. She was an inspiring person, very much on the lines of, you know, international culture, co-operation. One thing that is now common in all schools but was very new then – it was a very democratically run school. We had a Students' Council which was responsible for discipline, for running the shop – we made a lot of money in the co-operative shop – for running all sorts of student affairs. The teaching was very stimulating and very liberal-minded. There were two language streams, one French, the other English. Religion was taught as "comparative religion" and geography as "international culture". As I say, now it's quite a common thing, but in those days it was very revolutionary. I made a lot of friends and acquired an international outlook. There was a Lithuanian girl in the school and I ran up to her with sort of open arms – "*Oh, hello, we come from the same country*" – and she threw an inkpot at me! The point was that from the Lithuanian point of view the glorious period of the Polish/Lithuanian Empire was not that at all – they felt they were under Polish occupation! So I suddenly realized that, you know, there's always another outlook on everything.

JMQ: I wonder if the contacts you had at the Geneva International School with so many languages and so many people from different countries influenced you later, because you are an analyst who has travelled a lot.

Oh yes, I think it did a great deal. I think my earliest childhood did form my character a lot both in relation to depressive anxieties and reparation and with a certain delayed heterosexual development. Physically, I was always attracted to boys but my emotional life was much more connected with girls – I never had crushes on schoolmistresses, for example, but always on sister figures – and for a long time my friendships with girls were more important and meant a deeper commitment than my relationships with men. These were not good, quite naughty in fact in my adolescence. But the International School gave me, I think, the deepest conviction of tolerance and curiosity – non-voyeuristic curiosity – about how things happen. I stayed there from about late 13 to about 16.

Being rebellious in that school, for a short time I went through a Catholic phase. I met a very intelligent Thomist priest with whom I had many philosophical conversations and I tried for a year or so to be a practising Catholic. It didn't take, because it was only a rebellion – in my case, against the school.

Discovering water sports and literature

JMQ: Where did you live in Geneva?

In Champel, Chemin de Champendal. What saved my sanity to begin with was the Lake. My parents bought me a boat. They were very, very poor but there was a chap called Condeveau – we knew of him because he was the Swiss champion of single rowing and he advertised his practice boat for sale. My parents couldn't afford to buy it outright, but when he saw how keen I was he allowed them to pay for it in instalments. So before starting school I would just spend my time on the lake swimming and rowing. Once when I was older I nearly rowed to the far side of the lake, but I didn't quite manage to complete it. My hands were torn to pieces.

Also, literature drew me to analysis because I fell in love with Proust very early . . . and that must have been before I was 16 because I remember reading Proust already in French. It was also the germs of a certain duality in me, which was helped by analysis. On the one hand I was tremendously attracted to art, literature, mental functioning, things of that kind, and on the other hand – and that would go back probably to my sister – I had a very acute social conscience, so I had to do something that would be socially useful. Not easy to reconcile.

An early interest in psychoanalysis

My father always had a big library and I had started reading some things about Freud. Then we had a visit from Madame Eugenie Sokolnicka. The French like to think that I was influenced by her to become an analyst, but if anything she would have put me off analysis. All the same, it's in connection with her that my father explained something to me. She was a very unhappy woman, desperately vain and always in search of a man. I first met her in Paris. She had seven black cats which I loved but which my mother was a bit phobic about, so that made me feel very superior. Then I remember Sokolnicka visiting us in Geneva and she was mad about men – terribly unhappy – and she always had with her a patient who went on holiday with her. I think it was Gaston Gallimard, the great publisher, and obviously terribly in love with her. So I asked my father, "*Look, if she is so mad on men why doesn't she marry that man who's running after her?*" Then my father explained to me about transference and why doctors are not allowed to marry one of their patients. My father was very good in that way – he opened my eyes to many things – and he said that when you have a psychoanalyst you get very attached to that person. He read everything that an enlightened and intelligent man would read in those days.

JMQ: You were between 13 and 16 at the time – isn't that exceptionally young to be interested in psychoanalysis?

That's when I first heard of it. It is young, but then I started reading Freud when my father explained it to me. So that's how I first heard about analysis and became interested in it. I was enthralled by Freud's *Beyond the Pleasure Principle* (1920g) and *Civilization and its Discontents* (1930a [1929]). And my father was more rehabilitated in my eyes, if you like, because the journal he was working for took up a very clear anti-fascist stance.

At 16, Hanna returns to Warsaw then begins her medical studies

Back to Warsaw

By 16, I was back in Poland. I had a couple of friends, one of whom later became an analyst too – her name is Lisa – and we read Freud avidly; we discussed his work and applied it to literature, quarrelled about him and so on. When it came to choosing a profession I was very much torn because my interests were literary, artistic and so on, but my conscience told me that I had to do something useful – and I was very politically engaged too. I started reading psychoanalysts on literature, for example a book on Baudelaire by René Laforgue, and I thought that this was really the answer to my prayers – becoming an analyst. I then realized that what interested me was human manifestations in all sorts of ways – in literature, for example, and in illness – and that analysis was an entry to that. I wanted to study psychology and law and work in the prison service, because I was working also as a volunteer in a home for delinquent girls when I was in Warsaw.

JMQ: You left Geneva and your parents in 1934 – at 16 years of age – to go back to Warsaw?

Well, it was a very civilized kind of adolescent rebellion. My father, who was a great patriot, was very open to the argument that I wanted to have a Polish qualification. But mostly I missed Warsaw, my friends – even though I had made very good friends in Geneva.

So, I went home alone and there I learned a lot. [. . .] I did two years at the *Lycée* for Catholic Polish Girls. [. . .]

In Warsaw I mixed mostly with the bourgeoisie and the intelligentsia. There was a tremendous cultural life, with many high-quality theatres – they were subsidized, so it was easy for penniless students to attend. The government was more and more right-wing, but political opposition was gaining in strength. When I joined the Polish Youth Movement I got in touch with what real poverty is and saw for myself the social problems and the restrictions on civil liberties. I was quite close to the Trotskyists. So those were my schooldays, if you like.

Hanna decides to study medicine

Then I had this choice – what to do in life? I wanted to do psychology and law and go into the prison service. I sought the advice of a Polish psychoanalyst, Dr Bychowski, who was later to become very well-known in the United States; he advised me to go to Vienna – which, given the circumstances of the time, would not have been a good idea at all! My father gave me good advice. He said: "Look, if you want to reform things, never depend on a salary from any kind of organization. Have an independent profession, so that you can do things on your own authority." I think that was very good advice, and I have followed it all the way through. Except while training to be an analyst, I have never worked for the NHS, even though I was very supportive of it. I have never worked for any organization – except, once, towards the end of the war, when I had a medical director in the hospital where I worked.

JMQ: Was it in Warsaw that you chose your future profession?

That's right. In a way I tossed a coin. It was very difficult to get into the Polish medical school – not only a competitive examination, but they were also very biased against women and even more so against people with a Jewish name. So I thought: "If I get in, I'll be a doctor; if I don't, I won't." And I did get in. So I started studying medicine, which I don't regret – it's a good preparation for analysis; I did three years of medical school in Warsaw before the outbreak of war.

Hanna's father is forced to leave Switzerland

JMQ: Why did your parents move from Geneva to Paris in 1938?

What happened to my parents was this. The *Journal des Nations* was mainly funded by the Italian [anti-fascist] opposition. There were two editors – my father and an Italian called Carlo, a lovely man. But Carlo was stateless, so Giuseppe Motta[1] kicked him out. He then went to the *Zone Libre* between Switzerland and France and he rang the *Journal* every day. My father wasn't stateless, so he was all right – until the Polish government decided to call all holders of what were called Consular Passports – a passport that allowed you to live abroad – to return to Poland for a review of their situation. My father didn't go back because by then Poland had become so fascist that they would certainly have refused him a passport. As a result, he lost his Polish passport, and two months later Motta kicked him out too. That meant that the *Journal* had to shut down, because with both Editors being out of Geneva it just couldn't go on.

   My parents went to Paris in 1938. My father had a very hard time even though he was a very respected journalist. The *Journal des Nations* was a very serious paper read by everybody who was interested in international affairs. There was such an influx of émigrés and doctors that they had a very hard time. Some of my father's friends in the press helped them out financially.

From 21 to 22: a reluctant refugee in France

Stranded in Paris at the outbreak of war in September 1939

By the time I returned to France for the 1939 summer holidays, my family had settled in Paris. The declaration of war in September of that year prevented my going back to Warsaw – I'll tell you what happened in a moment. I found myself stuck in France for the rest of the year.

   My parents were living partly off the international grant I had been awarded in order to continue my medical studies. In addition, I earned a little money by giving private tutorials for exams and French lessons. But it was a really difficult time. Round about then, I joined an illegal group of Trotskyist friends, but in spite of my pacifism I soon came to realize that I was playing a dangerous game – so I left the group.

Meeting Paul again

And that's where I met Paul again, my future husband; we used to know each other as children – we didn't like each other at all in those days – but when I met him in Paris in 1940 . . .

JMQ: What was he doing in Paris?

He had enlisted in the Polish Army. He too had a political history. He was a member of the Young Communists, a party that was illegal in Poland, and he was arrested for "shouting out anti-State slogans". In fact, he told me that he never raised his voice at all. I can quite believe that, because Paul wasn't the kind of chap who would go out and raise his voice! Anyway, they nabbed him and he spent nine months in prison awaiting trial. Then he was let out on licence pending appeal. One of his uncles was working in a tourist agency and he managed to get Paul on one of those tourist buses heading for Czechoslovakia. From there he went to Paris and he was studying physics when I met him. Later he changed to mathematics. And you see with my luck – of course, I didn't know then that it was luck – the pair of us fought like mad to get on the last train back to Warsaw, but to no avail, it was so full up. So, you see, I had more luck than reason.

JMQ: Did you understand the risk you were taking?

Oh yes, I understood. But, look, I had just turned 21, Hitler was invading Poland – how could I not be there!

JMQ: Were you to some extent attracted by the sheer dangerousness of the idea?

No, not by the dangerousness, by duty. But since I didn't manage to get on that train, I had a year in Paris. I think I've studied to become a doctor in more universities than anyone else I know!

JMQ: So you went on with your medical studies in Paris?

And I was already trying to find out how one becomes an analyst. That's what I went into medicine for.

JMQ: Did you meet any psychoanalysts during your stay in Paris?

Well, I knew a name – René Laforgue, whose book on Baudelaire I'd liked. So, I rang Laforgue and he said he had no time to see me: he was just about to evacuate Paris. That was a stroke of luck, really, because I learned later that he used to take his patients swimming every weekend in his pool. I would have fallen for it immediately – I love swimming. Later I met an English analyst who had been in analysis with him and she told me all the horrible things. And subsequently I learned also that he had collaborated with the Nazis. The French Society never accepted him. So, after that, I eventually reached England . . .

The last boat for England

JMQ: In what circumstances did you leave France?

Well, we stayed in Paris until the German army began marching on the city, in the spring of 1940. After crossing almost the whole of France, my parents and I managed to get on the very last Polish boat that was heading for England. It was transporting the Polish First Division, and accepted some civilians on board.

Survivor guilt

Hanna Segal: One of the main obstacles I had to overcome while I was growing up was my "survivor guilt" relating to various dramatic circumstances, long before the Shoah. Unconsciously, of course, it started with surviving the death of my sister when I was just 2 years old, but consciously it centred on three events in which I had the feeling of having failed in my duty.

The first was in 1936: the Spanish Civil War. While I was on holiday in Geneva, I had arranged with a friend, who knew people in the Spanish government, to go to Spain. But my parents caught me trying to sneak out of the house one night. I just could not ignore the distress they felt when they learned of my plan, especially since I was their only child.

It is difficult for the younger generation to realize the crucial importance, both symbolic and real, of that war. The fall of republican Spain was the real beginning of the Second World War.

The second time I failed in my duty was when I didn't go back to Poland at the beginning of September 1939, when war was declared. This time, my parents were not against my returning, because they understood my motives; but the last train to Warsaw was so overcrowded that I couldn't even fight my way in. Of those of my friends who did make it into the train, none, as far as I know, survived. Much later I would say that I have always had more luck than sense.

The third occasion was just before I left France for England, when I accompanied a schizophrenic girl to a mental hospital near Lourdes. I was offered a post as a house doctor in that hospital. This was also a great honour, and the hospital director was quite taken with me – and, of course, would have been only too glad to have another practitioner on his staff. I really did want to stay; I could have joined my comrades in the Resistance. But again, it was my attachment to my parents that held me back. They said that if I stayed in France, so would they – and, given the fact that they were Jews in addition to my father's political activities, that would have meant certain death. So, reluctantly, I followed them to England.

(Hanna Segal, autobiographical notes, February 2001)

Once in England, Hanna takes up her medical studies again

In London during the Blitz

JMQ: Once you reached England, were you able to go on with your medical studies?

In England, one university accepted me provided I took the university entrance exam, so I started swotting for that. Then I went to Manchester. By the way, it may be important to say that the year I spent in London made me love England, because I think I would have hated England before. Remember, this was the time of the "Blitz". England used to be tremendously reactionary, but the war brought about such a change. People never used to talk to one another in trains and so forth, every Englishman would be behind his newspaper. This was especially true of class divides – there were no bridges – but somehow the Blitz brought everybody together in a much more open society. Also, something that was really admirable: everywhere on the Continent food was in the hands of the black market, but in Britain most food was rationed and the black market was marginal – that meant that during the war there was less poverty in Britain than ever before. The birth weight of children almost doubled because everybody was fed the same rations.

JMQ: A big social and political change?

An enormous political and social change. And it's interesting when you compare it with the panic that occurred after 11 September 2001; during the Blitz, London was bombed every night, every single night. I used to move around a lot because I lived in Chelsea and I was teaching Polish colonels English way up past Regent's Park, so every evening I was on a man's bicycle that I inherited, a big one, trundling along right across London – this was just at the beginning of the Blitz. But I wasn't the only one. I never saw panic. Never. Because people helped one another. The ambulances worked. The fire service worked. Not like in England today. There was solidarity. There was much more democracy and of course after the war they chose a very reformist government in the early 1950s. So this is really what got me attached to England. When we first went to an air-raid shelter in Paris people started complaining that "those foreigners are taking away our oxygen".

Medical studies in Manchester

JMQ: And afterwards you went on with your medical studies?

I had a very interesting term in Manchester because Manchester medical school offered to take me provided I took the second Medical Board. I met a student counsellor, Miss Dorothy Emmet, and told her that I had a thirty-shillings-a-week scholarship – how could I live in Manchester on that? She replied, "Well, actually I've got a free room!" For a nominal rent she took me in, and she had another German girl staying with her, Elsa, who was supposed to work a bit in the house. What the work consisted of was – Miss Emmet liked her porridge made the night before for the next morning, so every other day either Elsa or I would do her porridge. That was the work we had! And through her I met the Manchester intelligentsia. She was a marvellous person. She produced a very beautiful book about Kafka's last love; when I read that book, I discovered also the marvellous things she did for Kafka's widow and child. She was a terrific person. She was only the second woman to be appointed a Professor. So I stayed with Dorothy Emmet, and she remained a friend until her death. She died in her late nineties, and produced her last book in her early nineties – about her reminiscences of philosophers who had influenced her. She was a fantastic person. She was a Quaker, and her whole life was Philosophy – and also social work and helping people. And she had a great sense of fun. So the time I spent in Manchester was quite happy.

With Fairbairn in Edinburgh

That wasn't the case in Edinburgh. What was excellent there was that they had opened a Polish section of the medical school, so that we were taken into our proper year which for me was Fourth Year. So I had only a year and a half to make up. They gave us an extra summer term to catch up. But, God, Edinburgh was very unpleasant in those days. It was what Glaswegians call West Endy and East Windy. They were so cold. If you had no money you could get nothing. At the weekend every shop, every coffee shop, every tea shop was closed. The free golf courses were shut. There was nothing. But if you were rich and belonged to a club, everything was open. They had their own golf course, they had their own bar . . .

JMQ: But wasn't meeting Fairbairn in Edinburgh decisive for your future?

Yes, but that is where my "trying to find out how to become an analyst" ended. I went to work as an unpaid helper in the Davidson Clinic which was one of the early sort of Tavistock extensions – it was actually terrible. What I learned from them, I learned from their mistakes. But I did meet Fairbairn and he was very fair because he told me how to become an analyst; you didn't even have to be a doctor. And he told me of the Institute, and that there was a split between Miss Freud and Melanie Klein – two names I didn't know at all. He gave me two books to read – Mrs Klein's *The Psychoanalysis of Children* and Anna Freud's *The Ego and the Mechanisms of Defence*. Well, it didn't take me long to make up my mind. I found *The Ego and the Mechanisms of Defence* quite boring really. But when I read Klein I was absolutely over-whelmed. I wanted to start analysis with Fairbairn, but his fee was £1 a session, that's £5 a week, and my whole scholarship amounted to just half of that sum, two-and-a-half pounds a week.

Meeting Melanie Klein

Why Melanie Klein?

JMQ: But what attracted you to Klein?

I tell you what – one of the things that happened. At one point in our evacuation from Paris, my parents and I took a train and, on this train, a young girl had an acute schizophrenic break-down. The only person anywhere near being a doctor on the train was me. So the girl's parents asked me to look after her. I did so and got her to hospital and so on; and she was talking non-stop and one of the things she was talking about was "I lost my lover in the loo, I lost my lover in the loo". I wondered what the hell that was all about. Later, when I started reading *The Psychoanalysis of Children*, I thought to myself "this is a language one can understand". After I read what Klein said about children's phantasies and devouring mother and all that, I thought, "God, I could have understood that girl!" It hit me so much because I think it must have reverberated with my own depressive experience and my interest in the human mind (including my own, presumably), but anyway with this discovery of the language of children I thought, "God, if I'd read Klein, I could have talked to that girl on the train . . ."

JMQ: Loss and depression were very much part of your life as a very young child. Could that go some way to explaining why you found Klein's ideas so attractive?

Well, I found reading Freud very exciting too. What I loved best was one of the first papers in which he speaks of the death instinct, the major one, *Beyond the Pleasure Principle* – that was my favourite, even though it has no clinical material. It brought back the excitement of the life and death instinct and, as you say, the mourning. So it was both the richness of the internal world and the seeing of this language that one can understand – and the whole experience, as you say, of touching on somebody who could understand, who could understand *me*.

It so happened that Fairbairn had a friend who was an analysand of Mrs Klein, a Dr Matthew, who was an associate member. He took me in analysis as his clinic patient for the year I spent in Edinburgh. Finally I came back to London, shortly before the end of the war. London was again being bombed, this time with what we used to call "doodlebugs", which were flying bombs. Without my knowing anything about it, my arrival was preceded by a letter of introduction – Fairbairn had written to Winnicott!

Beginning analysis with Mrs Klein

Winnicott at that time was still quite close to Mrs Klein and I had an interview with him. It was he who recommended me to Mrs Klein, but initially she wanted to send me to Paula Heimann. She said a younger training analyst would be very good for me. But I didn't want that. I told her I would wait until she was able to take me on. She took me as a patient in her clinic consultation until I managed to find a job in which I would be earning a bit more. At that time, all psycho-analysts – not just those in training – were required to have a clinic patient. I was a house doctor in Paddington Green Hospital, earning £10 a month. Shortly after this, however, both the NHS and the Polish Government-in-Exile appointed me as a consultant psychiatrist, and that helped finance my analysis. I think too that at that time Mrs Klein was particularly keen on having students who were both young and brilliant – that must have played a part, I think.

(Tape 4, side A, 1 February 2004)

First interview – and quite a surprising one – with Edward Glover

The first interview with a view to training as a psychoanalyst was with Glover. He absolutely astounded me because I had read the war things he had written – for example *War, Sadism and Pacifism* (1933). I admired him very much and I was very much looking forward to seeing him. Well, I arrived and he asked me the usual questions, whether I wanted to be an analyst for personal reasons as well as for scientific reasons. I said yes, as I had problems of my own to solve. He was a very impressive-looking, white-haired man. Then he asked me if I had thought about the person I wanted to have analysis with. I said yes, I've just started with Mrs Klein. He jumped out of his chair at that and said "Oh, they've got the wrong people. We've got our own people. I don't want to have anything to do with that!" It was like a bombshell to me. I remember telling Mrs Klein when I went the next day. I said: "Look, somebody's mad in this outfit and I'm sure it's not me." She didn't say much. She said something along the lines of, well, there are difficult changes in the Society and I'll get another interview – because Glover was still Education Secretary. He was at that time in an absolutely spiteful rage against Klein. Why? I didn't know anything about it at that time. Then I had an interview with Dr Payne. All that took place while the "Controversial Discussions" were going on, but since I was still in training, most of it went over my head.

Keeping clear of the Controversial Discussions

JMQ: But while the Controversial Discussions were going on, you must have heard that your own analyst was coming under attack. Did that affect you in any way?

Well it did hurt me. But Mrs Klein didn't say anything to me about it, nor about the difficulties entailed by the whole thing.

JMQ: People like Glover were quite openly attacking her . . .

Well, Melitta – Klein's daughter – attacked her own mother in that way. I had no idea what it was about. I was very disappointed because as I say I was looking forward to seeing Glover, and his early writings, I think, were still very Kleinian. Another thing that happened to me is that in my first year I made friends with a young colleague called Ruth Thomas. Thereupon, she fell ill with pneumonia, and when she came back she dropped me like a hot potato – she just wouldn't talk to me any more. Later I found out – Moses Laufer told me this – that her analyst had forbidden her to have anything to do with the Kleinians because that would only confuse her.

The "A" seminars and the "B" seminars

Well, anyway, Herbert Rosenfeld was a year above me and he told me much more about what was going on at the time I started my training. To begin with we were all in the one crowd, but when I started my clinical seminar we had already an "A" stream and a "B" stream . . . We had some theoretical lectures in common and an agreed curriculum, but others had different clinical seminars. The "B" section was Miss Freud, who didn't want her candidates to be "infected". The "A" section comprised all those who later became the Independents and the Kleinians. So, anything that wasn't "B" was "A". In fact, there were a lot of Independents who actually started as Kleinians – Winnicott or Scott would have been considered Kleinian. Scott had his first analysis with Klein.

I don't remember very much about the teaching. Actually, the students there – well, our life – were quite different from nowadays. There were many more parties, many more contacts outside, a lot more drinking . . . so I remember it as quite a good student time! You know, we'd go out a lot and drink illicit stuff and things like that. But I didn't have many more clinical seminars. Some of them were interesting, like Money-Kyrle's. I had Ella Sharpe too, but I found her not at all interesting, I must say – very disappointing in her clinical seminars. But she wrote a well-known book on dreams.

(Tape 4, side B, 1 February 2004)

Some thoughts on the underlying wish to be a psychoanalyst

I've just had a new idea about that. Elizabeth Spillius once made a survey, and she found that the majority of analysts are people who have been "displaced" in some ways – it's as though they were in search of a home somewhere.

JMQ: Well, that's true of Geneva and probably of a lot of other places too . . .

If I look at myself, I would say that what is perhaps important is a variety of good and bad experiences. If all your experiences were so continuously bad, it's probably very, very difficult to go beyond that; but, on the other hand, if they were always good, why – as Freud would have said – should you want to be an analyst? As you know, Freud says that the mature person has a combination of bad experiences that have been overcome and good experiences that have been regained; that may be the stimulus for trying to solve how a bad experience turns into a good one.

The second thing, even though Freud warned against therapeutic zeal, I think that some basic good disposition is necessary if you want to be an analyst; I speak often of absurd counter-transference and the unconscious counter-transference that the analyst must have in his internal world.

Sufficient good experience and good identification with the parental couple are the basis of a positive counter-transference. I think that what Freud calls therapeutic zeal probably has to do with manic reparation: "Either I'll get you better or I'll wipe you out." There is a kind of basic wish to have benevolent neutrality, but I don't think analysts are neutral; that's not true, they can't be neutral, they are committed to something – so it's "neutralized" rather than "neutrality". But the analyst is objective, in the sense of being able to look objectively.

JMQ: Would you say that for most psychoanalysts reparation is a significant factor?

Basically, a more depressive constellation than a narcissistic schizoid one probably makes for a better analyst, I think. It may be narcissistic on my part to say that you and I experience being drawn to Mrs Klein by depression, reparation and so on, so maybe that's why I think that. But from my experience of others what destroys analytical progress is narcissism. Somebody makes a discovery which is of some value and immediately wants to out-Freud Freud and out-Klein Klein. We are terribly ridden by a sort of narcissistic ambition.

JMQ: Perhaps there are many ways of being ambitious

On the question of ambition, people think that the British Society never split because of the English character being always ready to compromise. I don't believe that. I think our Society didn't split because neither Klein nor Anna Freud was motivated mainly by personal ambition. They were both ambitious, of course, but I think that for Melanie Klein – her work, her discoveries – and for Anna Freud – the memory of her father, preserving his inheritance – these were more important than private ambition. All the other Societies split not really on account of theoretical differences but on mad ambitions.

JMQ: That's exactly my impression. There are psychoanalysts who are very ambitious and seek power and others who are ambitious not for their own work but for the development of psycho-analytic knowledge. The former often think that the latter have the same narcissistic aim as they themselves do: they are in projective identification, often without realizing it . . .

I would say that neither Klein nor Anna Freud was primarily narcissistically ambitious. Within the Independent group, there were early Independents like Sylvia Payne and Marjorie Brierley who also were not motivated by personal ambitions . . . quite simply, they had their own views.

Donald W. Winnicott

JMQ: What memories do you have of Winnicott?

Well, my history with Winnicott is complicated. First of all, I'm really quite grateful to him because he gave me a job in Paddington Green: it was near to Mrs Klein and he gave me time off. . . . It was a very flexible job. Also, I was very deprived of books at that time. My father had an enormous library, but when we moved to Geneva he didn't bring his books with him. But he went on buying books, and I was always buying books. Winnicott lent me all the past issues of *The International Journal of Psychoanalysis*, so I could read everything. I was terribly impressed by what Melitta Schmideberg had written – I didn't know about the split with her mother [i.e. Melanie Klein] – and Winnicott himself has some lovely articles. Otherwise, however, I didn't like him and he didn't like me. [. . .] Winnicott was adored in Paddington Green . . . he was a kind of God-figure . . . "Oh, Dr Winnicott's coming!" But he never once stood up to change the hospital regulations and allow parents to visit more than for just two hours twice a week. [. . .]

JMQ: Later on, you disagreed also with Winnicott's technique?

I could go on for hours about that. It's part of the same thing. For example, with regressed patients he tended to act out. In his technique, if you like, he was the Ideal Mother, the all-giving mother [. . .]. But if patients didn't respond or became aggressive, he couldn't handle the negative transference. [. . .] But when you were with him it was very hard to dislike him, because of his smile.

JMQ: He began by working with Mrs Klein, then distanced himself somewhat – is that correct?

He had quite a strange relationship with Mrs Klein. You see, for him, she was so good. Mrs Klein herself was all right. But of course he was challenging her technique. He always said it wasn't Mrs Klein, it was the Kleinians.

JMQ: She never criticized him even though she disagreed?

What Klein did was to have big controversies with Margaret Little, but she never took on Winnicott directly. She attacked his technique through Little, because Little was very open about what he was doing (Little 1990). The point is, I think, that Klein always felt terribly guilty towards Winnicott because he asked her for an analysis and she told him: "Look there are many people who could analyse you our way, like Joan Riviere for instance." So he went to Joan Riviere. [. . .] I think he never forgave her for that, and she felt very guilty towards him. Mrs Klein liked him till the end.

(Tape 2, side A, 31 January 2004 and tape dated 6 February 2007)

Disagreements between the Middle Group and the Kleinians

The psychoanalytic approach in the case of "regressed" patients: a controversial topic

When Hanna Segal speaks of her memories of the early 1950s and of the controversies that followed the modifications to psychoanalytic technique introduced first by Balint then by Winnicott, Masud Khan and other members of the Middle Group, it is not surprising to note that, even today, she sometimes gives vent to some of the passion with which, in those far-off days, she defended the traditional psychoanalytic setting. From the end of the 1940s on, she was personally involved in the debates that opposed the Middle Group – made up of psychoanalysts who were followers of Balint and Winnicott and subsequently known as the Independents – and the two other groups within the British Psychoanalytical Society: the Contemporary Freudians, who were followers of Anna Freud, and the Kleinian group, led by Melanie Klein. The differences between these groups focussed mainly on the psychoanalytic treatment of so-called "regressed" patients – a controversy that came up against an initial stumbling-block in that the very concept of "regression" had no place in Kleinian thinking.

The debate in itself was not a new one. It goes all the way back to the one between Freud and Ferenczi in the 1920s. That controversy was reopened by Balint, when he took up Ferenczi's doubts about the validity of the classical psychoanalytic technique. Drawing on his clinical experience, Balint argued that, with a certain type of patient, the atmosphere of the analysis changed – interpretations no longer seemed to have any impact and were even felt to be persecutory or seductive. In his view, this regressed phase was a return to a primitive state of harmony with the object – "primary love" – from which the dynamic structure of conflict is absent; he called this phase the "basic fault" (Balint 1968). For Balint, this kind of object relation resembled similar states that had been described under different names by other psychoanalysts, as would be the case later with Winnicott and Kohut in particular.

As regards technique, Balint recommended that the analyst accept this regressed state and refrain from interpreting the patient's material in terms of the transference. He argued that the analyst should not present him- or herself as a separate and distinct object and should refrain from offering interpretations aimed at bringing the patient out of that regressed state. What was important in Balint's view was that the patient should discover his or her own way to a "new beginning". He thought also that there could be some degree of physical contact between analyst and patient – certain gestures such as holding the patient's hand during a session are necessary enactments if non-verbal communication is to be maintained when verbal communication is no longer possible. According to Balint, accepting the experience of regression and acting-out meant that the emphasis was placed on the mutual sharing of the experience in the analysis; he argued that this was an important therapeutic agent in its own right.

Kleinian objections

The psychoanalytic approach in the case of regressed patients which was adopted by Balint – and even more so by Winnicott – therefore differed substantially not only from the classical technique but also from the Kleinian approach, which found itself challenged on several points of technique. It could be said that the whole basis of the Kleinian approach lies in establishing a strictly-defined psychoanalytic setting, the essential prerequisite, Kleinian analysts would argue, for a complete unfolding of the transference. It is therefore necessary for the psycho-analyst to restrict him- or herself to the work of interpretation, without seeking to give any kind of reassurance – reassurance comes from the psychoanalytic situation itself and from the analyst's attitude, stability and capacity for relieving anxiety through interpreting the patient's material.

The disagreements between the two approaches had also to do with the interpretation of aggressiveness, destructiveness and envy. According to Balint and Winnicott, hate and sad-ism are secondary to the emergence of feelings of frustration, when the object is perceived to be separate and different. For Melanie Klein and her followers, however, the object is per-ceived from birth onwards, and from the very beginning there is a conflict between the life and death drives. Accordingly, hate and sadism are primary drives which must be interpreted directly in the transference relationship. As regards the idea that transference interpretations as such should be avoided, Kleinian psychoanalysts would argue that in cases of severe pathology the analyst must offer interpretations in order to open some doors that may help the patient move out of the impasse, because the patient alone will not be able to do so.

The differences between these two groups spring also from the fact that they have a different conception of narcissism, as I have pointed out in my discussion of interpreting separation anxiety in the course of the psychoanalytic process (Quinodoz 1991). For those psychoanalysts who follow Balint and Winnicott, narcissism is a normal developmental phase; it is therefore quite normal for narcissistic phenomena to emerge during analysis, so that, in their interpretations, they pay little attention to the conflictual aspects of the narcissistic trans-ference. On the other hand, Klein's followers see narcissism in a context of aggressiveness, destructiveness and envy; these psychoanalysts consider narcissism to be the outcome of a set of drives and defences that can be interpreted in all of their detail in the here-and-now of the transference relationship, in particular when breaks in the analytic encounter take place.

If the disagreements between the Middle Group and the two other groups – and in particu-lar the Kleinians – had simply involved questions that did not amount to challenging the clearly-defined psychoanalytic setting (Little 1990), the debates would probably not have taken on the kind of contentious and personal turn that at times became endemic. However, given that Balint, Winnicott and above all Masud Khan did not always follow the precepts of the classical setting, those analysts who belonged to the other two groups were in no mood to compromise; that issue, they argued, went to the very heart of the technique of psycho-analysis. Accordingly, they felt that enactments of that kind could well lead to damaging ethical transgressions on the analyst's part (Sandler 2002).

From the Middle Group to the Independents: opposing points of view

In his in-depth study of Balint's technique, Stewart (1992) expresses his reservations about Balint's approach to regressed patients – and that very fact highlights the extent to which opinions changed as the Middle Group evolved into that of the Independents. In Stewart's opinion, Balint underestimated the transference violence that is sometimes hidden behind the outward attitude of patients who have regressed to the basic fault stage. "In my experience, this description is not strong enough as it does not encompass the sheer malice, destructiveness and extreme envy that is also behind the lack of co-operation" (Stewart 1989: 223). Stewart goes on to discuss the difficulties that the analyst encounters in deciding which requests coming from the patient can be accepted and which cannot – one example being the patient's wish for the analyst to hold his or her hand during the session. Stewart's own experience, as well as that of some of his colleagues, taught him that although physical contact may at times have a positive therapeutic effect, at others the patient will subsequently have a frightening dream of being raped or sexually assaulted. "The inference is that the unconscious experience of the patient had been very different from that of an innocent physical contact" (ibid: 226). Stewart goes on to point out that the apparently calm atmosphere typical of this kind of regression may be due to the fact that persecutory sexual anxieties have been split off and evacuated. In spite of his reservations with respect to Balint – which show that he has moved away somewhat from his original position – Stewart still believes that, if the circumstances warrant it, there is room for a psychoanalytic technique that accepts regression (Bridge 1992).

But why so much passion?

Why did the controversy over these issues generate so much passion? André Haynal (1987) has attempted to answer that question. He says that part of the explanation for the intensity and at times tragic impact of debates among psychoanalysts lies in the intimate nature of the teacher–pupil/analyst–analysand relationship that is established in the course of analytic training, especially when the groups involved have a limited number of members. That emotional intensity is due also to the fact that the instrument which analysts – like artists – use in their work is their very own person (Haynal 1987: 153).

As I write, those passions of former days have somewhat subsided. It is important to note that very few Independents actually practise that particular kind of "holding"; most of them follow a strictly-defined (classical) psychoanalytic protocol. The Independent Group is no longer what it used to be – many of its members consider themselves to be "non-aligned" rather than direct followers of Winnicott or any of the other main protagonists. Also, the "gentleman's agreement" that governed relationships between the groups in the British Psychoanalytical Society is no longer in force. I would go as far as to say that those who belong to any one of the three groups that make up the Society today – Contemporary Freudians, Independents and Kleinians – would never have become what they undoubtedly are had they not been able to learn so much from one another.

Joan Riviere

JMQ: You were in supervision with Joan Riviere and Paula Heimann . . .

. . . and John Rickman of course. Joan Riviere had an enormous influence on me. She was an extremely impressive lady. Very very tall. Very beautiful. Very severe. It was said that in her lifetime she only wrote two good reports on students, one on Rosenfeld and the other on me! I know that isn't true. I know she wrote a good report on Henri Rey as well. She had a devastating wit. Students were very, very frightened of her and I'm not surprised. But she got on with me very well because we had interests in common, particularly in literature. She introduced me to a lot of English literature I didn't know. She let me have the run of her library – I was very deprived of books – and I introduced her to Guillaume Apollinaire. And so we had a lot of exchanges.

When I was in supervision with her she was extremely acute. You know, long before Mrs Klein described projective identification, advising not to interpret too directly to the patient because it would be like pushing back his or her projections, Joan Riviere said: "Don't be in a hurry to interpret the paranoid projections so much, just take them up in the material because the patient will tell you a lot more about his phantasies as long as they are safely lodged inside you, and that way you'll learn more." So, she had that intuition – don't just put the thing back. It was much later that we discovered the underlying reason.

Joan Riviere could be pretty cynical about things. She once told me: "You should always have one or two patients as a pot-boiler." I said: "What's a pot-boiler – is it to keep you thinking?" What she meant was for financial reasons – one or two patients who paid well! – as the English put it, "for the pot".

I wasn't married at the time but Paul was on leave and he stayed with me that first Christmas. Joan Riviere's husband had died shortly before, and she invited me along for Christmas day. I said I was sorry but I had a young soldier staying with me, and she said: "Well, bring him along." And they got on terribly well together because they had exactly the same sense of humour – normally, she didn't take to many people. She was quite a difficult person but she became very fond of Paul. It was a very good sign. They had similar cultural backgrounds. Very well read, and a similar, very sharp, very cynical wit which I'm completely deprived of! All my family has it, all Paul's children, but I don't. So she had a very deep influence on me.

JMQ: Did she have an influence on your clinical approach, for example on your acuteness in detecting the main issues for the patient?

Well, one's capacity to see that is more internal really. But she did develop it very much.

Paula Heimann

With Paula Heimann I learnt a lot too because I knew nothing, how to begin an analysis, etc. but it was a much more equal relationship. She was much more of a chum. Paul thought her very naïve which I didn't. I admired her, but I think he was right. [. . .] She was such an idealizer. You know, she would fall for things and not be able to deal with the consequences of what happened later. But he liked her and we got on quite well, but she never was the admired object, more like a senior colleague – and a good friend. We had good times together. It makes me think of some good Kleinian seminars, including with Paula Heimann, and Mrs Klein's child analysis seminar that I attended.

John Rickman

Certain things remain with me from other people. Two things about Rickman. One an anecdote: He was crossing a hospital garden to go to see a patient and a very disturbed patient, obviously murderous, rushed out at him, under some delusion or other. All Rickman said was: "Don't be afraid" and the chap stopped and just fell down.

JMQ: That reminds me of what my wife, Danielle Quinodoz, has described – interpretation in projection – mirroring what the patient says.

That's right. But now we have all the theory to back it. The other thing I remember of Rickman is his saying that when the patient keeps talking about one parent or has a transference of one parent – father or mother – always ask yourself: "Where is the other parent?" Otherwise I learnt mainly from my own work, from Mrs Klein and from Joan Riviere and Paula Heimann.

(Tape 4, side B, 1 February 2004)

Hanna Segal and Geneva

In 1955, Hanna Segal returned to Geneva in order to participate in the Congress organized that year by the International Psychoanalytical Association. Spurred on by Raymond de Saussure and Marcelle Spira, the small group of psychoanalysts in French-speaking Switzerland was expanding and becoming more international in outlook. Raymond de Saussure had lived in New York during the Second World War, and when he returned to Geneva he had many ambitious projects for developing psychoanalysis there – his active support and initiative were instrumental in enabling Geneva to host the IPA Congress in 1955. Marcelle Spira had just returned to her native Switzerland from Buenos Aires, where she had trained as a child analyst with the Kleinian group in Argentina.

The contacts that Raymond de Saussure and Marcelle Spira built up during that Congress no doubt provided the impetus for the current growth of psychoanalysis in that region of Switzerland. De Saussure was one of the founder members of the European Psychoanalytical Federation, and was elected its first President.

It was in 1955, at the International Congress in Geneva, that Marcelle Spira met Melanie Klein for the first time. As a result of that brief encounter, Marcelle Spira began to invite to Geneva several London-based psychoanalysts belonging to the Kleinian group – Melanie Klein herself and Hanna Segal, for example. After their meeting, Klein and Spira wrote to each other on a more or less regular basis between 1955 and 1960; the last letter is dated just a few months before Klein's death. In all, Melanie Klein wrote some 46 letters to Marcelle Spira and there are extant six rough drafts of letters from Spira to Klein. Their correspondence was made available to me after Marcelle Spira's death in 2006 at the age of 97.

My initial reading of that series of letters has encouraged me to make a much more detailed study of them. They contain discussions of several themes. Their content has mainly to do with the translation of Klein's *The Psychoanalysis of Children*; Marcelle Spira translated the footnotes into French. The work lasted many years, and in her letters Mrs Klein often asks how it is progressing. The exchange of letters mentions also the difficulties that Marcelle Spira was encountering in her attempt to spread Klein's ideas both in Geneva and more widely in Switzerland. Klein regularly encourages Spira to continue in this vein, and shares with her the difficulties with which she (Klein) had to contend in her own career. Here is an extract from a letter written by Melanie Klein to Marcelle Spira on 13 February 1956:

> I always thought it would be a very hard task to try to introduce into Switzerland and in particular Geneva where now de Saussure reigns, actual psycho-analysis, but I thought that you had not only the pioneer spirit to do that, but also the means to hold out for a longer time. Though difficult, I would not have thought it an impossible thing to do, but the precondition would be that you could wait until patients turn up, which I believe they would do in time.

A few months later, there seems to be rather better news of psychoanalysis in French-speaking Switzerland. Melanie Klein sent this reply to Marcelle Spira on 3 May 1956:

> I need not tell you how delighted I am that the Swiss are at last going to learn analysis, and my own experience has shown me that one person who has the perseverance, the capacity and the personality to stand up can produce the most far-reaching effect.

In her letters to Marcelle Spira, Melanie Klein mentions Hanna Segal

In the historical context of psychoanalysis as it was in 1956, Raymond de Saussure took the initiative of organizing an International Symposium in Lausanne devoted to the psychoanalysis of children. He invited, *inter alios*, Serge Lebovici and René Spitz. He invited Melanie Klein too, but she declined the invitation because she was unable to leave London at that time. Marcelle Spira wrote to Melanie Klein suggesting that Paula Heimann attend the Symposium since Klein herself could not be there. The following is an extract from the letter that Melanie Klein wrote to Marcelle Spira on 8 May 1956, in which she speaks very highly of Hanna Segal:

> In the meantime, we have had the Freud Centenary celebrations, and de Saussure, who was very friendly, approached me straight away and asked who could attend that special

meeting in Lausanne to represent my group. [. . .] I told him that I knew somebody more suitable and more capable to do this, and that is Dr Segal, who is also the one amongst us who can speak the best French.
[. . .]
I feel very happy indeed about this development and I was delighted that Dr Segal agreed to do it. I really think she is by far the best person both to explain my work succinctly and also not to be provocative, and de Saussure was very pleased when I told him that her way of presenting things was not provocative.

My impression is that he is quite determined to have her there, and when I remember his attitude one or two years ago it seems to me a tremendous achievement on your part. He was really very friendly and interested.

[. . .] I was delighted about Dr de Saussure's invitation to Dr Segal and also about her being so willing to accept it: the whole thing is the best news I have had for some time, and your part in it is fully appreciated by me and my friends [. . .]

With love,
Yours,
Melanie Klein

What struck me about Klein's letters was the warm and highly sympathetic manner in which she encouraged Marcelle Spira. It is a far cry from the emotional coldness and aloofness that is sometimes attributed to Melanie Klein. I would further point out that these letters are also one of the few instances we have of an exchange of correspondence between Klein and her colleagues. According to Elizabeth Spillius, in the *Melanie Klein Archives* in London, there is no trace of the letters written by her to other psychoanalysts; letters that Mrs Klein wrote to her family are still extant, but it would appear that she herself destroyed the rest of her correspondence.

Subsequent visits by Hanna Segal to Geneva

Hanna Segal's participation in the Lausanne Symposium was the starting point for her many trips to Switzerland. Since Marcelle Spira could not supervise her own analysands, she invited several London-based psychoanalysts – Melanie Klein, Hanna Segal, Herbert Rosenfeld, Betty Joseph and others – to Switzerland for that purpose. In her letters, Melanie Klein writes of the meetings Marcelle Spira and Hanna Segal had in London, during which they programmed the series of trips that Segal would make to Switzerland as well as Klein's own visit to Geneva (23–29 August 1957).

The fact that Hanna Segal speaks fluent French was no doubt a decisive factor in that series of invitations from French-speaking Swiss psychoanalysts in the 1960s and 1970s. In 1969, I remember attending the first Congress of the European Psychoanalytical Federation devoted to child analysis, which took place in Geneva. Hanna Segal was invited, as were Anna Freud and René Diatkine. I remember also that, during her stay in Switzerland, Anna Freud called on Herbert Graf – Freud's famous "Little Hans" – who was at that time Director of the Geneva opera house.

Later, from 1979 until 1989, Hanna Segal visited Geneva on a regular basis, once a month, for seminars and individual supervision. It was during this period that I got to know her better. I was impressed by the way in which she understood not only Klein's approach but also that of Freud himself. She explains and discusses the theories of different psychoanalysts in such a clear manner that her listeners can give a more solid foundation to their own thinking about psychoanalysis, linking theory and practice in a continuous to and fro movement. When, in 1989, she stopped coming to Geneva on a regular basis, I continued to meet her from time to time in London. That was when she agreed to preface my first two books *The Taming of Solitude: Separation Anxiety in Psychoanalysis* (1991 [1993]) and *Dreams That Turn Over a Page* (2001 [2002]).

Chapter 2

PSYCHOANALYSIS AND THE AESTHETIC EXPERIENCE

How Do Artists Succeed in Making Emotional Contact with the General Public?

As an adolescent, Hanna Segal was already passionately interested in art and literature. It is therefore hardly surprising that she devoted her first paper on psychoanalysis to that topic. "A psycho-analytical approach to aesthetics" was originally her dissertation paper for qualification as an associate member of the British Psychoanalytical Society; it was published in the *International Journal of Psycho-Analysis* five years later, in 1952. That paper was immediately seen to be a significant contribution to the the study of psychoanalysis and aesthetics. For Segal, the crucial issue that artistic creativity evokes is that of understanding how and by what means artists succeed in making emotional contact with the general public and in triggering an aesthetic response. Freud had discussed the question only *passim*. Segal took as her starting point Melanie Klein's work and her own clinical observations. She had discovered in the analysis of several artists suffering from inhibitions as regards their creative capacities that their inability to play freely with symbols was linked to the impossibility that they experienced with respect to the work of mourning. She suggested that working through the depressive position plays a decisive role in the symbol-formation processes that lie at the heart of the creative impulse.

In this chapter, I shall present the three major papers that Segal wrote on this topic, plus a short lecture that she gave in 2004. After "A psycho-analytical approach to aesthetics" was published in 1952, Segal wrote "Delusion and artistic creativity" (1974) in which, after drawing a parallel between psychotic delusions and artistic creations, she goes on to highlight the similarities and differences between them. For Segal, psychotics and artists share features that have to do with the depressive position, in particular the feeling that their internal world has been destroyed – hence the need to construct a new one. From that point on, however, their paths diverge: psychotics tend to create a grandiose and unreal self-image, while artists tend to restore their objects rather than their self and to stay in touch with reality.

In 1991, Segal wrote *Dream, Phantasy and Art*, in several chapters of which she explores the issue of artistic creativity and the aesthetic experience. She begins with a critical discussion of Freud's views on art in the light of her own ideas, then develops her hypothesis according to which the artistic impulse arises out of the depressive position: she argues that a work of art has its source in the existence of a destroyed internal world and the desire to restore it. The final chapter of the book deals with the relationship between imagination, play and art. In a public lecture she gave in 2004, Segal discusses artistic creativity in the field of dance, theatre and music. She describes in particular the part played by the body in these forms of art based on the artist's performance, a subject that she had not broached before.

Do Segal's ideas on creativity still have an effect on people today? It is always difficult to assess the significance of innovative ideas, but at times one comes across them again when least expecting to do so. So it was for my wife Danielle and me in March 2005, when we visited Ground Zero in New York. As we stopped in front of the murals that surround the hollow, we were surprised to read an extract from Segal's 1952 paper on "A psycho-analytical approach to aesthetics" beside a series of self-portraits drawn by children:

It is when the world within us is destroyed, when it is dead and loveless, when our loved ones are in fragments, and we ourselves in helpless despair – it is then that we must re-create our world anew, re-assemble the pieces, infuse life into dead fragments, re-create life. (Segal 1952: 199)

By what means did that extract find itself in such an unexpected place? Marygrace Berberian, the art therapist and social worker at the origin of the project, tells how it came about in an article entitled "Communal rebuilding after destruction: The World Trade Center Children's Mural Project" (Berberian 2003). She shaped the project in her mind in the immediate aftermath of the 9/11 attacks: "It was an almost insurmountable pain, which fuelled the fear, anger, and sadness that we felt as individuals and as a community. Artistic expression immediately alleviated the pain of a community struggling to make sense of an illogical sequence of events" (ibid.: 28). Children were the most affected; most of them imagined that a great number of buildings had been destroyed. Marygrace Berberian, who witnessed the collapse of the Twin Towers, was working at the time on an art therapy project in New York schools. "As an art therapist, I realized children needed to symbolically rebuild the Twin Towers. Children needed to rebuild what was destroyed" (ibid.: 30). Marygrace Berberian took immediate action and conceived the project of asking pupils to draw their self-portrait as a way of enabling them to express and process their feelings about the situation. Her project received huge support; March 2002 saw the inauguration, in the heart of New York, of this vast mural with its 3, 100 self-portraits of children and, amongst others, the extract from Segal's paper. The exhibition has been visited by large numbers of schoolchildren accompanied by their teachers or parents, in addition to the crowds of people who every day visit Ground Zero.

With her deep understanding of the spirit of the fundamental message contained in that extract from Hanna Segal's article, Marygrace Berberian gives this explanation for choosing that particular one: "Children were recreating life in their art. [. . .] Art is a creation; a recreation of past representations significant to the artist in the moment. The capacity to express oneself through line, colour, and form is a birth process. Creativity allows for describing, building and reconfiguring an injured object so that mourning can begin" (ibid.: 33).

A psychoanalyst reflects on the aesthetic experience

JMQ: What gave you the idea of writing about creativity in art and aesthetics?

Hanna Segal: I always had the impression that papers on art written by psychoanalysts were actually pretty simplistic, because they followed the content – which basically is always the same, whether it be a science fiction story or Oedipus Rex. They gave really no insight into the aesthetic values. Even Freud had nothing to say about aesthetic values.

How did it come to me that the creative process actually was reflected in the aesthetic value of the work? It must have been an inspiration. It so happened that at the same time I had in analysis a schizophrenic patient, a very inhibited writer of children's stories and a television director who was very grandiose. So, the similarities were in their processes of symbolization – that gave me the idea. I knew of course that concreteness plays a part in art. Now, the schizophrenic patient wasn't an artist. His sublimation – I couldn't say so at the time – lay in the fact that he became mad. He had this idea of a completely destroyed world. [. . .] The woman patient, the writer, became completely disinhibited. I don't mean disinhibited in the bad sense of the word but her inhibitions as regards writing were completely lifted. I do have the feeling, all the same, that the urge to address myself to the issue of aesthetics was because I wanted to link it up with my other interests. I had a strong feeling that analysis had a lot more to say about the creative process and the link between the creative process and the aesthetic value of the product than had ever been said before.

JMQ: One of your main ideas was the link you made between the creative process and the working-through of the depressive position.

Well, that would be my inspiration from Klein – the rebuilding of the internal world. In Klein's work there are a lot of ideas about that. When do you get a symptom and when do you get sublimation? In both, it's a case of working through the depressive position. So that wasn't a very big step I made; all I was doing really was applying this new concept I had borrowed from Klein to what impressed me in Proust and to various things I found in poetry – Rilke, for example, whom I quote in my 1952 paper on aesthetics: "Beauty is nothing but the beginning of terror that we are still just able to bear."

Where I think I went beyond Klein was in sort of putting Klein's work together as regards the restoration of the internal world. I think my original contribution was to show the degree to which such restoration is done and how it is actually reflected in the beauty of a work of art. The aesthetic experience of the person who is sensitive to this kind of phenomenon comes from an identification with the writer's or painter's ability to look at what lies in the depths, no matter how destructive, overcome it and turn it into a thing of beauty.

JMQ: I remember having had a similar aesthetic experience when I visited an exhibition of René Magritte's paintings. I wrote about it in my book Dreams That Turn Over a Page *(2001 [2002]). When I read about Magritte's life, I realized that much of what he painted was an attempt to overcome his anxiety states relating to his schizophrenic mother's suicide by drowning when he was just 14.*

Freud had the intuition that artists try to awaken in other people the same feelings that led them to create their work of art. You can see that the artist communicates at the same time both the destruction of the internal world and the capacity to repair it. It's as though he or she were saying: "I've been where you've been. And this is one of the ways out; this is what can be made of something you've gone through."

JMQ: We identify both with the artist's destroyed inner world and with his capacity to repair it.

And we feel uplifted. That's why tragedy doesn't depress you, but reading about concentration camps depresses you. Because the artist makes the unbearable bearable by giving it expression. That's why you don't find looking at Goya depressing – you find it uplifting.

JMQ: Indeed, in your 1952 paper on aesthetics, you make a link between creativity and symbol formation.

That's right. And I was interested in symbolism because I was treating artists and a schizophrenic and they were all having difficulty with symbols. The psychotic because he was psychotic, and the artists because their work consists in creating symbols. So, any disturbance in that field leads to disturbance in their work. In psychotics, the unconscious is sort of halfway between concrete and sublimated, but artists must be able to express the concrete in a much more symbolic manner. Art is very concrete – it appeals to our senses, to our eyes, to our ears, and so on . . .

JMQ: The work of writing also, perhaps?

. . . and reading. It's very very concrete. There must be an object, a real object. Either the play you're working on or the paper and pen you're writing with. The experience shows how to convert the perceptual impact in its most primitive form into the whole perception. One could say that the artist's job is to deal symbolically with the concrete while all the time being under threat from it.

JMQ: In Dream, Phantasy and Art *you significantly develop what you said in your first paper on aesthetics, and expand on Freud's views by adding some of your own new ideas.*

I don't know if I made much of it in the paper but a lot of it came after reading Stokes (1965) and through my own clinical experience – and also perhaps because of my own depressive tendencies. I think I undervalued the importance of the contribution from the paranoid-schizoid position. You know, there is in all artists not only a search for the ideal but also aggressiveness. I mention that in the papers. To what extent should a work of art reflect and admit aggressiveness, etc. But it's not only that. A work of art must transform very schizoid elements into art. Be able to include them, if you like. Something of that comes through in what nowadays we call action art and so on. But when it's let loose without any link to the depressive process, what you get may be just a black canvas or just a blue canvas or just a whatever . . . I think that is the contribution, if you like, of the schizoid state. But I still think that this has to be worked through and brought together in a depressive way, otherwise it just . . . well, it's a bit like pornography – pornography is not the same as art – so although all the pornography elements may be there they have to be transformed into something else. And I think I probably underplayed the significance of that.

JMQ: In that book, you explore also the part played by juxtaposing extremes in triggering an aesthetic impact. Could it be that at one of these extremes we find depressive elements and at the other paranoid-schizoid ones?

That's right. I think the contrast between the two and the conflict between the two give rise to a creative tension. After writing the paper on aesthetics, I discovered that Freud knew something about that. The "Minutes" of one of his Wednesday meetings has him saying that the *content* of a work of art is Oedipal but its *form* is dictated by much more archaic processes. And of course with Klein we have some insight into precisely those archaic processes. But Freud himself knew about that. And I think he knew that he was no good at that kind of thing – some people say that he couldn't understand the roots of creativity because they lie in those archaic processes.

JMQ: And that can be transmitted through the form of a given work of art, in music for example . . .

That's right, through the form. I think that the form a work of art takes is probably at least partly defined by innate abilities – when there is an inherited musical talent, let's say. Picasso's father was not a very good painter, but in the Bach family or the Beethoven family there were many musicians. So it's partly inherited, I'd say, and partly linked to infantile experiences. [. . .]

(Tape 6, side A, 12 March 2004)

JMQ: You emphasize also the fact that an artist has to work very hard because the integrative process demands a great deal of energy.

Yes and a lot of contact with reality. I have said that although an artisan may be an artist (sometimes he isn't, of course), every artist must be a first class artisan.

JMQ: And the influence of the artist's infantile experiences?

I think all artists must have their child part very much alive inside them, because they retain the child's early perceptiveness. They have this freshness, I would call it. It's only later on that the child is taught all sorts of rules, as it were. Such-and-such is pretty, such-and-such is this or that. I don't think I showed you the photo of my great-grandson at three or four months. You see these enormous eyes that are looking. And artists see things that other people didn't see before because they've managed to keep their own freshness of perception. They don't let perceptions be dictated to them. So they must be very much in touch with their child part, they must be very aware of internal realities and external realities – and also have a high degree of curiosity about the world and about perception. As a French writer once put it: "*Je suis un homme pour qui le monde réel existe*" ["I am a man for whom the real world exists"].
    I once had a patient who was a singer, but she was really too disturbed to make anything of her voice. It had partly to do with the fact that she loved herself and the image she had of herself so much that she had no love left at all for music. But she had a splendid voice and a powerful one at that, a very rare voice. But in her, it was clearly her transformation of a scream.

JMQ: Did she have inhibitions as far as singing was concerned?

Not quite in singing, but she did have too many inhibitions in her object relationships. She couldn't be in a choir, yet at the same time she couldn't learn enough from any of her teachers to be a soloist. She wanted to be born a soloist, so to speak. So she could never take it up as a career. [. . .] However, she still went on singing, joining this choir or that choir, singing for herself – but it was all so narcissistically centred that it didn't work. She wasn't an artist but, you know, she might have been.

JMQ: You lay particular emphasis on the relationship between reality and phantasy in the way both artists and psychoanalysts work.

I've always said that a psychoanalytic session is an aesthetic experience, because it deals really with the same problem – how to get in touch with terrible things and contain them and sublimate them and lead them to the point of restoration. I don't think psychoanalysis will ever become a science in the way that "science" is understood in a rather simplistic sense – you know, everything's "objective", and there are no emotions involved. It isn't quite like that, of course. Mathematics, for example, is certainly not science. Thought is in itself an aesthetic experience.

JMQ: The moment of insight – that is really an aesthetic experience.

And it is true also of science at a certain level. It has the same elements as in art.

(Tape 6, side B, 12 March 2004)

"A psycho-analytical approach to aesthetics" (1952)

Segal, H. (1952) "A psycho-analytical approach to aesthetics", *International Journal of Psycho-Analysis*, **33**: 196–207; reprinted (1981) in *The Work of Hanna Segal*, New York and London: Jason Aronson.

Segal's first contribution to psychoanalysis

Segal begins her paper by reminding us that, very early on, Freud wondered how a work of art succeeds in arousing emotions in us, and that his discovery of unconscious phantasy life and of symbolism made it possible to attempt a psychoanalytic interpretation of works of art. Although he wrote around twenty papers dealing with artistic production and made numerous references to the topic in many other writings, Segal observes that Freud was never particularly interested in aesthetic problems. If we examine more closely what he did write, we see that he approached the question of artistic creativity only indirectly; as is clear from *Leonardo da Vinci and a Memory of his Childhood* (Freud 1910c), Freud was more interested in elucidating the unconscious conflicts and phantasies which the artist expresses in a work of art. Other psycho-analysts have continued his exploratory work, including E. Jones and M. Klein; most of these papers show that works of art express in a symbolic way the infantile anxieties that we all experience.

In her paper, Segal approaches the problem of aesthetics in a different way from that of Freud, in her attempt to answer certain questions: "*What constitutes good art, in what essential respect is it different from other human works, more particularly from bad art?*" (Segal 1952: 196). These initial questions lead to others, such as: "*Can we isolate in the psychology of the artist the specific factors which enable him to produce a satisfactory work of art? And if we can, will that further our understanding of the aesthetic value of the work of art, and of the aesthetic experience of the audience?*" (ibid.: 197). Her observation that in artists who are in analysis there is a link between the inhibition of their creativity and their inability to go through a proper mourning process helped Segal to discover fresh answers to these questions. In her view, Freud did not have the necessary conceptual tools for finding the answers. In Melanie Klein's work, however, Segal discovered a certain number of features that shed new light on the origins of creativity in artists and on the aesthetic impact of works of art.

The aesthetic experience and the work of mourning

For Hanna Segal, the detailed description that Melanie Klein gave us of the work of mourning and its aftermath helps us to understand better the various stages in the artist's creative process, as well as the effect that a work of art has on the audience. According to Segal, the aesthetic emotion arises because the audience identifies with the artist – with the internal suffering that impelled the artist to create all the way through to the actual production of the work of art, the sign that working-through has succeeded. From that point of view, the introduction of the idea of the "depressive position" by Klein shed new light on how the mourning process – and the creative process – is worked through.

First of all, it must be said that the process of mourning and its working-through are not exclusive to artists. From birth onwards and through all the stages of life, human beings are confronted with a series of separations from and losses of objects, and these experiences have to be adequately processed. The manner in which adults process the work of mourning is closely linked to the way they manage to work through the losses and depressions that have occurred in early infancy. Melanie Klein gave the name "depressive position" to this early phase in child development in which the main anxiety concerns the loss of the loved object, both in the internal world and in external reality. She chose that term, with its connotations of depression, so as to highlight the fact that this developmental phase is the fixation or regression point for depression in adult life.

In her 1952 paper, Segal refers to the depressive position in order, above all, to explain the creative process in artists and the aesthetic emotion aroused in the audience. Later, she would supplement these ideas with her study of the relationship between artistic creativity and another developmental phase in early infancy, that of the "paranoid-schizoid position", a concept defined by Klein in 1947, the year in which Segal actually wrote "A psycho-analytical approach to aesthetics".

Working through the depressive position

Before setting out her own ideas, Segal summarizes what Klein meant by the "depressive position". It is a stage in child development that is reached when the infant recognizes his or her mother and other people – especially the father-figure – as complete persons, each different from the other. Where beforehand infants had only a partial and fragmentary perception of those in their immediate circle, these are now seen as real people. As a result, the infant's object relations undergo a fundamental change – and this generates an entirely new form of anxiety: as the infant discovers the importance of the loved object, the idea that that object might be lost creates intense anxiety. To this fear is added the feeling that it is the infant's own greedy and aggressive drives which will bring about this loss. The infant thus has to deal with a double danger: the fear not only of losing the loved object in external reality but also of seeing his or her internal world collapse because of the guilt feelings that are generated by the infant's phantasy of having caused the destruction of the object.

How can the depressive position be processed?

The infant comes out of this phase by remembering the good situation that prevailed earlier and wanting to re-create the loved object that has been lost inside the self and in the outside world.

> *The memory of the good situation, where the infant's ego contained the whole loved object, and the realization that it has been lost through his own attacks, give rise to an intense feeling of loss and guilt, and to the wish to restore and re-create the lost loved object outside and within the ego. This wish to restore and re-create is the basis of later sublimation and creativity.* (Segal 1952: 197)

Depressive phantasies thus give birth to the wish to repair and restore the loved object, but they stimulate further developmental growth only on condition that the ego can tolerate the depressive anxiety. "*If the object is remembered as a whole object, then the ego is faced with the recognition of its own ambivalence towards the object; it holds itself responsible for its impulses and for the damage done to the external and to the internal object*" (ibid.). On the other hand, if the infant's confidence in his or her ability to restore the good object inside and outside is too weak, the object is experienced as lost and destroyed, so that the internal situation is felt to be without hope: "*The infant's ego is at the mercy of intolerable feelings of guilt, loss and internal persecution*" (ibid.). To protect him- or herself from total despair, the infant has recourse to manic defences, a mechanism of which the essential features are denial of loss and separation and of the consequences that these may have, both in psychic reality and in the external world, as well as to other primitive defence mechanisms such as splitting, omnipotence and idealization.

A successful working-through of depressive anxieties has far-reaching consequences: the object becomes more personal and unique, and the ego reaches a more integrated state. "*Only when this happens does the attack on the object lead to real despair at the destruction of an existing complex and organized internal world, and with it, to the wish to recover such a complete world again*" (ibid.: 198).

Taking as her starting point the idea of the depressive position as presented by her, Segal draws a parallel between, on the one hand, processing the work of mourning in individuals who wish to restore their lost loved objects – represented by the internalized parental couple – in order to work through their depressive despair and, on the other, the creative impulse of artists who wish to restore, through a work of art, an earlier world that they thought was irreparably lost. In other words, re-establishing the parental couple in the internal world, which lies at the heart of the mourning process and reparation, is a feature both of the depressive position and of the work of creation.

All creators produce a world of their own

For an artist's work to be original, he or she has to create a world which is fundamentally "personal". From that point of view, what differentiates a work of art from any other production that is not artistic is the artist's capacity to create an entirely new reality. Even completely "realist" artists do not simply faithfully reproduce the external world, they impart something eminently personal in creating their work of art. For example, two authors living more or less at the same time, Zola and Flaubert, portrayed life as it was then – but they give us in fact two widely different pictures. This would also be true of two painters taking as their model the same landscape.

Segal is well aware of how difficult it is for a psychoanalyst to put into words the sheer variety of emotional experience that describing a concept such as the "depressive position" implies, whether in psychoanalysis itself or in art. That is why she often lets artists speak in her stead, artists who work in various fields and come from different backgrounds, in order to illustrate how she understands what the creative impulse is all about.

Marcel Proust: the need to re-create a lost world

For Segal, the French author Marcel Proust is, of all artists, the one who gives us the fullest description of the creative process. In his masterpiece *À la recherche du temps perdu* [*In search of lost time/Remembrance of things past*], Proust shows that the artist is compelled to create by his need to recapture his lost past. This is not, however, a purely intellectual memory of the past; what has to be recovered is the full emotional vividness attached to that memory. Proust manages to do this thanks to sensations and chance associations that bring back into his mind a forgotten fragment of his childhood. For example, it took him years to recapture the memory of his grandmother; when he succeeds in reviving her image, he can experience loss and mourn her. He notes that as soon as they reappear, such memories tend to disappear, so that only shadows remain. Proust then has the impulse to give them a new life; to do this he has to create a work of art: "*I had to recapture from the shade that which I had felt, to reconvert it into its psychic equivalent. But the way to do it, the only one I could see, what was it – but to create a work of art?*" (Segal 1952: 198). Thus, over the years, Proust brought back to life all his lost, destroyed and loved objects: his parents, his grandmother and his beloved Albertine.

The experience of mourning as a condition of the creative process

The foregoing extracts show that, for Proust, only the past and the lost or dead object can be transformed into a work of art. Segal insists on the unconditional necessity of acknowledging loss and mourning if the creative impulse is to exist: "*It is only when the loss has been acknowledged and the mourning experienced that re-creation can take place*" (Segal 1952: 199).

Proust confirms that point of view in his description of how he came to devote the final years of his life to writing. One day, after a long absence, he came back to look up some old friends, but when he found them, they all appeared to him as useless and ridiculous ruins – many of them, indeed, were already dead. At that point, something triggered in his mind: realizing that the whole world that had been his was about to disappear or was already destroyed, Proust decided to write in order to re-create the dying and the dead, with the idea of making them – and himself – immortal in the process.

Proust's writings are a magnificent confirmation of Segal's hypothesis: he was in a situation of mourning in which he could see that his loved objects were dying or dead. "*Writing a book is for him like the work of mourning in that gradually the external objects are given up, they are re-instated in the ego, and re-created in the book*" (ibid.). According to Segal, Proust himself describes how mourning leads to the wish to re-create the lost world. She says that this wish to restore is rooted in the depressive position as described in 1934 by Melanie Klein; Klein showed how mourning in adult life is a reliving of the similar work that had to be done in early infancy.

Inhibited creativity and failure of the depressive position

If, as Segal argues, the capacity to create depends on a successful working-through of the depressive position, it follows that any failure in this process will lead to inhibitions of artistic activity. Several artists whom she had in analysis confirmed that hypothesis; their inability to acknowledge and process the depressive position gave rise to inhibitions in their artistic activity or to the production of something other than a work of art. Segal goes on to give two examples of this.

Inhibition of the creative impulse in a painter

Case A was a young girl with a definite gift for painting. An acute rivalry with her mother made her give up painting in her early teens. After some time in analysis she started to paint again – but as a decorative artist would rather than "real painting", because her work failed to produce any significant aesthetic effect. For Segal, the patient had internalized a mutilated and destroyed father, after the unconscious sadistic phantasy attacks she made on him. However, the patient denied in a manic way any attempt at interpretation. One day, she reported a dream in which she saw a picture which represented a man lying wounded and abandoned. She felt quite overwhelmed with emotion and admiration for that picture: if only she could paint like that, she said, she would be a really great painter. For Hanna Segal, that dream meant that if the patient could only acknowledge her depression over the wounding and destruction of her father, she would then be able to express it in her painting. In fact, however, she was unable to do this, given the sheer strength of her sadism and the fact that her depression had led her to manic denial – in other words, as though everything was fine in the best of worlds. In addition, the dream showed that her denial of her father's death resulted in a complete absence of depth in her work, since all aesthetic feeling had been removed. It was as though neither ugliness nor conflict was ever allowed to disturb the neat and correct form of that young girl's work.

A writer's inhibition of the wish to write

Patient B was a journalist in his thirties who wanted to be a writer; he suffered, however, from an increasing inhibition as regards writing. An important feature of his character was a tendency to regress from the depressive to the paranoid-schizoid position. In his internal world, he had introjected an extremely tyrannical father-figure by whom he felt persecuted. He tried to defend himself by placating and serving that terrifying internal figure. As a result, he was often driven to do things of which he disapproved and which he disliked. He had a dream which showed how this conflict interfered with his writing: in the dream, he found himself in a room with some Nazi leaders who were going to poison him. In order to avoid being put to death, he said he could write something about them and thus make them live after their death. Of course, he had no wish to keep such hateful characters alive, and as a result he was inhibited in his capacity for writing. The patient complained also that he had no style of his own; in the course of his analysis, it became clear that the style of his writing belonged to the internal father-figure who dictated to him what he was to write. His submission to a terrifying internal figure was a chronic situation that prevented him from having any internal freedom to create: "*[H]e was basically fixed in the paranoid position and returned to it whenever depressive feelings were aroused, so that his love and reparative impulses could not become fully active*" (Segal 1952: 200).

Artistic creativity: an equivalent of procreation

According to Segal, creating a work of art can be looked upon as a psychic equivalent of pro-creation and the psychosexual genital dimension is a fundamental aspect of artistic creation. In support of this hypothesis, Segal states that all the patients she mentions in her paper suffered not only from inhibited creativity but also from sexual difficulties. She goes on to argue that working through the depressive position is a decisive factor both in achieving psychosexual maturity and in using the creative impulse.

> *Creating a work of art is a psychic equivalent of procreation. It is a genital bisexual activity necessitating a good identification with the father who gives, and the mother who receives and bears, the child. The ability to deal with the depressive position, however, is the pre-condition of both genital and artistic maturity. If the parents are felt to be so completely destroyed that there is no hope of ever re-creating them, a successful identification is not possible, and neither can the genital position be maintained nor the sublimation in art develop.* (Segal 1952: 200)

In her third example, patient C, Segal highlights the relationship between feelings of depression and genital and artistic problems. This artist, who was in his thirties, had suffered from depression since his adolescence and he complained of a complete lack of freedom and spontaneity. As regards his sexuality, he was physically potent but experienced no enjoyment at all in sexual intercourse. During the analysis, the constant pain he felt in the small of his back and lower abdomen – he himself described it as "a constant state of childbirth" – was seen to involve an identification with a pregnant woman representing his mother. This was not a happy identification, for he felt his mother had been destroyed by his sadism. Instead of producing a baby, says Segal, he felt he was destroyed like his mother. In this case, "*the inhibition both in his sexual and artistic achievements was due mainly to a feeling of the inadequacy of his reparative capacity in comparison with the devastation that he felt he had brought about*" (ibid.: 201). Unlike the other cases described, this patient recognized his depression, which is why his reparative drive was much stronger.

Symbol formation and the depressive position

The observation of patient E, a woman writer who had not been able to write for a number of years, allowed Segal to show how the patient's inability to experience depression led to an inhibition of symbol formation. This very disturbed patient suffered from depersonalization and food phobias leading at times to almost complete anorexia. One day she reported a dream which led Segal to think that the patient's main symptoms could be understood as a manifestation of her fear of death and that she tried to escape death by wearing various disguises. So far, she had mainly lived a "borrowed" life.

Some sessions later, the patient started complaining of her inability to write. Her inhibition was linked to the fact that she did not want to use words; for her, using words was tantamount to breaking an endless unity into bits, chopping things up, cutting things, making things finite and separate – all of which she experienced as aggressive acts. For Segal, this meant that using words was equivalent to a feeling of loss, and in particular the loss of the illusion of being at one with some endless, undivided world. The patient confirmed that hypothesis, saying: "*When you name a thing you really lose it*" (Segal 1952: 202). Consequently, using a symbol such as language meant accepting the separateness of her object from herself, acknowledging her own aggressiveness and losing the object. To protect herself against this, the patient had set up a system of defences that were aimed at avoiding separation and loss, including the loss of words as represented by writing them down. "*In order to write again, she would have to be stripped of her disguises, admit reality, and become vulnerable to loss and death*" (ibid.: 202).

Two years later, the patient had to put an end to her analysis due to external circumstances. Segal reports a session to which the patient came feeling very sad, for the first time since it became clear that she would be leaving her analyst. In the course of that session, the patient became able to experience a mourning process with respect to her analyst. In addition, after reporting a dream in which she was feeding the baby of another woman whose breasts had no milk, she said that words seemed once again to be meaningful and rich. She was able to experience sadness, guilt and anxiety over the forthcoming separation from the analyst – and also to discover that depending on the analyst could be a rewarding experience. Words acquired meaning and her wish to write returned again when she could give up the analytic breast as an external object and internalize it.

Sublimation, mourning process and symbol formation

That patient's material confirmed Segal's hypothesis that successful symbol formation is rooted in the depressive position. This is a topic that she does no more than outline in this paper; in her later work on symbolism, she develops the idea in more detail.

Agreeing with Freud's view that sublimation is the outcome of a successful renunciation of an instinctual aim, Segal goes on to suggest that such a successful renunciation can only happen through a process of mourning.

> *The giving up of an instinctual aim, or object, is a repetition and at the same time a re-living of the giving up of the breast. It can be successful, like this first situation, if the object to be given up can be assimilated in the ego, by the process of loss and internal restoration. I suggest that such an assimilated object becomes a symbol within the ego.* (Segal 1952: 202–203)

From that point of view, symbol formation, she says, is the outcome of a loss: "*it is a creative act involving the pain and the whole work of mourning. If psychic reality is experienced and differentiated from external reality, the symbol is differentiated from the object; it is felt to be created by the self and can be freely used by the self*" (ibid.: 203). Segal draws the conclusion that the creation of symbols, the symbolic elaboration of a theme, is the very essence of art.

What differentiates a successful artist from an unsuccessful one?

Segal approaches this crucial question from several different angles. In the first place, she says that artists must have an acute sense of reality, both as regards internal reality and in relation to the material of their art. On the first point, she gives the example of Proust who had a real insight into the phantasy world of the people inside him. On the second point, artists must have an acute sense of how to make use of their material, be it words, sounds, paints or clay. "*The real artist, being aware of his internal world which he must express, and of the external materials with which he works, can in all consciousness use the material to express the phantasy*" (Segal 1952: 203). What distinguishes artists from neurotics is the fact that artists have a greater capacity for tolerating anxiety and depression. The patients Segal describes in this paper could not tolerate depressive phantasies and made use of manic defences leading to the denial of psychic reality. In contrast to them, Proust could fully experience depressive mourning. "*The artist withdraws into a world of phantasy, but he can communicate his phantasies and share them. In that way he makes reparation, not only to his own internal objects, but to the external world as well*" (ibid.).

How are we to understand the aesthetic pleasure experienced by the artist's public?

For the artist, the work of art is no doubt the most complete and satisfying way of allaying the guilt and despair arising out of the depressive position and of restoring destroyed objects. But what makes a work of art such a satisfying experience for the artist's public? For Segal, the aesthetic pleasure proper – that is, the unique kind of pleasure derived from a work of art – is due to a process of identification. "*Aesthetic pleasure [. . .] is due to an identification of ourselves with the work of art as a whole and with the whole internal world of the artist as represented by his work*" (Segal 1952: 204). In other words, every aesthetic pleasure has to do with reliving the artist's experience of creation. Segal agrees with what Freud wrote in his paper on "The Moses of Michelangelo" (Freud 1914b): "*What the artist aims at is to awaken in us the same mental constellation as that which in him produced the impetus to create*" (Segal 1952: 204).

Segal then discusses the philosophical concept known as *nach-erleben* (which could be roughly translated as living an aftermath, reliving). For Segal, this concept is equivalent to unconscious identification; the unconscious reliving of the creator's state of mind is the foundation of all aesthetic pleasure.

To illustrate her thesis, she takes the example of "classical" tragedy. In a tragedy, the hero is impelled to commit a crime, the result of which is always complete destruction – this corresponds to a picture of the phantasies that are typical of the earliest depressive position where all the objects are destroyed. According to Segal, the audience makes two identifications: they themselves identify with the author, and they identify the whole tragedy with the author's internal world. Nevertheless, in spite of the devastation that runs through the tragedy, the author succeeds in making his or her destroyed objects alive again, and, through that very work of art, they have become immortal.

Excellence in art

Segal goes on to suggest that two factors are essential to the excellence of a tragedy: "*The expression of the full horror of the depressive phantasy and the achieving of an impression of wholeness and harmony*" (Segal 1952: 204). She notes that the external form of 'classical' tragedy is in complete contrast to its content, and suggests that the impression of excellence arises from the contrast between two extremes: on the one hand there is a terrifying depressive *content* and, on the other, a strictly defined *form* expressed through the rules of the unity of time, place and action. Thus it is that order can emerge from chaos. "*Without this formal harmony the depression of the audience would be aroused but not resolved. There can be no aesthetic pleasure without perfect form*" (ibid.).

Ugliness, beauty and the question of aesthetics

Having examined "classical" tragedy, Segal feels she can make a more general point. To do so, she needs to use the words "ugly" and 'beautiful". For Segal, "ugliness" is what expresses the state of the internal world in depression – the destruction of good and whole objects and their transformation into persecutory fragments. As for beauty, it could of course be thought of as the opposite of ugliness, but for Segal the antithesis of beautiful is, rather, unaesthetic or indifferent. If, however, we look at the situation in terms of what is aesthetically satisfying, ugliness is an important and, indeed, essential component of a satisfying aesthetic experience. Rodin had already noted the role played by ugliness in the experience of beauty: "*We call ugly that which is formless, unhealthy, [. . .] immoral, [. . .] vicious [. . .]. But let a great artist get hold of this ugliness; immediately he transfigures it – with a touch of his magic wand he makes it into beauty*" (Rodin quoted in Segal 1952: 205).

If we now look at comedy in terms of ugliness and beauty, we can observe the coexistence of two opposites: the outstanding comic heroes of the past are felt, at a later date, to be mainly tragic figures – Shylock and Falstaff are two examples of this. Comedy usually includes an element of manic defence, although never in its complete form: "*The original depression is still expressed and it must therefore have been to a large extent acknowledged and lived by the author*" (ibid.: 205).

Beauty, the experience of depression and of death

The idea that ugliness is an essential component of the aesthetic experience applies to practically all categories of the aesthetic, except one. In "classical" beauty – the Parthenon and the Discobolos are famous examples – there is no apparent sign of ugliness whatsoever. Classical beauty, however, must have some other element that is not immediately obvious. According to Segal, the very idea of beauty contains such an element: complete beauty, it is said, makes us both sad and happy at the same time, and it is awe-inspiring. Great artists themselves are very much aware of the fact that works of classical beauty – apparently so peaceful – nonetheless embody elements of depression and terror. Segal quotes Rilke on this point: "*Beauty is nothing but the beginning of terror that we are still just able to bear*" (1952: 206). For Hans Sachs, this terror is related to the very peacefulness of the perfect work of art, which is so peaceful because it seems unchangeable and eternal – to such an extent that it is hard to bear. For Segal, what is terrifying is the fact that this eternal unchangeability is an expression of the death instinct – the static element opposed to life and change.

The role of the death drive in works of art

These reflections lead Segal to restate her hypotheses in the light of the concept of the death drive. Thus far, her contention was that a satisfying work of art is achieved through access to the depressive position and the sublimation which enables that position to be processed, and that the audience relives the artist's experience. However, she argues, to express depression symbolically the artist must acknowledge the presence of the death drive, in addition to depression and mourning: "*the artist must acknowledge the death instinct, both in its aggressive and self-destructive aspects, and accept the reality of death for the object and the self*" (Segal 1952: 206). Restated in terms of the drives, ugliness – destruction – is the expression of the death drive, while beauty is that of the life drive. "*The achievement of the artist is in giving the fullest expression to the conflict and the union between those two*" (ibid.: 207).

From that point of view, we could say that all artists aim for immortality; their objects have to be brought back to life, and that life has to be eternal. "*And of all human activities art comes nearest to achieving immortality; a great work of art is likely to escape destruction and oblivion*" (ibid.).

"Delusion and artistic creativity" (1974)

Segal, H. (1974) "Delusion and artistic creativity: some reflexions on reading *The Spire* by William Golding", *International Review of Psycho-Analysis*, **1**: 135–141; reprinted (1981) in *The Work of Hanna Segal*, New York and London: Jason Aronson.

A common origin?

Continuing her exploration of the nature of creativity, Segal here takes up the question of a possible common origin to both psychotic delusions and artistic creativity.

She bases her study on the analysis of *The Spire*, a novel by William Golding (1964). The story is set in the Middle Ages and, put briefly, describes the megalomaniac delusion of Jocelin, Dean of the Cathedral, who is convinced that he has been chosen by God to build an exceptionally high spire. At first, the reader is carried along by Jocelin's exultation, but little by little the outrageousness of the project becomes obvious. Paying no heed to the fragility of the soil – the church is built on a subterranean gallery – Jocelin forces his collaborators to carry out his unrealistic project and drags them, one after the other, into destruction, madness and death. In his description of the conflicts in which the protagonists tear one another to pieces, the author highlights their libidinal and aggressive phantasies – which, from the point of view of the unconscious, are particularly significant. The very richness of the phantasy content of the novel allows Segal to suggest a symbolic interpretation. She says that Jocelin's project was doomed to failure because it was based on two series of weaknesses. On the one hand, constructing the spire was simply a reflection of the grandiose aim that Jocelin had conceived – to have everybody doing *his* will, with no regard whatsoever for what they might be feeling. On the other, Jocelin's sadistic attitude towards the couples he was working with derives from his identification with a sterile parental couple, unable to create or to procreate, so that any project he may have cannot succeed. "*This structure cannot be maintained for reasons of guilt and reasons of psychic and external reality. The basis of his structure is that there was no sex between the parents*" (Segal 1974: 138).

Similarities and differences between delusions and artistic creations

For Segal, this novel is much more than a description of a manic delusion and its collapse. As in every work of art, it contains also the story of its own creation and expresses the conflicts and doubts the author himself has concerning his creativity: "*The agonizing question that the artist poses himself is: 'Is my work a creation or a delusion?'*" (1974: 138).

Segal argues that delusion and artistic creativity have both common roots and divergences with regard to mental functioning. They share aspects that belong to the depressive position insofar as both the artist and the delusional person have a vivid feeling of the destruction of their inner world and of their need to create a new one. That feeling springs from the hatred the infant feels towards the parents at an early stage in development when he or she is confronted with the loneliness of separation, jealousy and envy. But given that the infant also loves the parents and needs them, he or she feels guilty about having attacked them and wishes to restore them to their original state of wholeness. It is at that point that the reparative impulse comes into play. "*So both the artist and the person suffering from a delusion start with a common cellarage:*[1] *the destruction of the parental couple in their fantasy and their internal world; and both have the overriding need to re-create a destroyed and lost structure*" (1974: 139).

Here, however, the similarity between artist and delusional person ends and the differences begin. The latter wishes to create an ideal and omnipotent self-image, refusing to acknowledge that he or she was born of the creativity of a sexual parental couple. This is illustrated by Jocelin, who sought to satisfy his own egotism with no heed for the fate of those around him. The artist, on the other hand, is primarily concerned with restoring the object rather than his or her own self-image. That implies moving on from the paranoid-schizoid position, dominated by the fear of being attacked by the bad object, to the depressive position, dominated by the fear of damaging the object and by concern for the object rather than for oneself. "*From this difference, restoring the object rather than the self, follow the crucial differences between the artist's and the psychotic's relation to his creation and the means which he employs*" (1974: 139).

It follows that the artist can remain to some extent detached from the work of art since it primarily represents the object and not the self; the artist can therefore separate from it, finish it and move on to the next one. In addition, the artist, unlike the person suffering from a delusion, has a conscious perception of the difference between phantasy and reality: "*In that way his work is not only not confused with him, it is also not completely identified and not confused with his phantasy objects. He can see it as a symbol, and as a symbol it can be used for communication*" (1974: 140).

Segal's influence in the field of aesthetics

David Bell is the editor of two books which bring together contributions from several of Hanna Segal's followers, *Reason and Passion. A Celebration of the Work of Hanna Segal* (1997) and *Psychoanalysis and Culture. A Kleinian Perspective* (1999). In his Introduction to *Reason and Passion*, Bell writes: "'A psychoanalytic approach to aesthetics' has had a very wide influence far beyond the reaches of psychoanalysis" (1997: 12). I asked him to say something about the influence that Hanna Segal's work has had in the field of aesthetics.

JMQ: What was the response of artists and psychoanalysts to Segal's hypotheses?

David Bell: This is not something that can be answered in a general way. There are many in the field of English literature/aesthetics who are very involved in Kleinian ideas and are influenced by Segal. But there are others who won't have heard of her, and there will be some who would be hostile towards even the idea that psychoanalysis has anything to do with aesthetics. I don't think there is a broad answer.

The philosopher Richard Wollheim, whose main interest centred on the philosophy of mind and aesthetics, particularly painting, certainly viewed Segal's contribution as fundamental in terms of really providing a full aesthetic theory (Wollheim 1998). Building upon Klein, Segal's work added a new perspective and Wollheim drew particular attention to the way in which Segal's model linked the work of the artist and the aesthetic response of the audience within the same explanatory framework, and he viewed this as a considerable strength of her model.

The audience responds by recognizing (not of course consciously) the struggle of the artist to give form to his inner world through the medium of his work.

JMQ: And psychoanalysts: how did they react to Segal's ideas on the origin of the creative impulse? Did they develop her ideas further? Or did they develop other hypotheses in different directions?

I think that in the history of ideas, very good ideas do not occur very often. Take for example Klein's paper on symbol formation. However great Hanna Segal's work in this area, it is still a development of Klein's foundational work. But it does add something new, particularly the distinction between "symbolic equations" and "symbols proper" and also the link she later establishes between symbolization and projective identification. She wrote again on the same theme in the 1970s, where she developed her original idea even more.

She was asked at a subsequent conference, some ten years later, about her "new thinking" on symbolism. I remember her replying along the following lines: "Well, I haven't really had another good idea since then . . . I've developed my ideas in the sense of illustrations and clarifications and applications. But the fundamental idea has not changed very much. Good ideas don't come that often." Segal's answer brought to mind what Einstein said when asked a similar question. This is the story about someone asking Einstein, at a conference: "I always keep a notebook with me, to write down my ideas in case I forget them. Do you keep your ideas in a book?" Einstein is supposed to have replied: "I don't get good ideas very often; in my life I have only had two! And I tell you, I am never going to forget them!" There is something of that in what Segal was saying.

JMQ: Would you say that there is general agreement as to Segal's ideas within the British Psychoanalytical Society (BPAS)?

I would say that within the Kleinian group and broadly within our Society her influence remains very substantial, not only in terms of her written work but also as embodying a very rich tradition of thought. Within the Independent group the situation is variable, some people are very influenced and involved, others less so and others more critical. And similarly in the Contemporary Freudian group, leading figures like the Sandlers or the Laufers were very interested in Segal's views. But there will be others who take a completely different kind of perspective on the same topic.

I see Segal as very much a classical Freudian psychoanalyst in the sense that she is rigorous about technique, views insight as the fundamental aim and that her world-view is wedded to the tradition of thought, which both Freud and Klein so exemplify, that gives centrality to a tragic vision of the human condition. There is a dialectic in psychoanalysis between what one may call a "Romantic" and a "Tragic" view of the human being. Some take what I would call a more romantic view, or even a more spiritual view. For Klein love and hate are always dialectically related and the link between all creative activity and the need to repair internal damaged objects, i.e. the activity of "reparation", remains fundamental.

JMQ: Are other people in the British Society interested in aesthetics?

Yes, I would say that there is a great deal of interest in aesthetic questions, but I am not an expert on this. There is a strong Winnicottian tradition on aesthetics, which is different and doesn't give so much emphasis to that dialectic between love and hate; it locates more the source of creativity in the transitional object, in the transitional space and gives centrality to the capacity to play.

JMQ: Isn't a work of art always the expression of internal conflicts?

I think that there is a kind of difficult tension as the Klein/Segal perspective may seem somewhat tautological. That is, if we think of a great artist who was clearly very disturbed, then Segal would say however ill the person was, the fact that he could represent and symbolize his inner world in such a deep way shows that he had the capacity for sanity. This may represent itself *only in the work* and perhaps not in life. Artistic work, from this perspective, comes out of the capacity of artists to confront the destructive and mad impulses within themselves, and to give them representation. The tautology might be that one proposes that the work demonstrates sanity – but the only evidence for this sanity is the work itself. However, I do not think one can get away from that. Some may suggest that the work does not represent sanity but comes directly from the disturbance and this would, in my view, create a serious theoretical difficulty.

I think Segal's view makes sense theoretically. Segal is stressing that imagination isn't the same as fantasying or day-dreaming, i.e. imagination is real *work* (here she would be very much in accord with Winnicott, who makes the same distinction). The artist has a very sharp sense of reality – the reality of his own internal world, which he gives representation to, and also he knows very precisely the reality of his materials, the paint, the brushes, the canvas, what he can do with them, where the limitations are. This is evidence of his capacity for "reality orientation", sanity. However "mad" he is, the fact that the artist knows *his inner world and his material* is evidence of this sanity. Maybe in many artists, there is a particular capacity for being in touch with, even overwhelmed by, a quite powerful level of disturbance, a capacity to give this disturbance its place in the mind, to know it, rather than deny it (of course this is not something that can be consciously brought about). But – and this is obviously crucial – this is linked to a highly developed capacity for that kind of sanity that can grapple with the disturbance, hold the tension between being on the one hand completely overwhelmed and, on the other, denying the existence of the disturbance, and thus give it form and representation.

Some might take the critical view that what is being said here is that *by definition* the capacity to produce art represents their sanity. I think Segal would say yes, that's what I'm saying, by definition.

JMQ: I have often appreciated the clinical value of Segal's ideas in relating creativity to the depressive position. Do you think that this hypothesis centred on an internal drama can be generalized to all creative impulses, or can a creative impulse be based on the perception of beauty, for example of Nature or of an ideal?

I think it is true that Segal's work centres on her elaboration of the alive functioning of unconscious phantasy and her very substantial development of our understanding of the paranoid-schizoid and depressive positions. But to turn more specifically to your question, I feel pulled both ways. One could imagine that inspiration and artistic work might come solely from an apprehension of great beauty, that this apprehension results in the wish to give form to that beauty. This makes a kind of sense, but it is in my view too linear. I think there is no human act that doesn't take place within the dialectical tension of love and hate, the wish to create and the wish to destroy. Goethe describes this duality when he has Faust say: "Two souls, alas! Dwell in my breast." So the perception of beauty and the wish to give it form is also, I think, always linked to a wish to stop it from being destroyed (arising, that is, from an inner perception of a wish to do just that) so that it can be maintained, be given its place. So I don't think that there is any human act that does not reflect this tension (that is, between the wish to create and the wish to destroy).

I can remember reading a long time ago an article by John Berger, the novelist and excellent writer on art. He wrote that when an author writes, one of the deep inner motives derives from the fear of things disappearing into oblivion. He said that what we call "the fear of death" is not the fear of death per se, it is the fear of dying *with the unborn babies still inside us*. That is, we die with the things that we might have given birth to, left unborn, dying inside us. I thought this was a very profound comment and also one that one can link up with from a psychoanalytic perspective. If the artist can let his ideas go, give them a place in the world, then he, so to speak, can die, can be aware of his death without it being so persecuting. If he omnipotently holds on to his work, won't let it go – say because he feels that it is never good enough – then he dies with it and thus gives in to his wish to destroy his unborn babies, and that is the tragedy. So I think inspiration can come from the perception and the capacity to perceive great beauty, to be moved by it. But then the impulsion to do something with it, I think, must come also out of the recognition that there are always forces in us that aim to stop precisely that.

(Interview, October 2006)

David Bell is a training analyst and supervisor with the British Psychoanalytical Society.

Dream, Phantasy and Art *(1991)*

Segal, H. (1991) *Dream, Phantasy and Art*, London: Routledge.

Freud and art

A detailed study of Freud's ideas on art

In this book, Segal explores three topics that have always interested her – dreams, phantasies and art – and, in the final three chapters, she discusses a topic she had already broached in 1952 in her paper "A psychoanalytic approach to aesthetics", that of artistic creativity.

In one of the chapters in the book, Segal makes a detailed study of Freud's ideas on art. What he was predominantly concerned with was the eliciting of unconscious phantasies embodied in works of art. For example, in *Leonardo da Vinci and a Memory of his Childhood* (Freud 1910c), Freud attempts to reconstruct Leonardo's psychosexual development as a child; this led him to new discoveries: another form of narcissism and narcissistic object-choice, and the transformation of the nipple into a penis. He showed also that artists have the ability to endow their characters with an unconscious without the artists themselves being aware of it. For Freud, this kind of intuitive knowledge is part of the equipment of the artist and makes the work of art intuitively right.

However, says Segal, in most of Freud's writings the actual problem of artistic creativity is touched on only tangentially, i.e. the source of aesthetic emotion. What we enjoy in the poet's imaginary world or day-dreams are the wishes that are expressed in the work of art. These are not conscious wishes, but repressed wishes that are unacceptable to consciousness. We find them acceptable, Freud argues, because they are disguised, and the aesthetic pleasure we feel bribes us to accept the hidden thought. "*One could say that Freud, in describing the aesthetic satisfaction as no more than a bribe, a kind of wrapping for the real, instinctual satisfaction, makes light of the aesthetic experience itself*" (Segal 1991: 77).

What is an "aesthetic emotion"?

If what Freud describes as the emotions aroused by art are not the aesthetic emotion proper, what then is the true nature of this emotion? Art arouses in us a great variety of feelings, some of which are "associative emotions"; we feel moved because the work of art reminds us of some event or other or of a memory we have. For example, we may feel moved by a tune because we first heard it when meeting a lover. But there exists a particular emotion, distinct from these associative emotions, which Segal calls the aesthetic experience proper. The specific pleasure experienced in this kind of emotion can be attributed to the "significant form"; this pleasure derives from the relations between, and combinations of, the shapes, lines and colours that we find in visual works of art. "Significant form" is thus a quality common to all visual art.

Art and wish-fulfilment

Segal agrees with Freud that wishes are fulfilled through art, but this is not simply a matter of the fulfilment of libidinal or aggressive wishes. "*It is a fulfilment of the wish to work through a problem in a particular way, not what is understood by wish-fulfilment, namely, omnipotence*" (1991: 79). Segal goes on to suggest that a work of art is an expression of the working-through by the unconscious ego, the part that processes conflicts. Consequently, "*[the] nature of the psychic conflict and the way the artist tries to resolve it in his unconscious ego may throw light on the significant form*" (1991: 80). However, content and form, like the associative and the purely aesthetic emotion, cannot really be separated from each other without impoverishing the aesthetic experience as a whole.

According to Segal, the powerful impact of a work of art lies in the artist's ability to mobilize not only associative and aesthetic emotions but also deeper unconscious emotions. In order to do this, the artist has recourse to symbolism. "*I think that form, be it musical, visual, or verbal, can move us so deeply because it symbolically embodies an unconscious meaning. In other words, art embodies and symbolizes and evokes in the recipient a certain kind of archaic emotion of a preverbal kind*" (1991: 81).

Segal states that artists do not operate mainly according to the pleasure/unpleasure principle and then find their way back to reality, as Freud originally thought. She argues that the artist never actually departs from reality. *"The artist seeks to locate his conflict and resolve it in his creation"* (1991: 82); this is not the case of the day-dreamer, who tries to avoid conflict by a phantasy of omnipotent wish-fulfilment and a denial of external and internal reality. To accomplish this, artists make use of all the means that belong to their particular art form, as we can see with Rodin, for example. Rodin says that, in sculpture, emotion is expressed through the suggestion of movement, each position containing the remnants of the previous position. This, according to Rodin, is a general aesthetic law.

Art and the depressive position

Reparation: the search for an original new world

In this chapter, Segal notes that Melanie Klein's first paper on art, "Infantile anxiety situations reflected in a work of art and in the creative impulse" (1929), addresses itself to the sources of the creative impulse. In that paper, Klein bases her argument on the idea that anxiety, in particular persecutory anxiety, is modified by reparation. She gives two examples of this. The first is that of Ravel's opera *L'Enfant et les Sortilèges* [*The Bewitched Child*]. In that libretto, a little boy hurts a squirrel. The objects in his room come alive, are angry with the little boy and begin to attack him. They stop attacking him when, on an impulse of compassion, the little boy takes the squirrel into his arms. The second example is taken from the biography of a Swedish painter who felt compelled to take up painting because of the intolerable anxiety she felt when faced with the empty space left on her wall once a painting had been removed from it. These two examples enabled Klein to emphasize the link between reparation and the creative impulse; she would later show that this involved the shift from the paranoid-schizoid to the depressive position.

Segal then goes on to develop the hypothesis she put forward in her 1952 paper, "A psychoanalytical approach to aesthetics", according to which the creative impulse is rooted in the depressive position. The need artists have to create comes from their deep feeling that their internal world is shattered and from their wish to re-create that lost world. Segal emphasizes the idea that all creation is in fact a re-creation of a lost world, even though artists themselves may not be aware of this. They do not, however, re-create the same world but an entirely new one, a world of its own. In this chapter, Segal says that the paranoid-schizoid position plays a more important role in artistic creativity than she had thought in her earlier work. The dynamics of creativity involve the reparative impulses of the depressive position, which in turn implies that earlier mental states have had to be worked through – in particular the integration of the perception of chaos and persecution.

How can an aesthetic emotion be communicated?

By what means do artists capture and engage their audience? According to Segal, artists do not aim to evoke in the recipient of their art the same constellation of unconscious feelings that motivated them, as Freud had suggested. She says that the artist must find the means to communicate both the internal conflict and the reparative attempt at resolution, thanks to the symbolic expression that belongs to each art form.

In *Dream, Phantasy and Art*, Segal takes another look at what we experience as "beautiful" as opposed to "ugly". She argues that "beautiful" cannot simply be equated with aesthetically satisfying: *"The aesthetic experience is in my view a particular combination of what has been called 'ugly' and what could be called 'beautiful'"* (1991: 90). She develops her earlier point of view, no longer seeing, for example, in classical tragedy, the ugly as largely in the content and beauty as mainly in the form of the play. Ugliness is everywhere present, as are the destruction and death of the participants. The violence, however, is counter-balanced by a feeling of inner consistency and psychological truth, as well as by a certain harmony of form. It is the artist's work which produces the transformation. Taking the example of Picasso's *Guernica*, Segal shows how the painter managed to establish connections between the various elements of his painting, creating formal wholes and finding a rhythm, thanks to his constant work of integration. *"There is also an uplift – contrasting with the horror of the scene there is an upward lift of light towards the centre right, giving a feeling similar to that of a Gothic cathedral. The ugliness of the breaking up and devastation is transformed into an object of beauty"* (1991: 92). In other words, we may find that something is "pretty", but not "beautiful" unless the dark side of life also is taken into account, albeit unconsciously.

The role of aggressiveness in artistic creation

Segal points out that true reparation, in contrast to manic reparation, must include an acknowledgement of aggression and its effect. She cites several works of art in which aggressiveness and destructiveness are initially very much to the fore, then give way to re-creation. The first step in starting artistic work contains aggression, hence the writer's anxiety in facing the virgin page and that of the painter before putting the first brush-stroke to a virgin canvas. *"Once the first line has been written or drawn something flawless has been infringed and it has to be made good"* (1991: 93). For a work of art to feel alive, there must be some "flaws" in it – as in classical Greek art, for example, which never actually keeps to perfect proportions.

Other essential elements are that the artist's reparative work is never completed and that the finished product bears traces of this incompletion. According to Segal, it is extremely important that the resolution of reparation should never be quite complete, so that our imagination may complete the work internally thanks to the mental effort we put into it. *"Hence, I think, the feeling of inexhaustibility – we can look at a picture, or listen to a piece of music, read poetry again and again. We do not exhaust the possibilities of completion"* (1991: 94).

The reparative act lies in the creation of symbols

Segal observes that, in artistic creativity, the whole reparative act is in the creation of the symbol. She would later say that reparative impulses are in all of us, whether we are engineers or artists, but it comes most powerfully into art because art is basically symbol-making. *"All art symbolizes something. This is a speciality of the artist. You don't make bricks, you make symbols. Without symbolism there is no art"* (Segal 2004). By means of symbols, artists carry out the reparative reconstruction of their internal world, which becomes a new creation. Works of art have often been thought of as the artist's symbolic baby. The symbol is not a copy of the object; it is not equated with it, as Segal pointed out in her work on symbolism. It is a re-creation that is felt as having a life of its own. Artists not only re-create something in their internal world, they must also bring it to life in the external world.

Artists are creators of symbols, they are not dreamers. Quite the contrary, in fact: the artist's relation to reality has to be very highly developed – as we see with sculptors or with writers. They must have an acute awareness of internal and external realities and be able to differentiate between them. This is how Segal summarizes the artist's qualities:

> *The artist must have an outstanding reality perception of the potential and of the limitations of his medium, limitations which he both uses and tries to overcome. He is not only a dreamer, but a supreme artisan. An artisan may not be an artist, but an artist must be an artisan. And he is usually acutely aware of it.* (1991: 96)

The art of the biographer

Segal takes another example, that of writing a biography, in order to highlight the two main stages of this process that are difficult to reconcile. The first stage is that of a more or less conscious identification with the subject, which is an essential motive for following in the hero's footsteps. In the second, there is a kind of fusion or merging between the self and the ideal object. The artist must, however, break free of that state of fusion in order to be creative. It is for this reason that the true biographic process begins precisely at the point where this kind of identification breaks down and makes way for the creative impulse based on the need to restore a whole object experienced as separate and distinct from the self.

The breakdown of idealization and identification generates a depressive pain linked to disillusion – but it is also the stimulus for creation. This was the case, for example, of Richard Holmes, who wrote a biography of Shelley to which Segal often refers. Holmes's comments on the role of the biographer illustrate many aspects of Segal's hypotheses. For Holmes, the subject of a biography does not exist in isolation – such people exist very largely in and through their contact with others. The biographer is like an observer, who has a real knowledge of the object with its good and bad aspects, a reality-testing which is an achievement of the depressive position. Segal adds that Holmes describes both the schizoid search for the ideal object with whom one identifies and merges, and the depressive pain the author feels in renouncing it in order to achieve truth. "*And in the description he seems to convey the sense of the need of separateness, the acceptance of the triangular situation from which one is excluded and the need to bring to life again not just the beloved object, but the whole world that object is related to. This is biography as art*" (1991: 100). Although biography may be an imaginative re-creation, it must be as close as possible to what might have been the actual truth.

Imagination, play and art

The relationship between imagination, play and art is the topic of Segal's final chapter in this book. Play and art both need imagination, but to different degrees. Unlike play, artistic creativity involves much pain and the need to create is compelling. Play, of course, may involve frustration and pain, but if it stops being predominantly pleasurable, children especially will abandon it. Art, however, cannot easily be abandoned; abandoning an artistic endeavour is felt to be a failure, sometimes a disaster. "*Artistic creativity has a lot in common with play, but it is anything but 'child's play'* " (1991: 109). Play has a lot to do with day-dreaming, but it is only incidentally a communication, whereas art is not only an internal communication, it is a communication with others. The artist, after all, must arouse an interest and make an impact on his audience.

In her conclusion, Segal writes:

> *All children, except the illest, and all adults, play; few become artists. Neither dream, day-dream, nor play involve the work, both unconscious and conscious, that art demands. The artist needs a very special capacity to face, and find expression for, the deepest conflicts, to translate dream into reality. He also achieves a lasting reparation in reality as well as in phantasy. The work of art is a lasting gift to the world, one which survives the artist.* (1991: 109)

"Motivation: the artist and the psychoanalyst" (2004)

(Unpublished lecture and discussion at the Royal Festival Hall in London, on 21 September 2004.)

A dialogue with artists on the theme of the performing arts

In this public lecture, Segal returns to the themes that she had discussed in a seminar in which a few artists from various fields – dance, theatre, sculpture, for example – had taken part. She begins by summarizing the main points of her ideas on art in a very lively and easy-to-follow manner, beginning with the notion that artistic creativity is rooted in a reparative impulse. However, she says in reply to an actor's question, the need to repair is not the only factor; for Segal the predominant motive force in artistic creation is the search for symbols. To this is added, firstly, the artist's talent – which springs from his or her identification with the parents' talent – and, secondly, the artist's innate talent, his or her personal capacity to express the most extreme psychological states.

In the ensuing debate with the artists, Segal discusses the difference between the plastic arts and those based on performance such as dance, music or theatre. These kinds of art share with the plastic arts the fact of being rooted in artistic creativity, but there are a certain number of differences, the most significant being, says Segal, the importance of the role played by the body in these art forms. Here the aim – which is never actually achieved – is to have complete control over one's body; this is the case not only of dancers but also of actors, who must at all times control their facial expression and their bodily attitude. Violinists have to be able to control their fingers, singers their voice. In comparison with those in the performing arts, artists who work in the field of the plastic arts are more independent of bodily expression.

In addition, the performer has a particular kind of relationship to the composer of the musical score or the playwright. Performers do not make their own world come alive, but that of the composer or author. From a symbolic point of view, then, what performers do is restore parental creativity rather than their own. And yet, every performance is a new one, whether it be dance, music or theatre, and the performer has to be true to the text – otherwise, says Segal, it is simply perversion. Actors have to project themselves into a character different from themselves in order to become that person – so that the great danger is that they become completely identified with that character.

In concluding her talk, Segal comes back to the importance of the body. What strikes her, she says, is the fact that the performing arts also somehow seek immortality, just as the plastic arts do. However, although the pyramids are still standing in Egypt, she adds, that can never be the case of a performance, which does not live on after the performer. Performance always comes to an end.

I was wondering if it is associated with the relation to the body, because the body dies. I don't mean that I believe in immortality, and that a great writer is immortal except in a symbolic way. But the body dies, and therefore the performance dies. That is a recognition that our body will die. You will never see the same performance again, even if there is another performance.

Taking another look at Hanna Segal's views

Like Hanna Segal, Daniel Widlöcher has studied the relationship between psychoanalysis and the aesthetic experience, in particular as regards communication between artists and their audience. I therefore asked him what, in his opinion, are the points of agreement and of disagreement between their two approaches to this question.

JMQ: How relevant, in your view, is Hanna Segal's psychoanalytic contribution to the field of aesthetic experience?

Daniel Widlöcher: When we look back on Hanna Segal's work on aesthetic emotion, we cannot fail to be impressed by how comprehensive her writings on the subject are. In the first place, she takes care not to adopt a purely psychopathological point of view – the one adopted by Abraham, Freud and those who came after them. Just think for a moment of Abraham's seminal paper on the Italian painter, Segantini, and of the way in which he stressed the melancholic aspects and feelings of abandonment – features, as we know, of crucial import- ance for Hanna Segal. We can appreciate the sheer cogency of her approach through the significance she attaches to the depressive position and to the experience of loss of the object (especially loss of the internal object). There is a connection here between the psychoanalytic influence of Melanie Klein and the literary one of Marcel Proust. In Proust's writings, reparation after a loss is closely linked to the process of association and re-creation of memory traces of the past as a way of inventing a new kind of aesthetic sensitivity. With a more "Kleinian" approach, Segal over the years gave more weight to the protective function of the depressive position against persecutory attacks arising in the paranoid-schizoid position, as well as to the part played by the death drive identified with its aggressive component. She does not pay much attention to infantile sexuality as such – it is more taken into account in terms of the secondary gains arising from the eroticization of the work of art rather than as the primary motivation behind the creative act itself. Much the same could be said as regards her concep- tion of sublimation – for Segal, it relates to the constructions of the imagination in the service of repairing loss rather than to a displacement in the choice of object and aim of the drives.

She does not, of course, underestimate the manic component of reparative creation, but she ignores more or less that of melancholic megalomania. Her focus is indeed on the depres- sive position, not on the psychopathology of melancholy. It must be said, all the same, that Hanna Segal, as her observations make plain, deals with these issues as they impact on adults, without much reference to a possible ontogenetic hypothesis based on the infant's early development (I am thinking here of Meltzer's writings on the "aesthetic object").

JMQ: Does your own idea of "co-thinking" (Widlöcher 2003) have any relevance to the aesthetic experience?

I have indeed been wondering about that: does psychoanalysis open up any interesting perspectives as to the nature of aesthetic sensitivity rather than simply as to its effects? My feeling is that Hanna Segal makes no attempt to differentiate the creator from his or her audience. She does of course talk about empathy in her discussion of the relationship between the emotionally moved person and the creator (or performer) of the work of art – but in terms of identificatory processes in the widest sense of the term. What she finds more complex is the relationship not with the artist but with the work of art itself and the material used to create it. She is quite right to emphasize the cogency that exists between the organization of a work of art and the intentionality that lies behind it, but she goes back to the theory of "fore-pleasure" without paying too much attention to the idea of technique as opposed to that of tendency – Freud had a great deal to say about that. I would say, in fact, that what seems particularly significant in Hanna Segal's approach is the idea of symbolism. That outlook could perhaps be challenged, at least from a psychoanalytic point of view; it seems to me that we have to differentiate between symbolism in children's play and that in a work of art.

What I find lacking in Segal's papers on aesthetics is the notion that one of the functions of a work of art is to convey a message, and that function has two aspects – the work of art is, as it were, "addressed" to someone else, and that person "receives" it. Perhaps from that perspective we could establish a more significant relationship between aesthetic sensitivity and psychoanalytic communication, in regard to the "co-thinking" that is one of its main features.

The remaining issue is that of ugliness, a topic that would be worth going into in more detail. The idea that ugliness is the opposite of beauty does not strike much of a chord with me. Hanna Segal quite rightly relates beauty to Eros – but does that imply a link between ugliness and the death drive? In my view, Thanatos has to do with chaos, and chaos is not the same as ugliness. Like Hanna Segal, I would tend to think that ugliness is simply beauty that has ended in failure. But then, does that way of looking at the subject still have anything to do with psychoanalysis?

(Interview, February 2007)

Daniel Widlöcher (Paris) is a psychoanalyst and full member of the Psychoanalytic Association of France.

Chapter 3

THE PSYCHOANALYTIC TREATMENT OF PSYCHOTIC PATIENTS

The very first case of schizophrenia treated by the psychoanalytic method

In 1950, Hanna Segal wrote a paper in which she describes the treatment of a schizophrenic patient using a strictly psychoanalytic approach with only minimal modifications to the setting. Called "Some aspects of the analysis of a schizophrenic", that paper is of considerable historical value since it is the first-ever account of the treatment of a confirmed schizophrenic, suffering from a delusion and hallucinations, by the psychoanalytic method. Segal began by seeing him five times a week in a hospital setting and then at home; after some six months, she succeeded in establishing a true psycho-analytic situation similar to that of neurotic patients – the patient lying on the couch with the analyst seated behind him. Before Segal, other psychoanalysts had undertaken the psychoanalytic treatment of psychotic patients – but only after making significant modifications to the setting. Segal's approach was made easier thanks to Melanie Klein's work on the nature of the psychotic mechanisms she had discovered in early infancy. Here, I am thinking in particular of Klein's concepts of the paranoid-schizoid position and projective identification about which she had written in her 1946 paper, "Notes on some schizoid mechanisms". At that time also, two other pupils of Klein had begun analysing psychotic or borderline patients – first Herbert Rosenfeld and then, shortly afterwards, Wilfred R. Bion. In the 1950s, Segal, Rosenfeld and Bion collaborated closely and created an atmos-phere of research that was particularly favourable for the development of innovative ideas in a field of psychoanalysis that had for so long remained unexplored.

"Some aspects of the analysis of a schizophrenic" happens also to lie at the origin of Segal's later work on symbolism. At the very beginning of the analysis, she realized that Edward, her patient, found it extremely difficult to make use of symbols; he usually had recourse to concrete symbols, a type of thinking that is characteristic of schizophrenic patients – they cannot differentiate between a symbol and the thing it symbolizes. For example, when Segal spoke to him of his anxiety about being castrated, the patient felt that she was quite literally castrating him: for Edward, the *word* "castrated" was equivalent to *being* physically castrated. Later, Segal would develop her own ideas on symbolism and in 1957 she introduced the concept of the "symbolic equation", a primitive form of symbolism that she differentiated from true symbolic representation, which is the developed form of symbolism.

In the years that followed, Segal wrote several other papers on the psychoanalytic treatment of psychotics. In 1954, in "A note on schizoid mechanisms underlying phobia formation", she showed that ordinary neurotic symptoms may be governed behind the scenes, as it were, by early psychotic mechanisms of a schizoid nature. In 1956, she wrote "Depression in the schizophrenic", a remarkable paper in which she describes the tendency that such patients have to draw back from their depressive anxieties and get rid of them by projecting them into the transference. In 1975, Segal wrote "A psychoanalytic approach to the treatment of psychoses", a clear and concise presentation of the Kleinian approach to the psychoanalytic treatment of the psychoses in the light of her experience of 25 years' work in that field.

The three forerunners: Segal, Rosenfeld and Bion

JMQ: In what circumstances did you and Herbert Rosenfeld begin treating psychotic patients psychoanalytically?

Hanna Segal: How to speak about those years and to convey to you the atmosphere . . .? Two things, from my point of view. They were two marvellous years: I married, I had my first baby, I read my first paper. It was the time I was settling down in London and everything was going well for me in my private life and in the excitement of starting a practice.

You asked me about my relationship with Rosenfeld. We both started analysing psychotics and we helped each other: if he was away I could look after his patients or he could look after mine and we discussed things together quite a lot. Bion came later, most people don't realize that. But there were other people, younger people, interested in that area too so there was a tremendous atmosphere – particularly with Mrs Klein's new paper in 1946 – a tremendous feeling of discovery. Everything was going well. Politically, England came out of the War a much more progressive country than it ever had been before. So everything was sort of opening up and flowering.

JMQ: What was the impact of all these new ideas on psychoanalysis?

You see, Mrs Klein never analysed a real psychotic. But her idea of projective identification and splitting and the importance of the shift between the paranoid-schizoid and depressive positions – all this was an enormous input. It took years, and we still, I think, haven't fully understood all the variations as regards creativity and delusion. And certainly we haven't approached anywhere near enough the pathology of the paranoid-schizoid position. That only started with Bion really. It's not "excessive" projective identification, it's two different forms of that mechanism, the one pathological, the other normal. And our technique changed gradually in that, in my day, many of our interpretations had to do with phantasy; we sort of went along with that, not quite realizing that there were different levels of phantasy, and so to some extent we were colluding a bit with the patient.

I wrote a paper, "A note on schizoid mechanisms underlying phobia formation", in which I describe a patient who brought a whole quantity of dreams. [. . .] But in fact I was colluding with her all the time. She was bringing those fragments, I was interpreting them, without taking up how bringing this whole crowd of dreams was really an attack on my mind, dispersing my mind.

JMQ: As you say, we have to interpret not only the content but also the function of dreams in the transference.

Not just dreams, but all the various goings-on. And even though I knew that by then – it was after I wrote my paper on symbolism or about that time – I was still doing it. It takes time.

JMQ: The idea is still very widespread that the paranoid-schizoid position is "bad" because it corresponds to a regressive phase, while the depressive position is "good" because it corresponds to a more mature stage in development.

That's right. And there is a tendency to idealize the depressive position. There is a whole paranoid-schizoid world which is indeed a stage of development; people sometimes function by cutting off and operating – up to a point – on the depressive level, but the repressed anxieties are still there.

JMQ: Would you agree that there is a normal as well as a pathological paranoid-schizoid position?

Yes, indeed. You have to be able to establish a normal paranoid-schizoid position. We needed the theory of container and contained to help us work that out. It's normal for the child to project because that, after all, is his or her first means of communication. The infant cries, stirs mother's anxiety and mother reacts – after transforming, thanks to her capacity for reverie, the content of what she has taken in, she sends it back to her infant. Projecting into the mother's mind is part of the normal paranoid-schizoid position.

(Tape 4, side B, 1 February 2004)

JMQ: In your 1950 paper "Some aspects of the analysis of a schizophrenic", not only did you show for the first time that it is possible to treat a schizophrenic patient by psychoanalysis, but also you introduced the idea of concrete symbolism – a forerunner of what you would later call the "symbolic equation".

That was certainly very much acknowledged by everybody, including Klein. It had, of course, long been described as a schizophrenic mode of thinking; it wasn't that people didn't know about concrete thinking. Freud and Jones spoke of symbolism but Melanie Klein addressed herself to symbol formation and its vicissitudes. She was the one who really opened up the subject of symbolization and symbol formation. Her paper on Dick, the psychotic boy, opened up a whole new field: symbol formation in the development of the ego.

I pointed out to her that it wasn't true to say that Dick did not form symbols at all; his symbolization was extremely concrete. He would say *"Poor Mrs Klein!"* when she was sharpening a pencil, because he thought that it was herself that she was cutting! That's concrete thinking. Then I made the link between projective identification and symbolization. That was partly because I had a schizophrenic patient in analysis – the first time *that* had ever been attempted. Rosenfeld refers to his first case as psychotic, but his patient was really borderline.

JMQ: So Edward was the first schizophrenic patient to be treated by psychoanalysis?

Yes, that was, I think, the very first analysis, without any major modification to the setting, of an actual schizophrenic who started as acute but by then had been ill for some 18 months. His illness was becoming chronic and he was given up as a hopeless case – he was being treated only by electric shocks and medication, which in those days was virtually useless. With that patient, I discovered an enormous clinical problem: if I spoke to him of his anxiety about being castrated, I realized that he felt I was actually castrating him and that was it. Whenever he spoke, he was doing something very concrete – once he had left the hospital, we were not allowed to speak about any patients in the hospital because that meant they would be chewed up. You see, if he and I *talked* about them, we were felt to be actually chewing them up. So, if I was to analyse that man I had to go very deeply into it.

And then with my woman writer, her inhibition also had to do with concreteness. She would say that words would come out of the page and bite her. The originality of my contribution was to link all this with projective identification in the sense, as I put it in my paper, that symbolism is a tripartite relationship: the subject, the object and the symbol. It requires a person. Symbols don't exist per se, as Jung thought – as though one could list them in a dictionary. For something to be a symbol, there must be a person for whom it symbolizes that particular thing.

Now, if you project a part of your ego into the object then the object is equated with that; you cut it off from yourself and it becomes part of external reality. So in order to be able to speak to a schizophrenic patient you have to know this mechanism and be able to show him how he attributes to the analyst his eyes or his ears, cutting himself off from them; then he feels them to be part of the external world and not a product of his own thinking. That idea had a great influence, not only on the Kleinians, but on others too. I think, all the same, that this view of mine was very much enriched by Bion because I was thinking in terms of "excessive" projective identification – and he changed the quantitative into the qualitative. It's not really a question of being excessive or not, it's something different. Bion introduced the idea that there is a *qualitative* change in the projective identification. He did this in his first paper on the differentiation between psychotic and neurotic forms of mental functioning, pointing out that the nature of the projective identification in each case is different. Identification includes the perceptual apparatus, and that is very important – he shows primarily that the perceptual apparatus is fragmented and forms what he calls bizarre objects which are bits of the object plus bits of the projected self, imbued with hostility and very fragmented. So you don't have thoughts but fragmented hostile objects inside you. Later, of course, he extended the idea with his concept of the alpha and beta elements of container and contained.

JMQ: Did you work closely with Rosenfeld and Bion?

The work the three of us did in that period was very interlinked. I don't usually claim priority, but for some reason I do get annoyed when people think that Bion preceded me – because it looks as if I was doing all this work without ever referring to what he was doing! But in fact he wasn't yet on the map at that point; I was already a qualified analyst when he started his training.

Rosenfeld made an enormous contribution with his early papers about the superego of the schizophrenic. His understanding of the erotic transference is a tremendously important element. You know, a lot of the suicides that took place were misunderstood in those days – I'm thinking also about Hermine Hug-Hellmuth, one of the first child analysts, a real pioneer, who was killed by her nephew. Then there was this other quite promising Hungarian poet, who killed himself and everybody blamed the analyst – a woman – because all he wanted was for her to become his lover and people couldn't understand why she didn't give in to him; had she done so, they thought, he wouldn't have killed himself! You see, people just didn't have a clue. They treated this kind of erotic transference as though it were Oedipal. . . . But it's not, it's completely different. An erotic transference is a projection into the breast of a sexualization of the breast on a terribly primitive level, it has very little to do with the true Oedipus Complex. . . . If you suggest to a patient who is in an erotic transference an interpretation in terms of Oedipal feelings, the patient will experience that as a sexual act on your part.

(Tape 4, side B, 1 February 2004)

JMQ: Tell me about your 1956 paper on "Depression in the schizophrenic". That too was an original contribution you made, was it not?

Yes, and there are two historically important points I would make about that. I wrote that paper just before Bion published his article on the differentiation of the psychotic from the non-psychotic personalities. I had noticed this phenomenon beforehand in one of my own patients, but Bion was already working on his theory about this kind of differentiation. He was very impressed by my work, but I don't think it influenced him in any way because he was already writing his own paper on the topic – and it is indeed a fascinating paper. As I have said, we were very close – then, later, it all changed so much . . .

JMQ: And counter-transference? Weren't you something of a trail-blazer in that field too?

Yes, that's the second historical connection. [*Dr Segal's voice takes on a sad note here.*] It always amuses me to think about it . . . We had a little group around Mrs Klein when we sometimes discussed cases, papers and so on. And I was preparing this paper for the Congress – it was a little bit too long and needed cutting. I started with a lot of stuff about the counter-transference and Bion said, "Cut that out – nobody's interested in your feelings – they can see it in the material." A few years later he brought out a theory of counter-transference which became extremely important to us. You see, I think Mrs Klein agreed with most of our developments – but she was very cautious about counter-transference. Anyway, Bion's work was very illuminating for us in showing how the counter-transference works.

JMQ: In your paper on depression in the schizophrenic this plays an important role because your schizophrenic patient really pushes her depression . . .

I think I do say in that paper that I felt depressed. I felt like an audience watching Ophelia. And that was really my clue. In the original version, all the same, I make much more of the counter-transference – in those ten minutes that I was advised to cut out. I spoke about the fragmentation in my mind and the difficulty of this and that and the other . . .

(Tape 7, side B, 13 March 2004)

"Some aspects of the analysis of a schizophrenic" (1950)

Segal, H. (1950) "Some aspects of the analysis of a schizophrenic", *International Journal of Psycho-Analysis* **31**: 268–278; reprinted (1981) in *The Work of Hanna Segal*, New York and London: Jason Aronson, pp. 101–120.

An extraordinary observation of considerable historical value

The value of this paper resides in the fact that it is an account of the very first psychoanalytic treatment of a schizophrenic patient in which the analyst's approach is strictly psychoanalytic. What does "strictly psychoanalytic" mean when it comes to treating a schizophrenic patient? First of all, it means that Segal's patient suffered from a clearly diagnosed schizophrenic illness and, secondly, that Segal's approach was strictly that of a psychoanalyst – interpreting the material with only minor deviations from analytical technique.

The diagnosis of schizophrenia is absolutely certain

There can be no doubt that Segal's patient was indeed schizophrenic. At 18 years of age, when he was posted to India to do his national service, Edward began having delusional ideas about being imprisoned and suffered from aural hallucinations. Up till then, his childhood and adolescence had seemed relatively well-adjusted. In India, he was placed in a psychiatric hospital. When he returned to England, the consultant psychiatrist diagnosed "rapidly-deteriorating" schizophrenia, with a poor prognosis. Segal saw him for the first time in a military hospital in London. In that interview, he was completely withdrawn, retarded and apathetic. He felt that it was not he himself who had changed, but that he "had been" changed, thus expressing his feelings of persecution.

A strictly psychoanalytic approach

As regards what Segal calls a strictly psychoanalytic approach, this means, firstly, that she took great care not to step out of the role of the analyst who interprets, unlike some other psychoanalysts who tended to take on that of an ally or educator. On this point, Segal disagrees with Federn who, with his psychotic patients, took only the positive transference into account, recommending that the treatment be interrupted as soon as the transference became negative. For Segal, such an attitude would only deepen the split between idealized object and persecutory object – a split that is characteristic of the transference with schizophrenic patients.

Secondly, a strictly psychoanalytic approach means that from the outset Segal offered the patient five sessions per week, with the patient on the couch and her sitting behind him. With Edward, she was able to begin a five-session-per-week analysis when he was transferred from the military hospital to a private nursing home. At first, there was no question of asking him to lie down on the couch. After three months' analysis in the nursing home, Edward went home to his parents' house and the analysis continued with patient and analyst sitting opposite each other. In the sixth month of treatment, the formal analytical situation was finally established. "*The patient lay on the couch, associated and, at least consciously, expected nothing from me beyond analysis. From that time on my problems were the same as those of the analysis of a neurotic, i.e. the analysis of the patient's system of phantasies and defences*" (Segal 1950: 273).

Reassure the patient or interpret the negative transference?

When he returned to his parents' home, Edward was surprised to find that he was still having delusional ideas and hallucinations. He was full of rage and despair, because he thought that he had managed to leave his illness behind, in the hospital. Segal realized that Edward wanted her to be an unchanging good figure, and that he was afraid that he might damage that good image if she got too close to him and to his madness. Obviously he wanted her to reassure him, to become an ally against his persecutors – his parents and the hospital doctors whom he blamed for not having got rid of his madness.

At that point, Segal was faced with a problem that often gives rise to controversy: should a psychoanalyst reassure a very ill patient in a moment of crisis, when the patient is crying out for reassurance? Segal argues that reassuring the patient amounts to presenting oneself as the idealized object – but at the cost of reinforcing the split between good and bad objects. As the split deepens, the patient comes to idealize the analyst and to displace unconsciously the hostility that normally would be aimed at the analyst on to other people in the patient's immediate circle, who are less equipped than the analyst is to cope with such hostility.

In order to avoid reinforcing the split between good and bad objects, it is essential for the analyst to accept the negative transference and interpret it, linking it to the positive transference. That is the option which Segal chose: instead of reassuring Edward, she interpreted his fear of going mad and his suspicion that the analyst had turned into an enemy now that, since he was back at home, she was equated with the hated hospital doctors: "*In a way, we were alone with madness: it was either in him or in me. If anyone was driving him mad, it could only be I*" (Segal 1950: 272).

The interpretation of the negative transference has proved to be an essential feature in the analysis not only of Segal's schizophrenic patient but also in that of neurotic patients, because it is one way of avoiding a negative therapeutic reaction. As Segal points out, that is a decisive contribution of the Kleinian approach compared to other techniques that resort to reassurance.

> *By giving sympathy and reassurance the analyst becomes, for the time being, the good object, but only at the cost of furthering the split between good and bad objects and reinforcing the patient's pathological defences. The unconscious suspicion of the analyst is then not analysed but is acted out, and sudden reversals may occur when God turns into the Devil and the negative transference may become unmanageable.* (1950: 272)

While the analyst is experienced as "ideally good" the progress of the analysis is interfered with by repression into the unconscious of phantasies about the "bad" analyst.

Concrete symbolism in schizophrenics

From the very beginning of Edward's analysis, Segal observed that he would make use of symbols in a very peculiar way that she calls "concrete symbolism" – which is one of the significant features of schizophrenic thinking. What does Segal mean by this term?

Freud explored the language of schizophrenics in one of his metapsychological papers, "The Unconscious", written in 1915. He noted there that in these patients word-presentations are treated as though they are thing-presentations, and quoted the example of one of Tausk's patients who was both terrified and inhibited by the fact that he had a "hole" in his sock – for that patient, a "hole" actually *was* the female genital aperture (and not simply "like" the female genital).

As far as Segal's patient is concerned, she notes that he consistently made use of concrete symbolism and that this was a serious difficulty all through the analysis. She noticed it initially when she realized that, for Edward, being in hospital actually meant being in prison – and not being in a place *like* a prison: the hospital actually *was* a prison. "*The significant point which emerged in this session was his equating of the notion of 'being like something' and 'being something'. There was no distinction between the symbol and the thing symbolized*" (1950: 269). In the same way, when she interpreted Edward's castration anxiety, the mere mention of the word "castration" was felt by him as though she were actually and physically castrating him. In other words, for Edward, language was not a way of expressing symbolic representations, because he experienced words as actually *being* things in concrete reality. Segal says that failure in symbol formation often results in the poverty of thought habitually displayed by schizophrenics. I shall come back to this point later.

After this case study was published, Segal continued her exploration of symbolism and, in 1957, introduced the idea of the "symbolic equation" – a primitive form of symbolization which she differentiates from symbolic representation, a much more evolved kind of symbol formation, as we shall see later.

Defence mechanisms in psychosis

In her account of Edward's analysis, Segal describes the principal defence mechanisms used by her patient – in particular, splitting between an idealized figure and a bad one, disintegration of the ego and a series of rapid introjections and projections. Segal describes also his use of manic denial: after collaborating for some time, he would suddenly reject an interpretation. His "no" unconsciously meant that he was abolishing any experience he felt to be unpleasant. Segal therefore had constantly to pay careful attention to her patient's reactions. "*I had always to follow carefully what he was doing inside himself with any interpretation to discover how far he was trying to invalidate it or do away with it*" (1950: 273). In addition, Edward's persecutory delusions and hallucinations were linked to the omnipotence of his thinking. For example, in his delusion about being imprisoned, Edward felt that he was being punished because of a particularly agonizing phantasy: he felt himself to be a greedy child who had exhausted all the world's food supply so that, in his unconscious omnipotence, he feared that he had destroyed the whole world. Segal says that the schizophrenic has recourse also to repression: of course the phantasies of the psychotic, especially of the schizophrenic, are much more archaic and primitive. "*But that does not mean that in the psychotic repression does not operate and does not have to be analysed*" (1950: 278). That said, although Segal gives many examples of her patient's projections – in particular Edward's projection of his illness into his analyst – she never at any point mentions projective identification, a concept that is, all the same, implicit in her case study.

Evolution in the course of the analysis

Thanks to her work with this patient, Segal showed that typical schizophrenics could be treated by psychoanalysis with only minor deviations from strict analytical technique. At the beginning of his analysis, Edward was a deeply regressed psychotic and his behaviour was very infantile. Later, he became more like a latency child. He began to acknowledge that his delusions and hallucinations were not shared by everybody, and that, if he did not hide them, he would be considered mad. He thus became more able to distinguish between phantasy and reality. With time, the rigidity of his defences lessened and he gradually became capable of tolerating consciously some of his phantasies and conflicts.

Towards the end of the first year of treatment, there was a marked improvement. All his conscious delusional ideas disappeared. Edward was leading an apparently normal life and following a course at university. He was still preoccupied with his phantasies about soil erosion, but these were giving rise to sublimations. This improvement was in part genuine, but some of it was the outcome of a magic denial of his madness and to a splitting off and "encapsulating" his illness in an insignificant little buzz located in his ear.

After 18 months of analysis, Edward had a temporary relapse: his hallucinations returned, in the form of "voices" that he heard. Although that relapse showed that some schizophrenic mechanisms were still operating, it became possible to make a detailed analysis of the mechanisms underlying his hallucinations by bringing them into the transference relationship. For Segal, that incident might have brought about a complete breakdown had Edward not been in analysis.

Shortly after this, Edward began once again to have anxieties linked to splitting, idealization and persecution. The continued analysis of this kind of splitting led to a gradual bridging of the gap between the persecutory object and the idealized object. This process was manifested in many ways in Edward's clinical material. At the same time, there was a general improvement in his relationships. "*While he became freer to admit that in his phantasies I appeared in various persecutory figures, his relationship to me became incomparably more confident and warmer. I think he feels that he has found in me a friend, and if that is so, this is the first intimate relationship that he has ever experienced in his conscious memory*" (1950: 277).

Schizophrenic narcissism can be analysed

For Segal, that part of Edward's analysis shows clearly that schizophrenic narcissism is accessible to analysis, whereas Freud saw in schizophrenic narcissism a factor precluding analysis. For Freud, the transference neurosis was all that could be analysed – so that patients suffering from narcissistic disorders could not be cured by psychoanalysis, because they produce no transference. The later work of Melanie Klein showed that, in every case, there exists in such patients a relationship to phantasied internalized objects, and that a state of narcissistic withdrawal can be approached in terms of a relation to internal objects. Through his hallucinations and narcissistic withdrawal, Edward was able to have an experience of internal persecution in the transference. "*My voice appeared in the hallucination, asking for dreams. Canalized into the transference situation, the process became accessible to analysis"* (1950: 276).

A new approach to the analysis of schizophrenics

In concluding her paper, Segal highlights what was specific to the technique she used at that time – in 1950 – and in what ways it differed from that employed by other psychoanalysts, in particular by American practitioners who also treated schizophrenics. Frieda Fromm-Reichmann and Paul Federn, for example, argued that the analyst must not give interpretations that would introduce into consciousness any new unconscious material, since the ego of the psychotic is anyway submerged by it. Segal shows that she proceeded differently, bringing into the patient's consciousness new unconscious material whenever it was warranted. For example, at the beginning of the treatment Edward had very intense castration anxieties which were much less repressed than is usually the case with neurotics. It was not enough simply to interpret his castration anxiety; this did not diminish until Segal introduced new and more archaic material into Edward's consciousness. *"I had to interpret to him the underlying and entirely unconscious phantasy in which he identified himself with both his pregnant mother and her unborn child. His castration fear was partly a result of this phantasy in which he ceased to be a man and which his masculine self felt as a castration"* (1950: 277).

The differences between neurotics and schizophrenics

Unlike neurotics, says Segal, schizophrenics tend to repress the link between different trends of thought. That astute observation foreshadowed the idea of "attacks on linking" that Bion would introduce several years later, in 1962. As Segal put it in her 1950 paper: *"Schizophrenics, more than others, repress the links between different trends of thought. They often tolerate in their ego thoughts and phantasies which would probably be repressed in the neurotic, but on the other hand they repress the links between the various phantasies and between phantasy and reality and those links have to be interpreted whenever possible"* (1950: 277).

Another difference between schizophrenics and neurotics springs from the fact that the psychotic's phantasies are much more archaic and primitive. Repression, however, continues to operate in psychotics. That is why, over and beyond the material brought into consciousness by the return of the repressed, the analyst has to identify and analyse the repression mechanism in operation at a deeper level.

> *To take an instance: my patient produced consciously primitive phantasies of being poisoned, overfed or starved. These were not repressed, but what was repressed was the fact that these phantasies referred to his mother in the past and to me in the present [. . .]. The delusions about being poisoned cleared up after those other unconscious phantasies were interpreted and connected with the conscious delusions.* (1950: 278)

Segal says that she tried to analyse in this psychotic patient all the important resistances, and to interpret the unconscious material at the level of the greatest anxiety, much as she would have done with a neurotic patient. In her conclusion to this paper, written in 1950, Segal says that in her view the analysis confirmed the diagnosis of schizophrenia and that, even though after three years of treatment Edward seemed to have recovered, his defence mechanisms remained psychotic. In her postscript to this case, written thirty years later, in 1980, Segal tells us that, after four years of analysis, Edward put an end to his treatment in a hypomanic manner, under the pressure of external and internal factors. He remained well for approximately twenty years, then had another breakdown. At that point he began analysis with another psychoanalyst.

"A note on schizoid mechanisms underlying phobia formation" (1954)

Segal, H. (1954) "A note on schizoid mechanisms underlying phobia formation", *International Journal of Psycho-Analysis*, **35**: 238–241; reprinted (1981) in *The Work of Hanna Segal*, New York and London: Jason Aronson, pp. 137–144.

Interpreting the underlying schizoid mechanisms is helpful

In this paper, Segal shows how common neurotic symptoms may be underpinned by early psychotic defences based on schizoid mechanisms. If interpretations are aimed exclusively at the neurotic level without taking into account the underlying mechanisms, they will have little effect. Segal here gives the example of a phobic patient who brought an endless stream of dreams to her sessions. Segal interpreted the content at a particular level without realizing that, at another level, she was unconsciously colluding with the patient. Gradually Segal began to realize that, by constantly reporting dream fragments, the patient was unconsciously attacking the analyst's mind with the aim of fragmenting it. That is why it is important to interpret the schizoid mechanisms typical of psychosis which may underlie a patient's neurotic symptoms.

Published in 1954, this paper outlines one of the themes that Segal was to develop some time later: that it is sometimes essential to interpret the function, in the transference, of a dream before interpreting its actual content. In her comments on this paper twenty-five years later, in 1980, Segal observed that her technique had evolved quite considerably since she wrote this case study.

> *I thought I was analysing the transference when I was interpreting to the patient her phantasies about me. Now I think I completely failed to analyse the transference properly. [. . .] Today, I would be more concerned with showing her what she was actually doing in the session in the moment-to-moment interaction between us. I would concentrate less on the detailed content of her phantasies and dreams.* (Segal 1981: 143–144)

Relations between Melanie Klein and her closest followers

JMQ: And when you discussed your work with Mrs Klein and Bion and others in the small group, what was Mrs Klein like with her pupils?

Hanna Segal: She was very open-minded and she had no difficulty. I'll tell you what she said once which amazed me. I had problems with a patient who was suicidal; there was an awful lot of splitting and projection and in discussing this Klein said: "Of course, your generation (she meant me, Bion and Rosenfeld) do it so much better than I could." Go into so much more detail, you see. In some ways she was, one could say, arrogant when it came to her ideas. You couldn't disagree. A paranoid-schizoid/manic-depressive position. But within those terms of reference she was very open-minded. And, for instance, Rosenfeld too spoke about counter-transference, so did I – all of us who spoke about schizophrenics did so, because we couldn't avoid it – so much of it is counter-transference. Klein was very sceptical but she never turned against it or inhibited it. It was a development that she was suspicious of, but she never . . . When people say that she quarrelled with Heimann because Heimann wrote a paper about counter-transference, that can't be true. She never attacked Heimann.

She told Bion she disagreed, she thought about it a great deal . . . For example, yes, when we spoke about the mother who transformed beta-elements into alpha-elements, Klein said: "Well, what else do you expect a good mother to do!" But she never inhibited Bion's work. So this idea that Heimann left because Klein couldn't tolerate differences is rubbish – it's just not true.

JMQ: Didn't some people give her the reputation of being severe and curt?

She was extremely tolerant, within those limits. If you disagreed with her about the paranoid-schizoid and depressive positions – she did lose some followers. She had a lot of followers after *The Psychoanalysis of Children*, but she lost some over her formulation of the depressive position. That would be Glover and Melitta. And later she lost some over the paranoid-schizoid position. That would be Heimann and others and, later, over what she said about envy. Those were fundamental things that she was quite strict about. But within those parameters she was extremely encouraging to the young. Unlike some great analysts, you know, who actually chose to have a mediocre following because they couldn't tolerate rivalry . . . Klein nurtured the creative people very much. [. . .]

JMQ: She lost followers also with her concept of envy?

I don't know how many but a lot of people were put off – too near the bone.

JMQ: That's surprising, because many people start reading Klein with Envy and Gratitude *and they do seem to appreciate it.*

And many artists, from that book, took a lot . . . It was extremely popular. But envy's not a nice thing. People want analysis so that they can be nice and feel comfortable. Many of my supervisees, when I have to start with ABC, will say: "I didn't say that because the patient doesn't feel comfortable with it", or "I didn't say that because *I* don't feel comfortable with it". And I tell them, look, if you and your patients feel comfortable, then you are in collusion.

JMQ: And how do your supervisees react to that?

I say that quite a bit. Some can understand it and go along with it, but others can't get rid of the habit of always wanting to cajole the patient – make the patient feel good . . . I say sometimes: "You're just bloody lazy. You like to relax and be comfortable. Because the other way is hard work – the patient will hate you and evade you and attack you. You have to work at it – not be comfortable."

(Tape 7, side B, 13 March 2004)

JMQ: Donald Meltzer was also one of Mrs Klein's pupils – and yours, too, isn't that so?

Meltzer's problem was that he was the favourite son. He was my favourite son, as a supervisee. I supervised his first case. I supervised his first child case. He was my most gifted supervisee. And the whole group idealized him a bit. [. . .]

JMQ: What did you think of his book The Psychoanalytical Process?

Well, already in that book I pointed out to him that he equates parents with analysts. I said to him: "Donald, the analyst *isn't* the parent. The analyst *represents* the parents." [. . .]

(Tape 5, side A, 1 February 2004)

"Depression in the schizophrenic" (1956)

Segal, H. (1956) "Depression in the schizophrenic", *International Journal of Psycho-Analysis*, **37**: 339–343; reprinted (1981) in *The Work of Hanna Segal*, New York and London: Jason Aronson, pp. 121–129.

The schizophrenic's anxiety when faced with the depressive position

In this highly original paper, Segal shows that in the course of their development, schizophrenics reach the depressive position, which is an indication of better psychological integration. But they find it intolerable and tend to get rid of depressive anxiety by projecting it into the analyst – so that they lapse once again into persecutory anxiety linked to the paranoid-schizoid position.

This can only be done by projecting a large part of their ego into an object, that is by projective identification. [. . .] By projective identification I mean that process in which a part of the ego is split off and projected into an object with a consequent loss of that part to the ego, as well as an alteration in the perception of the object. (Segal 1956: 339)

This paper proved highly significant for the technique of psychoanalysis. Segal shows how important it is to be in close touch with any depressive feelings that emerge in the patient and to examine how they are projected in the transference; the analyst will then be in a position to interpret this process and thereby avoid any negative therapeutic reaction on the part of the patient.

Segal develops this thesis at some length, taking as an illustration the analysis of a young schizophrenic woman. To summarize the salient features of the patient, I would say that as a child she was exceptionally gifted, had hallucinations from the age of 4, then for a long time went into progressive withdrawal and a slow deterioration of her personality. When she began analysis at 16 years of age, she suffered from chronic hebephrenic schizophrenia.

Projection of depressive feelings into the analyst

In the first series of sessions, Segal shows how that young patient managed to emerge from her delusion, so that her mental health improved. However, she could not deal with the depressive position nor with the progress linked to it. She then got rid of her depressive feelings by projecting them into the analyst and lapsed back into madness. In the second series of sessions that I shall discuss later, the patient again managed to emerge from her delusion, but this time she did succeed in coping with her depressive anxiety; she could therefore recover her healthy part and differentiate it from her mad part.

Let us go back briefly to the first series of sessions. In the second year of her treatment, the patient had become very silent on her return after a holiday. She would say only one or two sentences in the whole session. Her behaviour showed that she was hallucinating God and the devil; they represented the good and bad aspects of her father who had committed suicide when she was 15. She wept, looked terrified and continually picked threads from the cover of the couch and broke them off. One day, she came out of her silence and, looking at the analyst suspiciously, put great emphasis on the words "pale and thin". Then she put her hand to the base of her throat and gave herself two very slight scratches. Segal knew that the patient was very concerned about vampires – which are supposed to bite their victims at the base of the neck and leave two small scratches – and suggested the following interpretation: "*I said [. . .] that she felt she was pale and thin because she was being sucked by a vampire, and I drew her attention to the way she looked at me and said she suspected me of being that vampire*" (1956: 340).

The patient then spoke, saying that she did indeed have the feeling that, by basing interpretations on what the patient said, the analyst was living on the patient's life and sucking her blood. "*Such a direct verbal admission of feelings about me was most unusual in this patient*" (1956: 340). The following sessions were devoted to working through the young girl's feelings in this vampire situation. For example, in one session she said that by keeping silent and making the analyst talk, she was slowly sucking out the analyst's life-blood. The tone of her voice was quite different – all through that session she looked depressed, thoughtful and far saner than ever before.

The next day, the patient greeted the analyst in an unusually open and friendly manner. However, as soon as she went into the consulting room, there was an immediate change: she started to behave in a delusional and hallucinated way. Segal was surprised at this sudden change, which was in stark contrast to the previous session in which she had manifested a much better integration of ego and objects. The analyst, who had secretly been delighted by the manner in which the patient had greeted her, suddenly began to feel depressed when she saw the girl become madder than ever. Segal then thought that the girl's behaviour was symptomatic of a negative therapeutic reaction to the insight which, thanks to the analysis, she had gained during the previous few days without being able to rebuild something good inside her. That insight had brought the patient – for a moment – closer to full mental health. She was, however, unable to tolerate such an insight, and in particular the guilt she felt at having unconsciously "vampired" the analyst without having made anything good out of it; she therefore immediately projected her depressed and sane part into the analyst. In this way, she got rid of it by projective identification and by becoming even madder than before.

Differentiating the healthy part from the ill part in order to integrate them

The second series of sessions took place a few months later. Here we see that the patient did succeed in overcoming her negative therapeutic reaction and that, consequently, her healthy part and her ill part became much more integrated.

The patient had come back from the summer holiday withdrawn and hallucinated. One day, as she was dancing round the room, picking some imaginary things from the carpet and making movements as though scattering them around the room, it struck Segal that the patient must have been imagining that she was dancing in a meadow, picking flowers and scattering them. Segal then had the idea that the girl was behaving as though she were playing the part of Shakespeare's Ophelia. It was as though her gaiety was designed to produce sadness in her audience. "*If she was Ophelia*", thought Segal, "*she was scattering her sadness round the room as she was scattering the imaginary flowers, in order to get rid of it and to make me, the audience, sad*" (1956: 341). When Segal said to her that she seemed to be Ophelia, the patient immediately stopped and said, "Yes, of course", and then added, sadly, "Ophelia was mad, wasn't she?" It was the first time she had admitted that she knew about her own madness.

In the following sessions, the analyst linked this material to the death of the patient's father, who had committed suicide when she was 15. The girl had felt guilty – she thought she had killed him because he had rejected her. Segal added that by behaving like Ophelia, she could get rid of her feelings of distress by putting them into the analyst and thereby losing her sanity. Since the patient was still hallucinating and felt persecuted, Segal added that when she got rid of her painful feelings in this way, she had the impression that, when the analyst interpreted this to her, these feelings were being pushed back into her – so that she was being persecuted by the analyst.

The following day, the patient looked sad and quiet. Segal saw that she again started picking threads out of the cover on the couch – but instead of breaking them off completely, she began to intertwine them. The patient said: "You know, when Ophelia was picking flowers it was not, as you said, all madness. There was a lot of other things as well. What was unbearable was the intertwining." Segal asked: "The intertwining of madness and sanity?" "Yes", answered the patient, "that is what is unbearable" (1954: 342). The analyst then pointed out the difference in meaning between breaking off the threads and intertwining them. Breaking off the threads represented her breaking her sanity because she could not bear the sadness and guilt that sanity seemed to involve for her. By intertwining the threads, she seemed to be saying that she had recovered the healthy part of herself, and that there wasn't just madness in her.

From a therapeutic point of view, what conclusion should we draw from this example? For Segal, the analyst has to follow closely in the transference the whole process concerning the emergence of the depression and its subsequent projection. In this way, the analyst helps the patient recover, retain and strengthen the sane part of the personality.

Telepathy – an unexplored phenomenon

JMQ: Psychotic patients are often said to be telepathic, but the phenomenon itself can exist even where there is no pathology. Do you have any experience of that?

Hanna Segal: I have already spoken about Osowiecki, the telepathic friend my parents had. An extraordinary experience with him. Well, one was this tragic experience with my father and another tragic one – I had a very beautiful young cousin, Sophie, and lots of boys were in love with her. One day, one of them disappeared and it was Osowiecki who found him – he had hanged himself in a park. Osowiecki was used by the Alpine mountaineering organizations to help them find people who were lost. When I look at it, I would say that it was always telepathic, it was always contact with another mind.

Osowiecki was very funny. I had very little money when I was a student in Poland because by then my father wasn't well off. I had what would be the equivalent of a fiver – a £5 note – in my pocket which I was keeping for my rent; it disappeared and I was devastated so I thought I'd go and see Osowiecki – I hadn't seen him since I was 13. So, I went to him, reminded him who I was, told him that I had had a £5 note in the pocket of my coat and that it had disappeared. "Ah, you're a socialist, aren't you?" "Yes." "I can see you on the May 1st demonstration in your black raincoat. You had it in your pocket. Now, I see a hand gliding into your pocket. That's what you get when you get mixed up with socialists!"

Anyway, I don't know how it operates but I had in my practice a few experiences which were incomprehensible unless it was telepathy. I had it with two patients – and each time twice. The first time I thought it was coincidence, the second time I thought "Where did she get that from?" The first incident was when I was a young analyst. I was invited to give a lecture in Cambridge and I couldn't change a patient's session and she dreamt of a big placard with my name on it in Oxford. Nowadays it would be understandable because I am always lecturing all over the place. I went to give this lecture and a Professor Z, who was chairing the meeting, was so depressed that I couldn't think in his presence. It was like a heavy burden. I come back to London and my patient fidgets about a bit, then says, "Oh, I don't know why, but what comes to my mind is 'Professor Z' and the terrible thing that happened to him and his wife: they lost a baby." She added, "I don't know why Z is on my mind. Maybe you were away and I wished you ill or something like that", she associated. And I had a feeling as though she came into my mind. She said, "Look you're thinking of Professor Z, stop thinking about him, I've told you what happened, so let's get on with my analysis!"

JMQ: I too have memories of surprising things like that, so I think there must be some kind of communication on that level.

How, we don't know – but I'm sure it's not God and not magic! I have noticed it particularly in patients who are extremely dependent and always in your mind. Always trying to get at what's in your mind.

I had a similar experience with another patient, and it also was in two parts. One was when I had my first baby. I wrote to the patient that I was coming back on such and such a date and that the birth was all right but didn't give the name of the child. And she dreamt of Daniel in a cave of lions. I interpreted that it must be my son but she said, "You never wrote me that his name was Daniel!" and she brought my letter to her session. And the other thing she did was the following: I had new curtains put in the room and she brought me a painting which was a painting of those curtains – before she even saw them!

Freud speaks of "The Uncanny" (1919h). It gives us a feeling of something uncanny, something that we can't know.

(Tape 3, side B, 31 January 2004)

"A psychoanalytic approach to the treatment of psychoses" (1975)

Segal, H. (1975) "A psychoanalytic approach to the treatment of schizophrenia", in M. H. Lader (ed.) *Studies of Schizophrenia*, Ashford, Kent: Headley Brothers; reprinted (1981) as "A psychoanalytic approach to the treatment of psychoses", in *The Work of Hanna Segal*, New York and London: Jason Aronson, pp. 131–136.

The communications of psychotics are meaningful

This short paper presents, in a clear and concise manner, the Kleinian approach to the psychoanalytic treatment of psychosis. Segal's first account of the psychoanalytic treatment of a schizophrenic was published in 1950, and, by the time she wrote the present paper, she had built up some twenty-five years of experience in the analysis of psychotic patients. She begins by pointing out that, in those days, the pre-Freudian attitude to mental illness persisted in many psychiatric approaches to psychosis. Patients could be classified and diagnosed, but the content of what psychotic or schizophrenic patients communicate was often considered to be incomprehensible. From a historical point of view, the psychoanalytic approach to psychosis is based on the same hypotheses as Freud had adopted for the treatment of the neuroses, i.e. on his conviction that the verbal and non-verbal communications of his patients could be understood. After neurotic patients, Freud tried to extend his attempts at understanding psychological manifestations into the area of psychotic mechanisms, as evidenced by his analysis of President Schreber's paranoid delusion (Freud 1911c). He never at any time attempted, all the same, the actual psychoanalysis of a psychotic patient. In his view, psychotics were wholly narcissistic and could therefore not form a transference, so that he could not visualize how any psychoanalytic work could be done with them.

The first psychoanalysts who treated psychotic patients had the idea that in every psychotic there are areas of the personality which are capable of forming an object relation. These analysts worked mainly in the positive transference, taking support from the healthier part of the patient's ego in an attempt to enable it to become dominant in relation to the psychotic part. That approach was adopted in particular by Frieda Fromm-Reichmann, Edith Jacobson and Harold Searles. Later, Segal herself, W. R. Bion and H. Rosenfeld would take a different line, basing the treatment of acute and chronic psychotic states on the technique introduced by Melanie Klein.

The psychoses are rooted in the pathology of early infancy

Although Klein herself did not analyse psychotic patients, with the exception of Dick (Klein 1930), she came to the conclusion that psychotic illness is rooted in the pathology of early infancy. In her analyses of very young children, Klein was struck by the prevalence of the mechanisms of projection and introjection over that of repression. She discovered that infantile neurosis is a defensive structure, protecting the child against primitive anxieties of a paranoid and depressive type which resemble those found in psychotic states. It is during the first year of life that the superego begins to develop, along with object relations and the capacity to form symbols, to think and to speak. In psychosis, these functions are disturbed or destroyed; there ensues a confusion between external and internal, a fragmentation of object relations and of the ego, a deterioration in perception, a breakdown of symbolic processes and a disturbance of thinking. Thanks to analysis, however, the resolution of anxiety can lead to a re-establishment of symbolic processes and ego development.

The need to establish a reliable setting

The organization and setting of the treatment must provide for the patient the kind of holding environment in which his or her relationship to the analyst can develop without being broken up by the patient's psychosis. Organized support for the patient outside the sessions must be ensured, and it can be essential for the environment to be well disposed or at least neutral towards the analysis, especially if the patient has to be hospitalized. "*It is often through a failure of arranging a sufficiently stable management that the analytic treatment comes to grief*" (Segal 1981: 133). An appropriate psychoanalytic setting would include such things as reliability and regularity of the sessions, a certain uniformity of the layout, and a feeling of physical safety if the patient is violent, etc. "*But the analyst himself is a very important part of the setting. He must remain constant and not vary his role so that the patient's phantasies of omnipotent powers over objects can gradually undergo a reality testing*" (1981: 133).

Psychotic patients develop an almost immediate and usually violent transference to the analyst, which is why it is difficult both to observe it and to withstand it.

> The apparent lack of transference or its peculiar nature when it manifests itself is due to the fact that the psychotic transference is based primarily on projective identification. By projective identification I mean here the patient's omnipotent phantasy that he can get rid of unwanted parts of himself into the analyst. This kind of transference is both violent and brittle. The psychotic tries to project into the analyst his terror, his badness, his confusion, his fragmentation and, having done this projection, he perceives the analyst as a terrifying figure from whom he may want to cut himself off immediately; hence the brittleness of the transference situation. (1981: 133–134)

Sometimes the patient may feel completely confused with the analyst, so that he or she seems to be losing any remaining sense of self-identity.

The failure of the symbolic function

The psychotic patient's experience of the transference is very concrete, as is the experience of the analyst's interpretations. "*When he is in the state of projective identification, and the analyst starts interpreting, the patient is apt to experience it as a projective identification in reverse, that is, to feel that the analyst is now putting into him, the patient, the analyst's own unwanted parts and driving him mad*" (Segal 1981: 134). This concreteness of experience is a technical point of the utmost importance, observes Segal. "*It is essential for the analyst to understand that, when he interprets anxiety, the patient may feel that he is in fact attacking him, or if he interprets a patient's sexual feelings, the patient may experience it concretely as the analyst's sexual advances, toward him or her*" (1981: 134).

The concrete aspects of the transference have to do with the failure of the patient's symbolic function; that is why, Segal points out, it is useless to interpret to the psychotic as though he or she were a neurotic. "*Ordinary interpretations of the Oedipus complex for instance, could well be experienced as a sexual assault and in fact make the patient worse*" (1981: 134). It is above all the schizophrenic's language – with its concrete symbolization, its confusion between object and subject – and the psychotic transference that have to be the subject of the analysis.

Containment

Segal goes on to develop her ideas on the Kleinian approach to the treatment of the psychoses with a brief presentation of the psychoanalytic model of the container/contained relationship as introduced by Bion. In this model, the analytical situation provides a container into which the patient can project his or her intolerable anxieties and impulses, but the setting itself cannot produce a change. The analyst has to receive these projected parts, tolerate them, understand them, and respond by an interpretation which makes the projected elements more tolerable and understandable. "*The patient can then reintroject these projected parts made more tolerable, together with the functions of the analyst with which he can identify, allowing for the growth of a part of himself capable of containment and understanding*" (1981: 135).

A valuable theoretical approach

In concluding her paper, Segal speculates as to the value of this procedure. The psychoanalytic treatment of schizophrenia concerns only a small number of patients. Nevertheless, it is important to differentiate here between the value to the patient and the value to the community. Segal argues that, for the patient, in the rare cases where all the conditions are right, psychoanalytic treatment is the treatment that gives the most hopeful therapeutic prognosis for the individual: "*when successful, it is the treatment that deals with the very root of the disturbance of his personality*" (1981: 135). From the point of view of society, she says, the value of the psychoanalysis of psychotics lies mainly in its research aspect. The knowledge of psychopathology that psychoanalysis can give has enabled the development of other psychotherapeutic approaches, such as supportive therapy, group therapy, individual psychotherapy and community care. As Alanen (1975) has made clear, psychoanalytic research can also contribute to methods of prevention as far as schizophrenia is concerned; these have been developed to some considerable extent in Finland. The research aspect is not confined to the treatment of illness; the analysis of psychotics has enabled us to go much more deeply into mental phenomena in general.

The extraordinarily creative activity of psychotic patients

Mireille Ellonen-Jéquier is a psychoanalyst in private practice in Geneva. Her expertise in the analysis of children, adolescents and adults is second to none. Her training was decidedly Kleinian in outlook – Marcelle Spira and other well-known pupils of Melanie Klein, including Herbert Rosenfeld and Hanna Segal, gave her a solid basis in that.

JMQ: Some psychoanalysts would say that psychotic patients cannot be treated by psychoanalysis. What is your opinion?

Mireille Ellonen-Jéquier: In my experience, it is quite possible to have psychotic patients in analysis. I have done so all through my career: psychotic children first of all, then adolescents and adults. Many have done really well, and others have made at least some progress. But it does demand some understanding of psychotic mechanisms, otherwise it gets too complicated. I'll give you the example of a 5-year-old autistic boy[1] who did not speak at all. The head of the psychiatric department referred him to me, saying that there really was nothing much that could be done for the boy, but perhaps psychoanalysis could lead to some improvement. I treated him for five or six years. He made a significant recovery: speech, contact with other people, all this improved. He was able to go to school, make good progress – he even went on to pass his Baccalaureate and then graduate from university! At present, he is married and has a high-level job. And as a child he didn't speak at all, he was autistic, and the psychiatrists thought him a hopeless case who could at best make some slight improvement thanks to psychoanalysis!

Then there was the young woman who was catatonic when the head of the adolescent department referred her to me for psychoanalysis. She wasn't yet 20 years old, but she'd already been in psychiatric hospitals many times, where she had electroconvulsive therapy and sleep therapy. She would not say a word either, and her parents accompanied her to her sessions for the first six months. She made slow progress, after a really serious suicide attempt that left her paralysed; her doctors thought she would never walk again. For several months I went to the hospital to keep her analysis going – they let me have a room in which to do this. She began to walk again – much to the surprise of her doctors who thought that, given what the X-rays showed, she would never walk again . . . When you analyse someone, you often wonder what is going on in the nervous system networks. Physiology? At present, that patient is coping well. I've had lots of similar experiences with psychotic patients.

JMQ: In that young woman's case, there was no doubt about the diagnosis – she was really psychotic, is that right?

Oh yes; the psychiatrists said she had catatonic schizophrenia.

JMQ: When you have psychotic patients in analysis, don't you have to modify somewhat the classical psychoanalytic setting?

Well, that depends, sometimes you have to come to some arrangement with the patient's parents and psychiatrist, sometimes not. In very serious situations, however, it is important to modify the setting as much as you need to. For example, with the young woman I have just mentioned, I worked very closely with the head psychiatrist in the adolescent department. I saw that patient in my own consulting room five times a week at first, then four times (I have always given my psychotic patients three, four or five sessions a week). For the first few months she sat facing me, then she was able to lie down on the couch – so that was how we did things until the end of her analysis. While I had that young patient in analysis, the head psychiatrist organized day-care facilities in the psychiatric department, a social worker took care of the young woman's family and financial issues, a psychiatrist dealt with her medication, gradually reducing it as the analysis progressed, and there was also a family therapist involved. We all met together, including the day-care staff, once a fortnight for an overall progress report.

That helped us to understand what that young woman was projecting into us, in the form of different parts of her self, and how she was trying to set us up against one another. Of course, we had to avoid falling into the trap which the patient set for us and try to understand the mechanism behind it. After these meetings, it was very difficult for me to analyse the patient's strategy because she wanted unconsciously to act out in that manner and because we were running counter to her defence mechanisms. In psychoanalysis, as you well know, we try to avoid meeting people in the patient's immediate circle in order not to generate any interference with the psychoanalytic relationship. The situation was all the more difficult for me in that we represented a persecutory element for her when we put all the parts together and tried to understand what was going on, because, unconsciously, she wanted to maintain the splitting. So I had constantly to analyse the persecution that this represented. Being able to analyse these mechanisms did speed up the process quite considerably, but I had to be very clear-headed all the time so as to be able to process the situation.

JMQ: Are there counter-transference issues that arise for the various carers, not only for the analyst?

As regards analysing the counter-transference, I would like to share a story with you. I was watching a presentation by Paul-Claude Racamier, who specialized in treating psychotics and who was telling us about one of his psychotic patients. He said that after every staff meeting concerning that patient, all those who had taken part would afterwards go for a drink or two. I said to them: "If you like having a drink or two, that's up to you – but maybe you should see it as acting-out. Shouldn't you be trying to understand why you need to have a drink? What did the patient do to you to get you into such a state? What's the message that the patient is communicating to you – in other words, what is the meaning of your counter-transference?" Up till that point, nobody in that group situation had even thought of the counter-transference dimension.

It is tremendously important to analyse your counter-transference when you treat psychotic patients. For example, I was analysing a young psychotic adolescent, very autistic; he too had been referred to me by the head of the adolescent department. After his sessions, I would go and have the soles of my feet massaged in order to get back in touch with actual sensations – I had the impression that I was slipping into a smooth and flat world in which there was no room for any kind of sensation. At first I didn't realize that I was having these massages immediately after that patient's sessions. One day I did realize that, and I began to wonder about my counter-transference. I could then understand that the patient was conveying "something about himself" to me – a state in which he had no sensations at all. I was able to relate that to what I knew of his childhood – he had often been left all alone in his cot, which was all white, in a world in which sensations no longer existed. That was what he was communicating to me unconsciously; I was able, thanks to my counter-transference experience, to let him understand that. He then began to report significant memories of his childhood, and that really helped him to turn things round in his analysis.

JMQ: Psychotic patients find it very difficult to communicate using verbal language. How do you manage to understand them and communicate with them?

Take the example of the young catatonic woman who had not said a word for months on end. For the first few months of her analysis, she sat facing me, then she lay down on the couch. In her initial sessions, she would not say anything; I gave her some paper and pencils and told her she could draw whatever she liked. All she drew was a straight line, and still did not say anything. I felt I was faced with a void: what was I to understand and analyse when she remained so silent? First of all, I showed her that I felt excluded; perhaps she was telling me that she did not want me to penetrate her world or know what she was thinking. I felt that the line she had drawn was like a shut-off universe, all smooth, so that when I said anything to her she was making me experience the fact that my words just slipped away, like water off a duck's back – there was nothing I could hold on to on that straight line. Little by little, I showed her how much energy and power she was putting into closing down her world like that, as shut-off as that straight line without any bumps – just like when she remained silent – and that it was her ego which was actively doing that. Thus nobody would be able to perceive anything in her or know anything about her – hence my feeling that she was leaving me with a void.

That is one of the paradoxes about schizophrenics, and it is often difficult to analyse it. They seem to have a weak, fragmented ego that is both empty and non-existent; yet at the same time their ego is very strong, because in spite of its so-called weakness, it works at creating this void by means of a highly complex defensive structure that often catches the therapist out. Some psychoanalysts, for example, say that the schizophrenic ego has to be strengthened. But that was my way of trying to get inside that young woman's world.

I had another schizophrenic patient who would never say anything except "I don't exist!" When she came to her sessions, before lying down on the couch, I noticed that she would hug the walls as though trying to disappear inside them. I pointed out to her that she did not simply *say* that she didn't exist; by hugging the walls like that so as not to be seen, she was actually *doing* everything she could so as not to exist. At the outset, all I could do was analyse her behaviour, because there was hardly anything else – so I tried to point out to her what she was actually doing. It wasn't that she didn't exist, she was doing everything she could to make people believe she didn't exist, so that they wouldn't see her: that is why she didn't *cross* the room but melted into the walls, as it were. Later that patient made excellent progress and is now completely normal.

JMQ: With psychotic patients, you often have to use a vocabulary that refers to the body, a kind of pre-verbal language . . .

Yes, I analyse everything that the various aspects evoke in me in my counter-transference and I try to relate them to the usually few things that patient has managed to express. Counter-transference plays a phenomenal role. Thanks to the counter-transference, you perceive things that have been transferred into you, things that the patient cannot put into words. Let me go back to the patient who used to hug the walls before lying down on the couch. One day as I was looking in her direction, she disappeared from sight! I was terrified at myself – I wondered if I was going mad. I then realized that she was wearing an outfit that exactly matched the colour of the couch and the wall. That made me think of mimicry; I told her that it wasn't that she didn't exist, but that she'd done whatever it took to find the outfit she was wearing. And that took some doing! What energy she must have put into disappearing like that – mimicry just like animals, so that she wouldn't be seen . . .

When she was younger, people always used to say that in school she was mentally retarded and that she didn't exist. I pointed out to her that, behind this feeling of not existing, her ego was putting in quite some work – she was being really quite creative in doing this and in shoring up her defences. At first, she was surprised when I said that. I added that all the intelligence and imagination she was putting into creating her defences proved beyond a doubt that she was certainly not mentally retarded! I should add that in analysing her defences, I always showed her how, in the transference, she might be experiencing me as a very dangerous person – maybe that was why she felt she had to hide away. At the same time, she wanted to get back in touch with herself and establish contact – she was, after all, coming for analysis – but she was very scared that I might see her, find her. In the analysis, I said, we shall try to find out more about why she was afraid to be seen and to be found. It is of course no use describing to patients the defence mechanisms that they use if we do not, at the same time, show them that other people terrify them and can be experienced as dangerous. That patient gradually made progress, but I'd have to describe the whole process in detail; it was really so interesting.

JMQ: We usually tend to see defence mechanisms as a sign of the weakness of the patient's ego – but, for you, they are also a manifestation of an extraordinarily creative activity, is that right?

If we look at how our thinking about treating psychosis has developed, I would say that Kleinian psychoanalysts have been a great help – but, to my mind, they have sometimes over-emphasized disintegration and the destructive aspects of psychotics. I don't quite agree with them there: it's not simply a case of the death drive dominating the life drive. I think, for example, that disintegration is not just the outcome of destructiveness – it is also the ego's attempt at saving itself. In the *Gulag Archipelago*, Solzhenitsyn says something like: "If only I could dissolve into tiny particles . . . The little particles would scatter and disappear into space, and so my enemies wouldn't be able to catch me, because when they catch one particle, they couldn't catch the others!" For Solzhenitsyn, it was a fantasy, but for psychotics it is actual reality. I have often experienced that in my analytical work with psychotics – they break up into little bits and scatter everywhere, not only to attack and destroy their own perceptions and other people but also to save their ego by projecting a destructive image on to an external object.

JMQ: Psychotic patients tend to set up an immediate and massive transference. Have you ever felt afraid?

It's always massive. What struck me with these patients was that, at the time, you feel so caught up in it, invaded by it, that sometimes you just can't analyse what's going on. So, often it's afterwards, once the session is over, that your capacity to analyse comes back to you. My analytical experience has taught me that it's the outcome of a splitting process due to the over-condensation that the patient carries out on representations. Let me explain. It's as though psychotic patients abolish all space between representations, condensing the whole set, as it were. That way, they prevent others from entering their world. (I'd like to give a clinical illustration of this, but it would take too long.) It is, therefore, a paranoid defence, just as disintegration may also be that kind of defence. Thereafter, in the patient–analyst relationship (it's also the case inside the patient) a kind of para-organization of space is set up. The space between representations is split off and put to one side – hence the void, the nothingness. At the same time, the analyst is faced with a closed-off world, shut-in, over-condensed.

All these highly amalgamated representations go to make up a world without space into which you just cannot penetrate (think of the line that my patient drew on the sheet of paper). And to this massive transference corresponds an equally massive counter-transference: just next to the emptiness, you sense an enormous weight that can make you feel anxious that you're going to be crushed, you don't know what it means, you don't understand a thing because all the representations are amalgamated. That often makes me think of those vehicles you squeeze into as small a volume as possible before getting rid of them: nothing left but tiny little cubes in which you can no longer distinguish the different parts. In my opinion, that is the reason why you can think better only once the session is over, because then you can put some space back in between representations. Understanding and analysing these mechanisms enabled me gradually to help these patients reintegrate the idea of space between representations.

Here is one example – a dream, coming after two years of analysis, that highlights these mechanisms. A patient dreamt that she went to the toilet; what came out of her was a shape-less lump which was grey-brown-blackish in colour and which she looked at in amazement. I said to her she was giving birth to her amalgam. She then reported another dream: she unfolded this shapeless lump and, and unrolling it as if it were a roll of toilet paper, she discovered pictures of different landscapes, some of which were beautiful, others terrifying, all in various colours. That was her very first dream in colour! It was as though the amalgam had become de-condensed: the now-separate representations (the different landscapes) had enabled colours to be laid out as in a spectrum, whereas, beforehand, all the colours were amalgamated, hence the grey-brown-blackish mixture.

In analysing these mechanisms, we are faced with a paradox that schizophrenic patients put before us: they are simultaneously empty and full (massive, condensed). Another paradox: they are simultaneously disintegrated (their bits and pieces are scattered in space or projected inside objects) and over-condensed. Thus it is extremely important to analyse these various mechanisms as they appear in the transference and counter-transference. If we don't do this, the risk is that we fall in with the patient's defences and start thinking that he or she is "nowhere to be found", as it were, and in any case impossible to analyse.

JMQ: Sometimes, when a psychotic child is in treatment, the parents act out by interfering in the relationship between their child and the analyst. How do you cope with such situations?

In general, we would want the parents to have help too, if possible with another therapist. Some parents don't agree; you therefore have to see them too and show them that they are in a very difficult situation with their child and that talking about it to someone could be quite helpful, etc. Then they are more ready to accept the idea. It's probably better not to say: "Well, you have a problem", because they could feel that to be a narcissistic attack. If they still do not agree to see someone else, I try to see them – but that is always a problem as far as the patient is concerned. Of course, you always have to tell the child what you discussed with his or her parents, but when the parents act out it becomes very difficult to talk to the child about it – yet it has to be brought into the rest of the analytical material.

I'll give you another example, an adolescent girl – but the same thing can happen with younger children. This young psychotic patient I had in analysis would never say a word. Every week I would receive a five- to ten-page letter from her mother describing everything that had taken place. I started off by reading them, but after a few weeks I'd had enough; I wondered what I was acting-in in the counter-transference. When the next letter arrived, I put it on the table without opening it. When the patient arrived, I said to her: "Your mother has written to me again, but I'm not going to read the letter. You can read it if you want, and then we'll talk about it. . ." Then that adolescent – who normally never said a word – began to speak: "You abso-lutely *must* read that letter! Do you realize what it would mean if you didn't", and so on. She insisted so much that I was able to show her how she was using her mother to talk about her own self, after projecting her voice and her affects into her mother, so that the patient herself did not have to talk any more. You have to find a way of bringing the parents' acting-out into the session so that the patient can recover his or her projected parts. When that patient began talking, her mother stopped writing letters.

JMQ: You need to be very experienced to analyse psychotic patients. What was your own training?

I began by graduating in psychology, then had a classical analysis that lasted three years, and then a much longer analysis with a Kleinian psychoanalyst. I had regular weekly supervisions in the context of my training to become a member of the Swiss Psychoanalytical Society, and in addition to that I had many years of supervision with British Kleinian analysts such as Hanna Segal, Herbert Rosenfeld, Betty Joseph, Isabel Menzies, Donald Meltzer, Turner and others. Also, I was in supervision for two years with Alberto Campo, an Argentinian psychoanalyst.

When I decided to start taking patients into analysis, I was afraid that I wouldn't have any because everybody thought of me as a Kleinian! One day, after I'd made various tentative approaches, one psychiatrist decided to refer a 5-year-old psychotic boy to me for treatment: "Anyway, there's nothing to be done with him, he is so autistic. Look, we'll send him to her and see what she can do with him!" Quite a difficult situation when you're just starting out. The family spoke a foreign language in which I was not particularly fluent. After about a year or so the boy began to speak, and the doctors were so surprised that the psychiatrist asked me to come to the psychiatric hospital and read a paper on the subject. That's how it all began. One day I was attending a clinical presentation about that patient in the hospital; he saw me in the room, looked directly at me and said "Jéquier is a real live wire". That meant "Contact!", lines of communication . . . How moving it was to see that boy come out of the depths of his autistic state. From then on, quite a number of autistic or psychotic children were referred to me and people began to say: "She's *the* specialist for schizophrenics!" In fact it was quite distressing for me to have so many referrals like that, but I did learn a lot from them and it allowed me to discover new worlds inside myself that I have always tried to understand, re-analyse and process. Later I took on adult psychotic patients – I would never have been able to analyse them, had I not had the earlier experience of all that work with child and adolescent psychotic patients.

(Interview, November 2006)

Mireille Ellonen-Jéquier (Geneva) is a member of the Swiss Psychoanalytical Society.

Chapter 4

FROM SYMBOLIC EQUATION TO SYMBOLIC REPRESENTATION

Innovative Ideas on Symbolism

In 1957, Segal wrote her seminal article, "Notes on symbol formation". In that paper she wrote for the first time about the "symbolic equation", a primitive form of symbolism that is typical of the schizophrenic's concrete thinking; she distinguishes it from true symbolism, i.e. symbolic representation. The originality of this paper comes not only from the innovative quality of the concept itself but also from the fact that in making the distinction between symbolic equation and symbolic representation, Segal links the transition between the two to the development of object relations and of the transference. It was Melanie Klein who first opened up that possibility when, early in her work, she linked the development of the ego to the capacity to form symbols.

In her paper, Segal notes that her approach to symbolism is different from that of much of the psychoanalytic literature on the subject. Symbolism as such had never really been examined in any depth by psychoanalysts. The notion had generally been used as a way of understanding the meaning of what patient and analyst were communicating, so that this could then be interpreted. Using the concept in that way went without saying, much as Molière's Monsieur Jourdain said that for some forty years he had been speaking prose without realizing the fact.

Segal's ideas on symbolism have resulted in several papers which now span several decades: in 1957, "Notes on symbol formation"; in 1978 she added to her then ideas a paper called "On symbolism"; in 1991 she devoted two chapters of her book *Dream, Phantasy and Art* to symbolism; and, finally, in 2000 she wrote a paper on "The Oedipus complex and symbolization" (Segal 2000a).

I should point out that the ideas contained in "Notes on symbol formation" have many points in common with those in Segal's papers on schizophrenia and on aesthetics. It is, of course, the case that several issues which concern symbolism are implicated also in schizophrenic thinking and artistic creation. Her work on these three dimensions really does amount to a trilogy. The fundamental intuitions she had on these topics were developed in the years that followed.

A pioneer in the exploration of symbolism

JMQ: You were the first to put forward the idea that patients who initially had little capacity for symbolization could in fact go on to develop one. Does that finding have repercussions not only for psychoanalytic theory but also for technique?

Hanna Segal: Well, things happen at a particular time. I started with my first psychotic patient just after Mrs Klein published her paper "Notes on some schizoid mechanisms" (1946). It's actually a very short paper, but it is the first proper introduction to the concept of projective identification and of paranoid-schizoid states preceding the depressive states – the depressive position. We were beginning to analyse psychotics. So there I was immediately confronted with their difficulty with symbolization in their sessions. When I made an interpretation in terms of castration anxiety, the patient actually felt castrated. I realized that what I said was taken as a statement of reality. He couldn't distinguish between the spoken word and actual reality. Also, he told me later, once he was back home, that we must never speak about or mention the names of any patients who remained in hospital because when we talked about them that meant we were chewing them up. So I was immediately confronted with that problem and to my surprise I had a couple of artists who were also struggling with that. I had a woman patient, an author, who couldn't write because she felt that the words were coming out of the page at her and biting her. And she felt that, for her, writing was like biting. So from two quarters I was concerned with that issue.

I then came to distinguish between two ways of symbolizing: in the one, a symbol *represents* something and in the other the symbol actually *is* something, concretely, I mean. I quote the example of a psychotic violinist in a hospital setting, who was not a patient of mine. An extremely talented young man, he could no longer play the violin. I asked him why he had stopped playing, and he replied: "Do you expect me to masturbate in public?"! At about the same time, I had a patient on the couch who also played the violin; for him too, because of its shape, it represented at various times either a penis or his mother's body. It never stopped him playing, however, because the instrument *represented* one or other of these – it wasn't *actually* a penis or his mother's body as such. It was a true symbolic representation.

JMQ: How did Ernest Jones contribute to all of this?

Jones wrote an absolutely fundamental paper on symbolism, in 1917 I think it was, in which he distinguished between metaphor, which is conscious, and true unconscious symbols. Actually, he read it at a meeting of the Psychological Society and an officer looked at his medal and said very angrily: "*And you dare call* this *a metaphor?*" For that man, his medal *was* the heroic action for which he had been awarded the distinction, it did not *represent* that action. If anyone were to think that his medal was simply a metaphor, that would, for the officer concerned, amount to a denial of the heroic action itself.

Jones made a couple of fundamental points which I always quote: that a symbol represents what has been repressed from consciousness, and that the whole process is unconscious. Later, he went on to say that symbolization occurs when sublimation has not been achieved. So, for Jones, symbolism is pathological. Nowadays, of course, we no longer think of symbolization as a pathological phenomenon.

JMQ: What about symbolism in Klein's work?

It seems to me that her approach to symbolism, without her being aware of it at all, is very different from Freud's. Freud, of course, didn't write anything specifically about symbolism. What helped me to bring things together were some papers of Klein, one which I think is one of her most important papers – "The importance of symbol-formation in the development of the ego" (1930), the paper in which she describes the autistic boy whom she calls Dick. In those days they called him schizophrenic – autism was not yet a diagnosis then. Dick was an autistic child, he didn't play, didn't talk, didn't relate and was interested only in door handles and trains. Those were the two little bits of interest that he had. Klein says that his inhibition as regards talking and so forth was due to a phantasy he had that his mother's body was full of dreadful things, so that he just wasn't interested in anything else.

Klein observed children in school and, as early as her first book, she treats symbolism as a constant occurrence in child development. School, for example, may represent the mother's body; the teacher could perhaps represent a penis or the father inside the mother's body. That kind of symbolism doesn't at all interfere with the child's capacity to symbolize. It's *not* being able to symbolize that is the problem, because for Klein creativity is also linked with age – you can't develop an ego if you can't symbolize.

JMQ: So it is possible to move from primitive symbolism towards a more evolved form?

I put all those things together, my own observations, those writings of Klein's that stimulated my interest in symbolism and in the role of symbolism in the creative process, and the concept of projective identification. This helped me to understand that, within the process that starts with concrete symbolism and goes all the way to the more evolved forms, symbolism is a tripartite relationship. The symbol, the object to be symbolized and the self, i.e. the person for whom the symbol is a symbol. But if you project a part of your self into the object, then you lose touch with its being your thought and it becomes a reality in the external world.

JMQ: That makes me think of the times in an analysis when, in the transference, the patient unconsciously sees us concretely as being some particular person or other. One of my female patients, for example, had been abused as a child – from time to time she would see me quite concretely as an abuser.

And whenever you opened your mouth you assaulted her.

JMQ: And the reverse also happened, because in the transference she behaved in an abusive way towards me, so that I was the person abused.

It's done so concretely, because if you project a bit of your perceptual apparatus then that part becomes a reality in the external world. That, I think, made a fundamental difference in the way we thought about this process, because we could then see that the major part of our work is reconverting, allowing the concrete to become symbolized. I'll come back later to Bion's work which is important too on this point.

I then went on to suggest a revision of our theory of repression. I suggested that repression sets in after the depressive position, or along with the depressive position, whilst concrete symbolization is – I thought at the time – excessive projective identification of a sticky kind, one that prevents any further development.

JMQ: Did you integrate Bion's views into your conception of symbolism?

Yes, I always refer to them because they take it sort of into more detail, and into qualitative rather than quantitative factors. Freud spoke of "excessive" repression. We say it's not excessive, it's a different kind of repression. [. . .] So that takes us a stage earlier than repression.

Later Bion also revised the theory of repression when he wrote of the "contact barrier", which is made up of alpha-elements, and of the beta screen. In his view, the alpha contact barrier is also a symbolization and a further development, whereas the beta barrier can only be split off. That led him to see repression in a dynamic way not only as a mechanism but also as the area of the personality in which beta gets transformed into alpha. For me, that way of understanding the process is really the basis of the Kleinian technique and particularly of the post-Kleinian technique. [. . .]

JMQ: It is so very concrete . . .

That was a very fundamental point. As you know, my first book of papers was published in America with the title *The Work of Hanna Segal* but I gave it a subtitle: "*Delusion and Creativity*" – because this is really the borderline zone in which we are constantly working.

JMQ: "Borderline" in a broad sense?

That's right. It's very important in artists, particularly in painters, because they actually have to be quite concrete. Artists say that theirs is a kind of process which lies somewhere between art and madness, and I do think artists have this problem of transforming what is concrete into what is symbolized – because, after all, they are very, very close to what is concrete. I quote in my paper the French writer Alexandre Dumas leaving his room crying and saying "*J'ai tué mon Porthos!*" ["I have killed my Porthos!"]

(Tape 3, side A, 31 January 2004)

JMQ: Bion's concept of "attacks on linking" seems to me to be another important factor in symbolization.

Yes, it is very important because the symbol is also a link to reality, isn't it? The link between our thoughts and what actually happens.

JMQ: The "attacks" of which Bion wrote aim to break the link between object and symbol.

On the Rorschach test, for example, the schizophrenic either takes up very minute details or the big whole-responses. Never the middle. Yet most of our life is not that tiny or that big; it takes place more or less in the middle, as it were.

JMQ: So the Rorschach test can reveal emotional links?

Yes, in the little details, in the little bit of concrete symbolization of a very disintegrated kind. Or when there's complete abstraction – a total cut-offness of any links, of any relationship to some big ideas corresponding to what are called the whole-response images in the Rorschach test. So there are people who are good at symbolization and abstraction, yet they may still be completely cut off from any emotional ties.

JMQ: You have called this concrete form of symbolization "symbolic equation". Sometimes you use also the term "concrete equation". Are they the same idea?

Yes, they are.

JMQ: I have heard some psychoanalysts say that the symbolic equation has nothing to do with symbolism. As far as you are concerned, we are still talking about symbolism, although of a very primitive kind; is that right?

I think that the difference is not really one of vocabulary, because you could call it something else if you wanted to. I think they really mean unanalysable. As far as I am concerned, once you understand the underlying dynamics, then it does become analysable.

JMQ: In his paper, "Some psychical consequences of the anatomical distinction between the sexes", Freud (1925j) uses the term "symbolic equation" to describe the equivalence between penis and child.[1] Is your use of the term the same as Freud's?

Klein uses it too. She always credits me with being the first to use the concept of symbolic equation, but in fact she herself uses it in one of her early papers when she says that things are equated one with another. However, I don't think Freud meant concreteness in quite the same way.

JMQ: Yes, Freud seems to use the term in a descriptive sense, without turning it into an actual concept. Another question: do you think there are different degrees of symbolic equation?

Yes, I do. Actually, when you and I talk together, we not only talk to each other but, at a different level, we actually have an impact on each other of a concrete kind. This is an example of Bion's idea of constant transformation: at one level we always react concretely and then transform it. Personally, I would certainly make a distinction between *anti-verbal* and *non-verbal*, because *anti-verbal* implies cutting the link concretely. The French are so very attached to language, but there's a whole world of experience which is not verbalized.

I speak about that with reference to Salman Rushdie's book for children, *Haroun and the Sea of Stories* (Rushdie 1991), in which there is a character who doesn't talk but dances. It's very beautiful and dance, after all, is the first language, the most ancient of languages (Segal 1994). But here the non-verbal fuses with the verbal, it doesn't contradict it, it doesn't attack it. If the non-verbal relationship is good then it gets verbalized much more easily; but if on the non-verbal level it's bad – due to a bad projective identification, for example – then there is no gradual transformation into a verbal form, simply a constant attack on verbal links. I would say that maybe 50 per cent of our ordinary conversational behaviour is concrete – especially when we talk to people with the idea of influencing them. It's not just the idea of understanding them rationally, it's taking possession of them through your tone of voice, the expression on your face.

JMQ: Have contemporary Kleinians developed your ideas on symbolism any further?

I think on symbolism specifically there is a contribution by Britton which is interesting. He says that there is a triangular relationship from the very beginning and that the father is also a "container". For Britton, there is a relationship between baby and mother with the father as an outsider, between baby and father with mother as the outsider, and between father and mother with the baby as outsider (Britton 1989, 1992). In other words, there is always a couple and a third person, and the relationship with that third person can be very bad. The third party can either be intrusive and bad, or be instrumental in bringing the other two together. Those are the links, I think, that are attacked in the container.

JMQ: Do you think that these ideas about the "third party" which we find in some British psychoanalysts could have been influenced by French psychoanalysts, who also stress the role of the father and so on?

Well, I think there was somebody called Freud before any French psychoanalysts came into the picture! I think actually that Klein brings in the father much, much earlier than Freud did. I know that people complain that in her writings it's always mother and baby, that she doesn't talk about the father, and so forth. But Klein places the Oedipus complex at the depressive position, all the same – and nowadays we place it even earlier. Right from the beginning there is a triangular situation in the container, with attacks on the parental couple.

(Tape 3, side B, 31 January 2004)

Segal: from symbolic equation to symbolic representation

Note: In order to make this section as clear as possible and to avoid cross-references, I have decided on this occasion to compile Segal's ideas on symbolism not chronologically, as in the other chapters of this book, but by general theme, based on the following texts:

Segal, H. (1957) "Notes on symbol formation", *International Journal of Psycho-Analysis*, **39**: 391–397; reprinted (1981) in *The Work of Hanna Segal*, New York and London: Jason Aronson, pp. 49–65.

Segal, H. (1978) "On symbolism", *International Journal of Psycho-Analysis*, **55**: 515–519; reprinted (1997) in *Psychoanalysis, Literature and War. Papers 1972–1995*, London and New York: Routledge.

Segal, H. (1991) *Dream, Phantasy and Art*, London: Routledge.

Segal, H. (2000a) "The Oedipus complex and symbolization" (unpublished).

Symbolism according to Freud, to Jones and to Klein

Freud: hysterical symptoms have symbolic meaning

Segal's work on symbolism is for the most part based on Freud's ideas, together with those of Ernest Jones and Melanie Klein.

The notion of unconscious symbolism is a fundamental tenet of psychoanalysis. Already in 1895, in *Studies on Hysteria*, Freud notes that hysterical symptoms are meaningful and that there is a symbolic determinism which decides on the form they adopt. That discovery would have been of only limited interest had Freud not thereupon used his knowledge of symbolism to treat hysterical symptoms successfully. He observed that hysterical symptoms disappeared as soon as the patient became aware of their symbolic meaning. Freud succeeded in doing this by decoding the indirect symbolic manifestations of the unconscious that are conveyed by means of linguistic expressions – following the "free association" method –, dreams, or bungled actions. In other words, symbolism holds the key to our knowledge of the unconscious. It is therefore easy to understand why symbolism is so crucial to psychoanalytic theory and practice.

As he explains in *The Interpretation of Dreams* (1900a), Freud was struck by the extent to which symbolism was used to represent dream material. He thought at first that dreams drew their material from universal symbolism and that each symbol had only one meaning. He quickly came to the conclusion, however, that this view was too simplistic, that any one symbol could have different meanings and that they were over-determined. He realized also that, in addition to universal symbolism, each dreamer has a personal or individual symbolism that has to be taken into account when dreams are being interpreted.

Jones: the symbolization process is unconscious

Basing his developments on Freud's groundwork, Jones wrote a key paper with the title "The theory of symbolism" (Jones 1916), one of the aims of which was to distinguish his points of view on symbolism from those of Jung. Jones's paper was significant in that it was an attempt to give a more precise definition to symbolism and sublimation, terms which, at that time, were somewhat vague. Segal quotes it because of its undoubted historical interest and because Jones's ideas are useful as reference points.

Jones's definition of symbolism is still widely accepted, writes Segal. "*A symbol represents what has been repressed from consciousness, and the whole process of symbolization is carried on unconsciously*" (Segal 1991: 32). The same is true of Jones's view of the origins of symbolism: "*Symbolism arises as the result of intrapsychic conflict between the 'repressing tendencies and the repressed'* " (ibid.). Segal summarizes Jones's ideas thus: "*One might say that when a desire has to be given up because of conflict and repressed, it may express itself in a symbolical way, and the object of the desire which had to be given up can be replace by a symbol*" (ibid.). Jones observes also that, in spite of the great number of symbols discovered by psychoanalysis, they actually cover quite a narrow field. They mainly have to do with the body, the parents and other close relatives, and topics such as birth, death and sexuality. This point of view was confirmed by later developments in psychoanalysis, which showed that infants are initially interested in their own or their parents' body, and that these objects and drives, present in the unconscious, are the source of all their subsequent interests through the workings of symbolization.

That said, some of Jones's ideas are no longer regarded as being valid. For example, he argued that only what has been repressed is symbolized, so that, because of this repression, symbolism as such is pathological. As Segal points out (1957: 392), Jones's definition, being too restrictive, excludes most of what is called "symbol" in other sciences and in everyday language. Also, for Jones, any given symbol had only one meaning, whereas nowadays symbols are seen to be polysemous and over-determined. Segal distances herself further from Jones when she says that there are very great advantages in extending the definition of symbols to cover those used in sublimation.

Klein: symbol formation and ego development go hand in hand

Melanie Klein's work with young children opened up a new approach to symbolism. Starting with Freud's ideas, Klein argued that the infant's play was an expression of his or her underlying unconscious conflicts, desires and phantasies. She showed that unconscious phantasy underpinned children's schoolwork and that both schoolwork and play are a symbolic expression of the child's phantasy life (Klein 1923b). For many children, the school building represents symbolically the mother's body, while the teacher inside represents the father. From that point of view, all school activity may be experienced as penetrating inside the mother's body and schoolwork itself may acquire a symbolic meaning: for example, numbers or letters may come to represent the genitals, with the letter "I" a symbolic representation of the male genital and the letter "O" the female one; in a similar vein, a group of two letters or numbers may represent sexual intercourse.

Klein went on to enhance her conception of symbolism. After a detailed exploration of the infant's relationship with the mother's body, she concluded that the child's epistemophilic drive gave rise not only to the wish to explore the maternal body and the phantasy of doing so, but also to wishes and phantasies of attracting and possessing it. The intensity of libidinal and aggressive desires is increasingly a source of anxiety and guilt feelings with respect to the mother; as a result, the child displaces his or her attention on to objects in the external world and endows them with symbolic meaning. Creating symbols thus becomes a way of reducing anxiety and guilt feelings with respect to the infant's primary objects. Thus, according to Klein, both libidinal and aggressive wishes with respect to the mother's body are the main source of the epistemophilic relationship to the world, and external objects are above all symbols of the infant's body, that of the parents, or parts of the body.

If anxiety is too intense, the entire process of symbol formation is inhibited, and this can have catastrophic consequences for the development of the ego. This was the case with Dick, a 4-year-old autistic boy who was unable to speak or to play and had little or no contact with his environment (Klein 1930). The analysis showed that he was terrified of his aggressive impulses towards his mother's body; he felt that, as a result of his attacks on it, he had transformed it into something bad. The result was complete paralysis of his phantasy life and of symbol formation. *"He had not endowed the world around him with any symbolic meaning and therefore took no interest in it. Melanie Klein came to the conclusion that if symbolization does not occur, the whole development of the ego is arrested"* (Segal 1991: 34). Once Klein managed to get hold of these phantasies, as Dick's unconscious anxiety diminished and became conscious, the process of symbol formation could begin.

The concept of symbolic equation

Two classic examples

As a starting point for her investigation, Segal takes the problem of symbolic functioning as she encountered it in her psychoanalytic practice through the transference/counter-transference relationship. She begins her 1957 paper by describing two patients in order to illustrate the difference she draws between two sorts of symbol formation and symbolic function. These two examples, now classic, are often quoted.

Patient A was a psychotic in a psychiatric hospital. Since his illness, he had stopped playing the violin. When Segal asked him why he had stopped, he replied with some violence: "Do you expect me to masturbate in public?"

The situation with patient B was quite different. When he was in analysis with Segal, he dreamt one night that he and a young girl were playing a violin duet. He associated to "fiddling" and masturbating, and it clearly emerged from these associations that the violin represented his genital and playing the violin represented a masturbation phantasy of a relation with a young girl.

> *Here then are two patients who apparently use the same symbols in the same situation – a violin representing the male genital, and playing the violin representing masturbation. The way in which the symbols function, however, is very different. For A, the violin had become so completely equated with his genital that to touch it in public became impossible. For B, playing the violin in his waking life was an important sublimation.* (Segal 1957: 391)

In other words, says Segal, the main difference between these two patients with respect to their use of the violin as a symbol for the male genital was not that in one case the symbol was conscious and in the other unconscious, but that in the first case it was felt to *be* the genital and in the second to *represent* it – and this in no way prevented B from using it.

What does "symbolic equation" mean?

These clinical cases led Segal to the conclusion that it was possible to differentiate between two kinds of symbol formation and symbolic function. This is how she put it in her 1991 paper.

> *In one, which I have called* symbolic equation, *and which underlies schizophrenic concrete thinking, the symbol is so equated with the object symbolized that the two are felt to be identical. A violin* is *a penis; playing the violin* is *masturbating and therefore not to be done in public. In the second case, that of true symbolism or* symbolic representation, *the symbol represents the object but is not entirely equated with it. To the patient who dreamed of the violin, the violin represented the penis, but was also differentiated from it, so that it could both embody unconscious masturbation phantasies and yet be sufficiently differentiated to be used as a violin as well, to make music which could represent intercourse but not be equated to intercourse.* (Segal 1991: 35)

Symbolism: a three-term relationship

For Segal, symbolism is a three-term relationship, bringing together the symbol, the object it symbolizes and the person for whom that symbol represents that object. If we put this in psycho-analytic terms, we could say that symbolism is a relationship that brings together a symbol, an object and the ego. From that point of view, Segal argues, if symbolism is seen as a three-term relationship, problems of symbol formation must always be examined in the context of the ego's relationship to its objects.

That innovative approach put forward by Segal in 1957 meant that she could then go on to make a detailed study of how symbols are formed and used in the course of the ego's development.

The formation of symbolic equations in the course of development

Early disturbances of differentiation between ego and object

Symbol formation begins very early, probably at the same time as object relations. Basing her description on the concepts of the paranoid-schizoid position and the depressive position, Segal notes that the child's first object relations are characterized by splitting the object into an ideally good and a wholly bad one. The aim of the ego is both total union with the ideal object and total annihilation of the bad one as well as of bad parts of the self. This initial splitting divides objects into good and bad, but there is as yet no clear differentiation between self and object.

If, in the course of the infant's development, disturbances occur in differentiating between self and object, these may be reflected in disturbances of symbol formation. "*In particular, disturbances in differentiation between ego and object lead to disturbances in differentiation between the symbol and the object symbolized and therefore to concrete thinking characteristic of psychoses*" (Segal 1957: 393). In other words, the formation of symbolic equations in schizophrenics is closely related to a blurring of the differentiation between ego and object in the early stages of infant development.

The role of projective identification

Segal mentions the fact that Klein had already linked symbolism to projection and to identification, as Ferenczi had suggested, but that in her early work she had not yet made a detailed exploration of the interaction between projection and identification. Klein would in fact do this in her 1946 paper on projective identification, "Notes on some schizoid mechanisms"; Segal based some of her own theories on that paper. Thanks to that major contribution and to her own observations with her patients, Segal was able to draw the conclusion that the more projective identification increases, the more concrete symbolism dominates. We shall shortly see the consequences of this.

Symbolic equations and early object relations

In the early stages of infant development, the child's mind creates objects which are then felt to be available. This phase is what Freud called hallucinatory wish-fulfilment. For Klein, that phase corresponds to hallucinosis in which, if ideal conditions are not fulfilled, the bad object is equally hallucinated and felt as real.

At this time too, the first projections and identifications are the beginning of the process of symbol formation. In projective identification, the subject in phantasy projects parts of him- or herself into the object, so that the object comes to be identified with the parts of the self that it is felt to contain. Similarly, internal objects are projected outside and identified with parts of the external world which come to represent them.

Early symbols formed in this way, however, are not felt by the ego to be symbols or substitutes, but to be the original object itself.

They are so different from symbols formed later that I think they deserve a name of their own. [. . .] I suggested the term "equation". This word, however, differentiates them too much from the word "symbol" and I would like to alter it here to "symbolic equation". The symbolic equation between the original object and the symbol in the internal and the external world is, I think, the basis of the schizophrenic's concrete thinking. (Segal 1957: 393)

Given that symbol formation is a three-term relationship, it collapses whenever projective identification increases.

> *In the absence of a person there can be no symbol. That tripartite relationship does not hold when projective identification is in ascendance. The relevant part of the ego is identified with the object: there is not sufficient differentiation between the ego and the object itself, boundaries are lost, part of the ego is confused with the object, and the symbol which is a creation of the ego is confused with what is symbolized. It is only with the advent of the depressive position, the experience of separateness, separation and loss, that symbolic representation comes into play.* (Segal 1991: 38)

Defence by annihilation and scotomization

When symbolic equations are formed in relation to bad objects, an attempt is made to deal with them as with the original object, that is by total annihilation and scotomization. This seems to have been the case with Dick (Klein 1930) who, says Segal, had perhaps formed numerous symbolic equations in the external world. Thereupon, in order to avoid the anxiety and feelings of guilt related to the original persecutory object, he would have had to deal with them by annihilating the object, that is, by a total withdrawal of interest. As the analysis progressed, Dick began to show interest in some of the objects in the playroom.

From symbolic equation to symbolic representation

The transition from the paranoid-schizoid to the depressive position

In the course of infant development, these early forms of symbol, symbolic equations, gradually change into symbols in the strict sense of the term, symbolic representations. According to Segal, this evolution in the function of symbols takes place during the transition from the paranoid-schizoid position to the depressive position; these changes are complex, but here Segal highlights only their main characteristics for the purposes of her demonstration.

In the depressive position, a transformation gradually takes place in symbol formation and use. Given that the object is felt to be whole, there is a growing awareness of separateness between self and object, and the symbol – in the narrow sense of the term – is felt really to represent the object. Because of ambivalence, the ego's relationship to the object is marked by guilt, fear of loss or actual experience of loss and mourning, together with a striving to re-create the object, repair it and restore it within the self and in the external world. In normal development, after repeated experiences of loss, recovery and re-creation, a good object is securely established in the ego. There is a growing sense of reality, both internal and external.

Simultaneously, there is a certain modification of drive-related aims. Earlier on, the aim was to possess the object totally if it was felt to be good, or to annihilate it totally if it was felt to be bad; in the depressive position, with the recognition that the good and the bad objects are one and the same, the drive-related aims are modified.

> *This situation is a powerful stimulus for the creation of symbols, and symbols acquire new functions which change their character. The symbol is needed to displace aggression from the original object, and in that way to lessen the guilt and the fear of loss. [The] aim of the displacement is to save the object, and the guilt experienced in relation to it is far less than that due to an attack on the original object.* (Segal 1957: 394)

In such circumstances, the symbol is not the equivalent of the original object.

Symbols are also created in the internal world as a means of recapturing and owning again the original object. But, in keeping with the increased sense of reality, they are now felt to be created by the ego and therefore never completely equated with the original object.

Segal follows Freud who, in 1923, postulated that a modification of drive-related aims was the basic prerequisite for sublimation, and adds that, in her view, symbol formation in the depressive position necessitates some inhibition of direct drive-related aims in relation to the original object "*and therefore the symbols become available for sublimation*" (1957: 395). Since the symbol is acknowledged as a creation of the individual concerned, unlike the symbolic equation, it can be freely used by him or her.

> When a substitute in the external world is used as a symbol it may be used more freely than the original object, since it is not fully identified with it. Insofar, however, as it is distinguished from the original object it is also recognized as an object in itself. Its own properties are recognized, respected, and used, because no confusion with the original object blurs the characteristics of the new object used as a symbol. (1957: 395)

Symbolization and the mourning process

Overcoming loss and separation with the help of symbols

As a result of the growing differentiation between the internal and external worlds, as the depressive period is being worked through, absence can be more easily accepted. Symbols are used to overcome the loss of the object and to protect the object against the individual's own aggressiveness. "*A symbol is like a precipitate of the mourning for the object*" (Segal 1991: 40). In this new situation, the function of symbolism takes on another meaning: the symbol becomes available for sublimation and makes ego growth that much easier.

For as long as the dead person is felt concretely to be a dead body, normal mourning is not possible. "*It is only if the dead person is symbolically represented in the mind that the symbolic internal reparation can be done*" (1991: 38). That internal reparation is necessary if mourning is to be successfully processed.

Segal then goes on to analyse the close relationship that can be observed between the capacity to symbolize and the ability to work through the mourning process. In pathological mourning, there is a concrete symbolic equation in which the symbol is not felt to be sufficiently differentiated from the object to enable the individual to use it freely. On the other hand, when the mourning process can be worked through, the symbol is created by the individual; in this case it represents the object and, being a creation of the person concerned, it can be freely used. "*Also, in that the symbol is not equated with the object, the proper characteristics and functions of a substitute used symbolically are fully recognized and acknowledged*" (1991: 41).

In order to illustrate the various degrees of symbolization, Segal reminds us that Freud is reputed to have said that every man marries his mother. "*But*", she adds, "*the sanity or otherwise of such a procedure depends on the type and degree of symbolization. The wife may symbolize and contain some aspects of the mother, or she may be felt to* be *the mother, in which case the marriage carries all the prohibitions and conflicts of the relation to the mother*" (1991: 47).

The relationship between primitive symbolism and more evolved forms

Coexistence is possible

Modification of the form of symbolization in the transition from the paranoid-schizoid to the depressive position does not mean that the highest form of symbolic functioning is established once and for all. Firstly, regression to the paranoid-schizoid position can always occur at any time in the individual's development, whenever there is recourse to pathological projective identification as a defence against anxiety. "*Then symbols which have been developed and have been functioning as symbols in sublimation, revert to concrete symbolic equations. This is mainly due to the fact that in massive projective identification the ego becomes again confused with the object, the symbol becomes confused with the thing symbolized and therefore turns into an equation*" (Segal 1957: 395).

Secondly, there are many modes of transition from concrete symbols to symbolic representation. These different kinds of symbol can coexist side-by-side in the same individual, in variable proportions. According to Segal, the mind does not function *only* with concrete symbols nor *only* with symbolic representations. "*I do not think I have ever seen a patient the whole of whose function would be on a concrete level or whose concrete symbols would ever be completely concrete; only predominantly so. Nor do I think the symbolism of the depressive position is ever free of concrete elements*" (1991: 43).

The aesthetic experience and the juxtaposition of the two forms of symbolization

In applying her ideas on symbolism to art, Segal suggests that the juxtaposition of these two forms of symbolization could be the source of the impact which a work of art has on the person looking at it. *"Any art, in particular, does embody concrete symbolic elements that give a work of art its immediate 'punch'; it has a concrete impact on our experience provided it is included in an otherwise more evolved type of symbolism, without which it would be no more than a meaningless bombardment"* (1991: 43). In Segal's view, working through the depressive position makes it easier to integrate primitive symbolism; in the case of the artist, this contributes to the fact that a successful work of art evokes an aesthetic emotion. *"One of the great achievements of the depressive position is the capacity of the individual to integrate and to contain more primitive aspects of his experience, including the primitive symbolic equations"* (1991: 43).

The role of symbols in communication

All communication is made by means of symbols

Segal goes on to examine the relationship between, on the one hand, these two modalities in which symbols can function and, on the other, the capacity to communicate. *"Symbol formation governs the capacity to communicate, since all communication is made by means of symbols"* (1957: 395). It follows that the capacity to communicate is disturbed when schizoid disturbances in object relations occur, and this for the following reasons:

> *First because the differentiation between the subject and the object is blurred, secondly because the means of communication are lacking since symbols are felt in a concrete fashion and are therefore unavailable for purposes of communication. One of the ever-recurring difficulties in the analysis of psychotic patients is this difficulty of communication. Words, for instance, whether the analyst's or the patient's, are felt to be objects or actions, and cannot be easily used for purposes of communication.* (1957: 396)

Internal communication and its inhibition

Symbols are needed not only in communication with the external world, but also in internal communication. This means that, when people have some awareness of their feelings, they are communicating with their internal world by means of symbols, since all communication is made by means of symbols. According to Segal, the difficulty in dealing with schizophrenic or schizoid patients is not simply that they cannot communicate with us – they cannot communicate with *themselves*, since there is no communication between the different parts of their ego.

Verbalization is a highly developed form of symbolism. *"The capacity to communicate with oneself by using symbols is, I think, the basis of verbal thinking – which is the capacity to communicate with oneself by means of words. Not all internal communication is verbal thinking, but all verbal thinking is an internal communication by means of symbols – words"* (1957: 396).

An important aspect of internal communication is the use of symbolization to integrate earlier desires, anxieties and phantasies into the later stages of development. Similarly, in the depressive position, the ego has the task of dealing not only with depressive anxieties but also with unresolved earlier conflicts – it does this thanks to symbolization. *"In the depressive position and later, symbols are formed not only of the whole destroyed and re-created object characteristic of the depressive position, but also of the split object – extremely good and extremely bad – and not only of the whole object but also of part-objects"* (1957: 396).

Lacan and Klein: similarities and differences

Hanna Segal often discussed issues of language and communication, particularly as regards symbolism. Lacan also dealt with this topic, but from a quite different angle. This is what Segal had to say to Jacqueline Rose, the distinguished professor of English, who interviewed her on the relationship between Klein, Segal and Lacan.

Jacqueline Rose: Is there any possible point of dialogue here between Lacan and Klein? I was interested to read in Phyllis Grosskurth's biography of Klein that Lacan offered to translate Klein's The Psychoanalysis of Children, *but then failed to do so. It seems to me that he was more dependent on her ideas than some of us realized before.*

Hanna Segal: Yes. A number of young French Lacanians told me at one point that I was the only analyst that Lacan thought well of, but that may have been before I became very explicit and said I didn't think the same of him!

There are similarities and differences between Lacan and Klein. I think that the similarity lies in the overcoming of concrete symbolism – what I call "symbolic equation" – and the passage to real symbolism which is related to loss; it has also to do with the acknowledgement of aggression and guilt, which Lacan leaves out a bit. Furthermore, he often reduces it simply to the loss of the phallus. Also, he doesn't make sufficient acknowledgement of the fact that this kind of work was going on before he appeared on the scene. He makes everything much more abstract, and I don't particularly like that aspect of his style. And he contradicts himself a lot. For example, at a conference one morning I heard a paper which said *"L'enfant ne connaît le père que par le discours de la mère"* ("The child knows the father only through the discourse of the mother"), and then that very afternoon another paper said *"Le discours est toujours le discours du père"* ("Discourse is always the discourse of the father"). It becomes a bit like the Bible, full of sayings and aphorisms. There is also a deification of language.

I think that the role of the father in the development, not only of language but also of symbolization, is to intervene into the state of projective identification where there is no third object and the child is in possession of the mother. The structural role of the penis in phantasy is to stop a stream of mutual projective identification between mother and child. In reality that is the role that a good father plays by stepping in as the third object. I think also that Lacan is phallus-obsessed and doesn't differentiate enough between, on the one hand, the phallus which is the urinary, exhibitionist, narcissistic object, and, on the other, the genital penis. The penis that serves its role in my scheme of things is the genital penis of the father in intercourse with the mother and in a psychological relationship with her.[2] The law is not so much "the law of the father" as a certain law of depressive versus schizophrenic relationships.

We differ too on narcissism, because for us narcissism is always based on object relationships and is related to projective identification and envy, whereas I think that for Lacan primary narcissism is a state from which we have to emerge.

The main differences between Klein and Lacan are of course technical. Seeing patients for 5 minutes, coming into a waiting room full of people and deciding "today I'll see *you*", [. . .] – well, that's just not the way we practise psychoanalysis.

(Interview, Jacqueline Rose, 1990)

Hanna Segal: "My sleepless night with Lacan!"

JMQ: You speak fluent French – did you ever meet Jacques Lacan?

Hanna Segal: Well, before I tell you about the sleepless night I spent with Lacan, I'd like to say a word or two regarding his famous phrase about the unconscious being "structured like a language". I think it's the other way round. Language is structured like the unconscious. There is a lot going on pre-verbally and it's only later that verbalization emerges, because probably there is some non-concrete phantasy – you know, in terms of the parents and their bodies and things that are already symbolized, with which little babies play very well. Babies play very early in life, and that's a kind of symbolization. Eventually they verbalize, and for me that indicates that it is language which emerges from the unconscious, not the unconscious modelling itself on language. That's why I say it's the other way round. When language eventually emerges, it reflects the structure of our basic functions: subject, object and action.

JMQ: What seems to have interested Lacan was above all the patient's capacity to become aware of the unconscious meaning behind what he or she says; unlike you, he didn't focus very much on the link between different levels of symbolization.

And was his idea of symbolism like Freud's – that all symbolism is pathological? Was that his idea? I don't know exactly . . . but with Lacan there is also a lot of action. He brings sessions to a close, cuts off the endings and so on. That's why I could never take Lacan very seriously.

Let's get back to my meeting with him. You'll remember that Lacan and Lagache were expelled from the French Society in 1953. What they hadn't then realized was that by that very fact they were no longer members of the International Psychoanalytical Association. So they turned up in London . . . and therein lies a tale – of how I got a beautiful scarf, and that for having spent a night with Lacan! This is how I came to be given that present. The IPA Council decided to give them 15 minutes to state their case at the business meeting. Paul and I were having tea with Mrs Klein and Lagache, who said that he and Lacan had a problem because neither of them could write English very well. So Paul and I said that, since we were both very bilingual, it wouldn't be a problem, just bring your stuff in French and it will be a matter of a few minutes to translate it. So Tuesday comes along, Lagache isn't free, but we invite Lacan for dinner. We have dinner. We retire to the study. Paul looks at the text and translates the first sentence. Lacan interrupts him immediately, saying: "Ah, well, you see, you can't understand all the implications unless you know the story behind the sentence." And he starts walking up and down, up and down, waving his arms all over the place. Now for the second sentence. Same thing . . . And this went on till seven in the morning!

[. . .]

Lacan came to see me another time too. That was when the Committee was already formed and everything. I knew nothing about it; I was a young member and I'd heard vaguely that there was this Committee appointed. [. . .] I said I had no time, I had a break for a bare 20 minutes to eat an egg or something. "I'll eat an egg with you", was his reply. [. . .] I just couldn't convince him that I had no influence whatsoever. He had some idea in his mind that I would save him. Anyway, ever since that night I have never been able to understand how people can listen to someone who stands and talks and talks and talks and talks without paying any attention to whether or not it means anything to the person listening. [. . .]

(Tape 3, side B, 31 January 2004)

Mental space and symbolism

In Chapter 4 of *Dream, Phantasy and Art* (1991), Segal takes a new look at what she had previously written on symbolism, this time in the light of Bion's developments, particularly his differentiation of normal from pathological projective identification and his description of the container/contained relationship. What Bion called beta-elements seem very close to Segal's description of concrete symbolic equations, to such an extent that we could be forgiven for thinking that symbolic equations are made up of beta-elements. For Segal, however, the concrete equation is more of a transitional stage between beta-elements and alpha-elements, since the meaning of symbolic equations is easier to detect insofar as they do have some degree of symbolism. As for alpha-elements, described as "unsaturated", they are closely linked to the symbolic function and are available for all sorts of transformation; this explains why there can be many symbols for any given object and, conversely, why any given symbol may have many meanings.

"The Oedipus complex and symbolization" (2000, unpublished)

In her paper "The Oedipus complex and symbolization", Segal begins by refuting the myth according to which Kleinian psychoanalysts are interested only in babies and breasts and ignore the Oedipus complex. Quite the opposite, in fact: Kleinian theory and practice attach great importance to the Oedipus complex and to its first beginnings, and Melanie Klein attributed to the father a more important role in early development than Freud did.

In Kleinian thinking, the Oedipus complex begins in the depressive position, a stage in development at which the infant perceives his or her mother as a whole person. But triangular relationships exist even before the depressive position is established. Some of these early triangulations go to make up the primitive roots of the Oedipus complex; here, splitting processes are uppermost, with the object being divided into idealized and hated parts. At this stage, there is also a third object, represented by the father's penis – the main receptacle for containing projections of unwanted parts of the self and of the object. This triangular situation forms the background to the early Oedipal configuration.

During normal development, splitting and projection diminish and the depressive position sets in. Mother is no longer perceived as a part-object; she is a whole object, a separate person with her own personality and her own life. This includes the acknowledgement of the father as her sexual partner. It can happen, however, that early processes of splitting and projection continue during later development, thus creating a pattern that seems to be Oedipal whereas in fact it is not. If we take a closer look at the clinical material, we can see that this is not a true Oedipal situation but the continuation of part-object relations that have more to do with envy than with Oedipal jealousy.

All this goes to show that the evolution of the Oedipus complex depends to a considerable degree on the integration of a certain number of basic mental functions in the course of infant development – a sense of reality, a capacity for symbol formation, the acquisition of speech and an expanding capacity for thought. Segal goes on to point out that, in her opinion, for symbolization to function properly, the depressive position has to be worked through and external reality has to be differentiated from internal reality. In her view, accepting the reality of the father and of the Oedipal couple is a crucial factor in this process. She concludes her paper by showing how R. Britton has expanded Bion's container/contained relationship by including a third object. Bion's description of containment is essentially that of a two-part relationship, whereas for Britton it is a triangular relationship revolving around three axes: father, mother and infant, with various combinations of links between them. Segal points out that Britton's conception is far from being a purely abstract idea – it is of great importance clinically.

More important than symbolism per se: the capacity of the mind to create symbols

What are we to think nowadays of Segal's concept of the symbolic equation? Have there been any further developments to it in recent times? Has it been taken up by any psychoanalytic schools of thought other than the Kleinians? Given that there now seems to be an ever-increasing "Babelization" of psychoanalytic concepts, I asked Jorge Canestri, who has made a detailed study of the history of psychoanalytic ideas within their various cultural contexts, what he thinks about these questions.

JMQ: Segal introduced a fundamental distinction between primitive symbolism – the symbolic equation – and a more evolved form of symbolism. One would have expected most psychoanalysts to use this innovative concept in their everyday practice – but that doesn't seem to be the case at all.

Jorge Canestri: As regards the difference between the primitive and the more evolved forms of symbolism, I would say that you have to go back to how the idea of the symbolic equation came about, both from the point of view of psychoanalytic theory and in terms of the history of ideas. I find the whole question very interesting; the historical aspect has recently been written up by Riccardo Steiner (2007).

The history of how the concept of projective identification evolved is closely linked to that of symbol formation in child development. If we draw an analogy with Bion's idea of a "normal" kind of projective identification used in primitive communication, we can imagine, as Steiner says, a "normal" kind of symbolic equation which would be a precursor of symbol formation proper. A similar analogy can be found in semiotics, as Peirce and Jakobson have pointed out. I would argue that, if we take into account Steiner's "normal" kind of symbol equation, we have to bring out, as Segal does, the difference between the symbolic equation and the more developed form of symbol formation, as well as the continuity that leads from one to the other. It is very difficult to understand why some psychoanalysts deprive themselves of a concept such as that – after all, its usefulness in all branches of psycho-pathology goes without saying.

I think Steiner is correct also when he says that Freud paid close attention to the topic in *Studies on Hysteria* (Freud 1895d), when he observed that, deep within any symbol, there is both verbal and non-verbal language. In his case study of Frau Cäcilie M., Freud writes:

> In taking a verbal expression literally and in feeling the "stab in the heart" or the "slap in the face" after some slighting remark as a real event, the hysteric is not taking liberties with words, but is simply reviving once more the sensations to which the verbal expression owes its justification. [. . .] All these sensations and innervations belong to the field of "The Expression of the Emotions", [. . .] as Darwin (1872) has taught us. [. . .] Indeed, it is per-haps wrong to say that hysteria creates these sensations by symbolization. It may be that it does not take linguistic usage as its model at all, but that both hysteria and linguistic usage alike draw their material from a common source. (1895d: 181).

In a footnote, Freud adds: "*In states in which mental alteration goes deeper, we clearly also find a symbolic version in concrete images and sensations of more artificial turns of speech*" (ibid.).

Steiner goes on to show that Ferenczi followed a similar path in "Stages in the development of the sense of reality" (1913). When Ferenczi argued that the body and internal perceptions are projected into the external world, he was drawing on a concept of the symbol which is very close to what Freud said in *Studies on Hysteria*, in the sense that pre-verbal and bodily aspects participate in the construction of symbols. I think that Melanie Klein followed that path too, because from the very beginning of her work on symbolism she referred to the body. In 1923 and again in 1930, when she wrote "The importance of symbol formation in the devel-opment of the ego", Klein argued that primitive unconscious phantasies are related to the body and that symbolization is very much linked to that aspect. In my view, that is a major element not only in Kleinian theory but also in Freud's work on hysteria and in Ferenczi's explorations too. There is a historical legacy there that I find particularly interesting; Steiner highlights it also.

I think it is all the more important to remember the history of the symbolic equation because it is part of the whole idea of symbols. It is a difficult question. In my view, however, the most important question for contemporary psychoanalysis – not just for psychoanalysis, in fact, but also for semiotics – is not the symbol as such, but the symbolic function of the mind.

JMQ: In other words, when you emphasize the symbolic function of the mind rather than the symbol as such, you are highlighting the possibility for psychoanalysts to make a clinical assessment of an individual's ability to grasp the symbolic meaning of unconscious phenomena?

Of course. An assessment of the quality, if that's the correct word, of the individual's symbolic function. In that sense, Melanie Klein's work is absolutely fundamental, as are the develop-ments we owe to Bion and to Segal. Hanna Segal, indeed, changed her conception of symbol-ism in her 1979 postscript and again in 1986 to take Bion's work on the container/contained relationship into account. That's the important aspect, because Bion too had things to say about the mind's symbolic function.

JMQ: Concepts such as the symbolic equation and the early stages of the Oedipus complex do not seem to be accepted in the same way throughout the psychoanalytic world: some do accept them under their original name, others seem to ignore them but in fact integrate them into their thinking, often under a different appellation. Is this tendency to "Babelization", which you have explored in some depth elsewhere (Amati-Mehler et al. 1993), specific to psychoanalysis or does it apply much more widely?

I think that some psychoanalysts find it difficult to accept a concept (or even a terminology) that was not born in their own particular psychoanalytic culture. From that point of view, I think we have to distinguish between two different issues.

The first is a question of theory: when analysts are at work with their patients, they try to create their own little world of theory and concepts. That is a good thing, because each patient is a unique individual, different from everyone else, and we cannot simply apply theory to practice in a mechanical way. That situation gives rise to a certain number of concepts, some of which may have more or less the same meaning as others although under a different name. That is inevitable as far as theory is concerned; although it contributes to a certain degree of "Babelization" within psychoanalytic circles, it does have its positive side too. I have tried to demonstrate this in my book *Psychoanalysis: from Practice to Theory* (2006).

The second issue has nothing to do with theory, but with the psychopathology of each individual psychoanalyst. If some psychoanalysts do not agree with what a given concept is called simply because it comes from a different psychoanalytic environment, that above all has to do with their own narcissism. There is also an issue around what I would call the somewhat idolatrous identification with a particular theory; in such cases, the theory functions as a kind of internal object and a sort of identity relationship is created with respect to theory, to the group to which the analyst belongs, to some of the leaders of the local group, etc. I think that this phenomenon plays an important role in the fact that some colleagues refuse certain ideas, especially in countries where psychoanalysis has its own specific culture – in France, for example, as well as in some other countries. It seems to me, all the same, that Green's tertiary process is linked to the symbolic equation, which could also be linked to what Arieti says about the schizophrenic's way of treating symbols.

JMQ: For Lacan, symbolism is an important aspect of both theory and practice; this is true of Klein and Segal also. What, in your opinion, are the points of convergence and divergence between these two conceptual approaches?

I think that there are many divergences and few points of agreement. It all hangs on a fundamental question. I think that Klein's conception, like Segal's, sees the mind in terms of its heterogeneity – and there I would agree with them. That aspect is important for their conception of symbolism and of the symbolic function. In other words, it is perfectly clear that Hanna Segal and Melanie Klein, like Freud and Ferenczi before them, do not believe that "the unconscious is structured like a language", as Lacan's famous formula puts it. If, like Lacan, we say that the unconscious is structured like a language, that implies that there is homogeneity between language and the unconscious. Conversely, for Hanna Segal and Melanie Klein, there is a significant degree of heterogeneity in the mind, which means that the unconscious cannot be structured like a language because that would imply bringing all the different factors together under the one heading, language – i.e. words and linguistic signs. In my view, the mind is *heterogeneous*; in symbols there is a constant integration of factors that come from the body, from the pre-verbal and from the non-verbal dimensions. You cannot encompass all that under the term "symbols" if what you mean by that is linguistic symbols alone. In my view, Segal and Bion state that very clearly. That is the major problem with Lacan's thinking.

There is all the same close convergence between Lacan and Bion on one point – the sign that takes the place of the absent object – and that is a good thing. But there is no convergence as regards their conceptions of the symbolic world, because, for Klein, Segal and Bion there is an iconographic factor – non-verbal, affect-related, emotional, etc. – which must be included in any conception of the symbolic world. For Lacan, the situation is quite different: in his view, the symbolic world has exclusively to do with linguistic symbols.

In my opinion, then, it is impossible to combine these two theories. They do converge on the point that, in order to think of the existence of a symbol, you have to think of the absence of the object; that convergence has to do with the logical basis of a conception of the mind. There too, there are some points of contact between Lacan and Melanie Klein – but not as regards their conception of the world of symbols as such. On that point, they are very far apart. That, to some extent, is what Green means when he says that "the unconscious is not structured like a 'language' but like a 'discourse' " – in other words, "discourse" includes everything I mentioned above: the body, pre-verbal aspects, affects, iconography, and so forth.

(Interview, September 2006)

Jorge Canestri (Rome) is a training analyst and supervisor with the Italian Psychoanalytic Association.

Chapter 5

THE FUNDAMENTAL CONFLICT BETWEEN THE LIFE AND DEATH DRIVES

A Theoretical Hypothesis Confirmed by Clinical Practice

As an adolescent, Hanna Segal read *Beyond the Pleasure Principle* and *Civilization and its Discontents*, so that she discovered Freud and the death drive at one and the same time. "*That was when it clicked with me!*" she says; she was immediately convinced of the value of Freud's hypothesis. Freud found it extremely difficult to share with even his closest followers his firm belief that the conflict between the life and death drives plays a decisive role in mental life. Melanie Klein was the only one who took the idea seriously enough to make use of it in her clinical work. Since qualifying as a psychoanalyst, Segal has never ceased to emphasize the usefulness of that hypothesis for the clinical practice of psychoanalysis. She maintains, of course, that she has not contributed anything particularly new to the concept in comparison with Freud and Klein; nonetheless her real contribution lies in her efforts to share her firm belief in its validity with other psychoanalysts, several of whom continue to question the importance of the fundamental conflict between the life and death drives.

Segal wrote only one article on the topic, several versions of which have been published, with slight variations from one to the next. Nonetheless, in various other papers by Segal there are many clinical examples of the manner in which she applies the notion in her everyday work with her patients.

"The death instinct: a protest against the pain of life" (Hanna Segal)

JMQ: In your conference papers and in your writings you lay a great deal of emphasis on the importance of the conflict between the life and death instincts. Do you think that psychoanalysts are nowadays more ready than in the past to accept that point of view, which both Freud and Klein advocated?

Hanna Segal: I really don't know. I say I don't know because I only discuss things in terms of their clinical usefulness. From a certain point of view theories are not absolute. One can't say that such-and-such a theory is *right* with a capital "R" – it can never be any more than a tenet. I think in an empirical science like psychoanalysis the point is that a useful theory is one which explains facts, clinical facts – one which fits the facts and explains them best, if you like. And also a useful theory is one which, if applied clinically, brings about a change in the material of the kind we expect. You see, there is probably a difference here between philosophers and psychoanalysts. Every theory – and that extends to scientific theories too – is only a hypothesis. At the moment, the concept of life and death instincts is to me the most satisfactory hypothesis for understanding certain dynamic processes. My husband was into philosophy and somewhat ambivalent about psychoanalysis, and he used to say: "It's not that psychoanalysis is a wonderfully scientific theory, but for the moment it's the only one on the market!" Maybe something better will turn up, but at the moment psychoanalytical theory is the one that best explains human behaviour and – thanks to Bion – behaviour in groups. You can't just apply what you get from the couch to a group as though the group was the patient. You have to

w do you see the link between, on the one hand, the conflict between the life and
ives and, on the other, narcissism?

ne link which Klein didn't make but which for me is absolutely basic is the link with
sm. Narcissism is the other side of the coin, if you like. Either I am the source of all life
is no life whatsoever.

Narcissism, then, would be the whole coin, as it were, with its obverse and reverse.
we put it this way: either I am the source of all life (narcissism), or there is no life
oever (the death instinct)? Anyway, let's get back to Klein: you say she didn't make a link
en envy and narcissism?

ith narcissism. That came later – with Rosenfeld, with me, and later still with Bion. As
rds the narcissistic structure – you can take it either that narcissism is primary and
secondary, or the other way round: that envy is primary and narcissism is a defensive
ture. That's the beauty of the thing.

Q: Could you be a bit more explicit?

ou are in a primary narcissistic position, you are the enviable object (because you are in a
te of non-differentiation as regards self and object). From that point of view, we could say
at we are born totally narcissistic. That would be Freud's primary narcissism. Thereafter, the
counter with the object produces envy, in which case envy is secondary.
   On the other hand, you could look at narcissism the way I understand it. The primary thing
the life and death instinct, and the narcissistic structure is a defence against envy. The object
as to be destroyed in order to avoid feeling envious towards it: "I shall forever be the enviable
bject!" I unconsciously project that envy into other people – so that they then become envious
nd destructive: "All that is good is in me, and all the bad things are in you!"

JMQ: So envy becomes a defence against, for example, perception of the qualities of
the object.

Yes, it is one manifestation of that. So long as you can maintain the narcissistic position
everybody is envious of you. You are not envious. That is what primary projection of envy is
all about. In other words, "I am all life and you are all destructiveness."

JMQ: When did you introduce these ideas?

I don't know really. John Steiner made a remark about my work which was very illuminating
to me. You know, when I wrote the Introduction to your second book,[1] I said that it was a
continuation of the theme that you had in your first book, The Taming of Solitude – and that
was something of a revelation to you. Well, in 1997, in his Introduction to my last book, John
Steiner said something about my work which was quite a revelation to me. He said that my
work centres on two themes: the life and death instincts on the one hand, and reality and
phantasy on the other. He goes on to say that there is a link between the two: since the death
instinct attacks reality, the reality of life, the reality of experience, the two themes are really part
of the same world-view. That was a complete revelation to me! You know from your own
experience as a writer, that when we write about something we are not archivists – we don't
think of our earlier papers and how they're all related and so on. Sometimes I refer to my
earlier work to explain certain ideas, but very often the underlying themes – well, it's other
people who unearth that kind of thing because we are too busy doing what we have to do in the
present.

JMQ: Would you say there is a link between artistic creativity and the death instinct?

Yes, there is a link with art because in my first paper on aesthetics I speak of the artist's search
for immortality in various ways. I think another thing which kept me close to the death instinct is
my understanding of art. How do you explain that Goya's war paintings and sketches don't
depress us but give us a feeling of satisfaction?

know something about the dynamics of the group. Tha
anything that would prove the contrary.

Personally I'm not sure I would have become a psych
and its Discontents and Beyond the Pleasure Principle wh

JMQ: You were really quite young when you began reading

I know the feeling I had when it clicked with me – "That's it!
didn't apply the idea of the death instinct in actual clinical pra
enough and precise enough. It was only Klein that took it serio
practice. I think partly because she was for a time analysed by ,
died prematurely – but she would have got something from Ab
And partly also, of course, because when you work with young

JMQ: How would you define the death instinct?

The way I see the death instinct – this is my way of putting it – is tha
against the pain of life. I quote in my 1986 lecture "On the clinical u
the death instinct" (published in 1993) the marvellous description by
Martin Eden, of a man dying by suicide, trying to breathe and feeling
of life". Freud spoke of the deflection of the death instinct, but Klein s
deal with the death instinct by projection – "*it's not me*" – and turnin
bad object – "*s/he is the bad one*". And of course that meets reality b
is good the more confirmation you get, as it were, of the strength of th
On the other hand, when the object is perceived as bad in reality, as
projection, that destructiveness is how the death instinct is manifested.

Now the things that I think make it more understandable is the link that
the death instinct and envy, because the death instinct is not directed only
world. Klein's theory is object-related; the death instinct is directed not or
self which wants life (and which therefore is vulnerable to pain), but also to
object. In other words, the death instinct manifests itself in envy because
breast which is hated and attacked for being the source of life. Also, I think th
enough attention to in my paper on the death instinct is the fact that the life ins
to reconstruct an object; it's always attached to objects. Freud doesn't say
object-related, but it undoubtedly is (the difference between Freud and Klein
the ego is aware of the object's existence from the very beginnings of life itsel

JMQ: Could you be a bit more explicit about what you mean by that?

I'll tell you a dream that I had recently which I found very amusing. I told it to Bet
she said, "Look, it's about the life and death instincts!" I read a lot of science fiction
that remained with me is about a chap who for some reason gets into a capsule
spaceship, maybe to make some repairs. At one point his harness becomes und
realizes that he's floating off into the void. For a time he is still in radio contact but t
gets cut off; that's when he knows there is nothing but void. It was years ago that I rea

But just a few weeks ago I had a dream in which, for some reason or other, I fou
getting out of a spaceship; I knew there was a little bit of atmosphere around still bu
all – the rest was void. Then somebody opened a hatch or something and told me
back, somebody got me back inside! And I thought it very funny when I woke up. I th
want to die – but not yet!" So Betty said, "Look it's clearly a dream about the life an
instincts." I thought, it's not only that – the life instinct is always object-related becaus
dream *I* don't turn back – somebody's there to pull me back. So you see our attachmen
is our attachment to the object.

*JMQ: In 1984, you gave a paper on the death instinct and Green, with his idea of the "de-
objectalizing function", developed some ideas close to those of Herbert Rosenfeld.*

We can all have theories. I think Green sees it as a much more passive thing. And I don't th
he links it with envy.

*JMQ: H
death d

I think
narciss
or ther

JMQ:
Could
whats
betwe

Not
rega
env
stru

JM

If y
sta
tha
er

is
h
c
a

*JMQ: Well, how do **you** explain that?*

I wrote about it in a paper on disillusionment – "The story of Adam and Eve and that of Lucifer" (Segal 2000b). It's based on Milton's *Paradise Lost*. In that paper I discuss the issue in some detail – the link between omnipotence and psychosis, I mean – and I explore the differences between the myth of Lucifer and that of Adam and Eve. The Adam and Eve myth is a depressive disillusionment which is in fact creative – you have to give up Paradise in order to live – and Milton actually says *"Maybe the fall of man was a good thing for us."* That disillusionment gave them life – the desire to work, to live, to procreate – whereas, in the myth of Lucifer, if he isn't Number One, if you like, everything is destroyed. He creates a world in his mind in which he would rather be King of Hell than Number Two in Heaven.

Well, when all is said and done, isn't it better to suffer all the pains of the Oedipus complex than to live in some kind of manic disposition – because then the whole world disappears and all that's left for you is to be King of Hell. That's where I think that the concept of the death instinct is most appropriate – in clinical practice and with its links to poetry. If you like, that would be my last – in both senses of the word: most recent, and probably final – formulation of the death instinct. I think it's one of my best papers.

(Tape 6, side B, 13 March 2004)

"On the clinical usefulness of the concept of the death instinct"

This paper was read as a Lecture given for the Freud Memorial Chair at University College, London in 1986 and published in 1993.

Segal, H. (1993) "On the clinical usefulness of the concept of the death instinct", *International Journal of Psycho-Analysis*, **74**: 55–62; reprinted in *Psychoanalysis, Literature and War* (1997), London and New York: Routledge.

All pain comes from living

Segal begins by evoking Jack London's *Martin Eden*, and quotes from it an example that quickly became a classic illustration of the conflict between the life and death drives in psychoanalysis. At the end of the novel, Martin commits suicide by drowning. As he sinks, he automatically tries to swim. Realizing that this was a sudden impulse emanating from his instinct to live, he felt contempt for the part of himself that still wished to live – and he stopped swimming. As he drowned, Martin felt a tearing pain in his chest, and Jack London brings out the last thought that went through his head: *"The hurt was not death. It was life – the pangs of life."* Segal draws the conclusion: *"All pain comes from living"* (1993: 56).

Freud was the first to describe the death drive, in *Beyond the Pleasure Principle* (1920g). He described it as a biological drive to return to the inorganic and postulated the existence of a conflict with the life drive; the aim of the latter is life and reproduction, while that of the death drive is destruction, dissolution and death. Freud at first tended to emphasize the biological aspect. In Segal's opinion, if Freud described his ideas about the death drive as a biological speculation, this was perhaps defensively, because he expected that this new idea of his would meet with great resistance. Segal gives this warning: *"We must not forget, however, that he was motivated in those speculations by purely clinical considerations about the repetition compulsion, the nature of masochism, the murderousness of the melancholic superego, etc."* (1993: 56). Later, in *The Ego and the Id* (1923b), Freud made clear the psychological aspect of the death drive and the relevance of the concept not only to depression and masochism, but also to the neuroses in general.

Annihilating the perceiving self

Nowadays we can formulate the conflict between the life and death drives in purely psychological terms. For example, both drives confront us with the experience of needs, but in different ways and in varying proportions. "*One [reaction is] to seek satisfaction for the needs: that is life-promoting and leads to object seeking, love, and eventually object concern. The other is the drive to annihilate the need, to annihilate the perceiving experiencing self, as well as anything that is perceived*" (Segal 1993: 56). Segal here makes an original contribution to this topic in that, for her, the death drive (or drive to annihilate) seeks not only to annihilate what is perceived in the external world, but also the experiencing and perceiving self – later, indeed, she would add the actual organ that does the perceiving.

In *Beyond the Pleasure Principle*, Freud (1920g) began by referring to the tendency to annihilate any disturbance as the "Nirvana principle", the idea being that this principle was related to the pleasure/unpleasure principle through its quest for constancy. Later, however, in "The Economic Problem of Masochism" (1924c), Freud changed his mind and argued that the quest for Nirvana was the equivalent of the death drive insofar as the Nirvana principle and the pleasure/unpleasure principle have the same aim: to do away with any kind of excitation. In his attempt to resolve this implicit contradiction, he suggested that the libido participates in the process by becoming fused with the death drive in order to play a part in the regulation of life processes.

Freud postulated also that the organism defends itself against the death drive by deflecting it, so that it becomes aggressiveness. According to Segal, destructiveness towards external objects is not simply a deflection of self-destructiveness to the outside, as described by Freud; from the very beginning, she argues, the wish to annihilate is directed both at the perceiving self *and* at the object perceived, hardly distinguishable one from the other.

In addition, Freud wrote that the death drive operates silently within the body. As a result, we can never see its pure manifestations, only manifestations in fusion with the libido – yet Freud speaks also of defusion between the life and death drives. For Segal, thanks to new technical developments, we have become more adept at identifying the components belonging to the death drive in that fusion. Also, in more disturbed patients, we can often detect the operation of the death drive "*in an almost pure form*" (1993: 57) and not simply in those processes in which it is fused with the libido.

"Pushing the button of annihilation"

Segal gives a clinical example to illustrate the manner in which the death drive operates in a psychoanalytic session. Patient A reacted extremely aggressively when faced with any emotional response, whether it involved other people or herself. She would have liked to annihilate other people immediately – "I want him dead. I want to kill all of them" – and, as regards herself, she constantly wished to get rid of her limbs and her organs so as to put an end to any feelings of frustration or anxiety. In one session, the patient spoke of her fear of nuclear war and wondered whose finger was on the button; what she could not bear was the thought of surviving in a post-nuclear-war world covered in devastating radioactive fall-out. The analogy between the patient's idea of "pushing the button", thereby detonating an atom bomb, and her destructiveness aimed at other people and at herself led Segal to the conclusion that all this was an expression of the death drive.

> *Pushing the button was an expression of the death instinct, but combined with immediate projection, so that the threat of death was felt to come from outside – the fall-out. I think that in that session she got in touch with an almost direct experience of her own wish for total annihilation of the world and herself. The interpretation on these lines immediately lessened the persecution and put her in touch with the psychic reality of her own drives.* (1993: 58)

Segal draws the conclusion that a confrontation with the death drive, in favourable circumstances, mobilizes the life drive as well.

Projection of the death drive during analysis

With her second example, Segal shows how the death drive can be deflected towards the outside world and projected on to the object; she had elsewhere expressed that idea in the terse formula "*Instead of dying, killing*" (Segal 1979a [1991: 20]). Patient B was nearing the end of his analysis. Normally, he manifested little anxiety. One weekend, he suddenly felt physically and mentally cold and progressively paralysed. Terrified, he felt that the coldness which was invading him was a sign that he was about to die and that the only way to get rid of this deadness inside was to go and kill his analyst, Segal. *"The experience not only made a shattering impact on him; it had a strong impact on me. One could dismiss it as a simple agoraphobic attack, but I had no doubt in the session that we were dealing with life-and-death forces"* (1993: 58). In the following sessions, the patient realized that the inner coldness he had felt had not come from outside but from himself, because he had wanted to die. Having experienced what it felt like to be invaded by death, he then realized that in fact he did not really want to die. The experience of the real consequences of giving in to the death drive mobilized his life forces. *"In those sessions, and subsequent ones, he could feel need, love, gratitude and anger with a strength and depth never experienced by him before"* (1993: 59).

Segal goes on to discuss the similarities and differences between Freud's and Klein's views on the subject. For Freud, the death drive is dealt with mainly by deflecting it outside the individual, where it becomes aggressiveness turned against objects. For Klein, although this deflection is converted into aggressiveness, the death drive is projected and directed towards the bad object created by the original projection. This mechanism accounted for the feelings of nuclear fall-out experienced by patient A in Segal's first example.

Projection of the death drive is often very powerful and has a direct impact on the counter-transference. It can take many forms; Segal often felt paralysed with patient B, while in other cases the analyst feels pessimism and despair invading the counter-transference. With certain patients, it is the life drive that is projected into the analyst, leaving all that is life in the analyst's hands and stimulating excessive protectiveness and concern as regards the patient.

Where does the pain caused by the death drive come from?

Segal then goes on to discuss the origins of the acute pain involved in the operation of the death drive. *"The question arises: if the death instinct aims at not perceiving, not feeling, refusing the joys and the pain of living, why is the operation of the death instinct associated with so much pain?"* (1993: 59). Segal argues that pain is experienced by the libidinal ego originally threatened by the death drive. It follows that the primary source of pain felt by the libidinal ego is the stirring of the death instinct within and the threat of annihilation. Once the drive is projected, dread and pain come from persecution and feelings of guilt, both of which are felt as coming from outside the individual. Freud described the superego of the melancholic as *"a pure culture of the death instinct"* (1923b: 53) and, in *Civilization and its Discontents* (1930a [1929]), he came to the conclusion that all guilt feelings arise from the operation of the death drive. For Klein too, anxiety and guilt have their origins in the death drive. *"So the operation of the death instinct produces fear, pain and guilt in the self that wishes to live and be undamaged"* (1993: 60). However, as we shall see, guilt is not a direct expression of the death drive. Guilt feelings arise from awareness of one's responsibility for the object, and that awareness has its origin in working through the depressive position.

The origin of pleasure in the experience of pain

This is a complex issue, and Segal evokes several aspects of the challenge that pleasure in the experience of pain represents for psychoanalysis – cf. Freud's study of masochism (1924c). According to Segal, the most satisfactory explanation is one which takes into account the conflict between the life and death drives, viewed from various perspectives.

In the first place, the pleasure experienced in pain is partly the sheer satisfaction of the drive. *"The death instinct, like the life instinct, seeks satisfaction and the satisfaction of the death instinct, short of death, is in pain"* (1993: 60).

It would seem also that in enjoying pain there is the satisfaction of the triumph of the death-dealing part of the self over the wish to live. This kind of triumph is not a direct expression of the death instinct. It arises from the destructive omnipotence aimed at the object. To a significant degree manic defences can explain this phenomenon. Segal pointed out this aspect when she evoked Martin Eden: surprised by the will to live that took hold of him without his realizing it, he sneered at that desire before letting himself sink. For Segal, this sneer of triumph, conscious or unconscious, is an important component of the negative therapeutic reaction, which is not only the sadistic pleasure of triumph over the analyst but also the masochistic pleasure of triumph over that part of oneself that wishes to live and to grow.

The pleasure in pain comes also from the fact that libidinization and sexualization are always present. This can be seen, for example, in people who are constantly searching for sexual pleasure. Here, the libido is used to cover up their unconscious sadism and masochism – the deep-down pleasure in inflicting pain and destruction on others and on oneself.

Generally speaking, libidinization is always present as a participating factor in the fusion between the life and death instincts.

In healthy development the fusion of the life and death instinct is under the aegis of the life instinct and the deflected death instinct, aggression, is at the service of life. Where the death instinct predominates, the libido is at the service of the death instinct. This is particularly evident in perversions. A delicate balance is established between the life and death forces and a disturbance of this balance in the process of analysis is perceived as a great threat. (1993: 60)

Envy also plays a significant role in the conflict between the life and death drives. In that sense, envy is one of the main manifestations of the death drive, although not, of course, the only one. As Klein (1957) pointed out, envy is necessarily an ambivalent feeling since it is rooted in need and admiration. Like all ambivalent feelings, there may be a predominance of libidinal forces or of destructive forces.

If the death instinct is a reaction to a disturbance produced by needs, the object is perceived both as disturbance, the creator of the need, and as the unique object, capable of disturbance removal. As such, the needed breast is hated and envied. And one of the pains that has to be avoided by self-annihilation and object-annihilation is the pain caused by the awareness of the existence of such an object. (1993: 60–61)

Segal evokes another clinical example to illustrate this point, then modestly concludes her paper by saying that, although she has not suggested anything new or added anything to what Freud and Klein had already stated, she did want to demonstrate the fact that the concept of the death drive is indispensable in clinical practice. "*Beyond the pleasure principle, beyond ambivalence, aggression, persecution, jealousy, envy, etc., there is a constant pull of the self-destructive forces, and it is the task of the analyst to deal with them*" (1993: 61).

The conflict between the life and death drives: a debate among psychoanalysts

In 1984, at the first Symposium of the European Psychoanalytical Federation held in Marseilles, I remember that Hanna Segal was able to confront her ideas on the conflict between the life and death drives with those of Jean Laplanche, Eero Rechardt and André Green. The debates showed that opinions on this topic are many and varied. Laplanche, for example, bases his point of view on "instinctual monism" – the death drive is quite simply part of the sexual drive. For Segal, on the other hand, there exists a dualism of the drives which can account for the life drive and the death drive. Another crucial question that arises is whether such a debate is of purely theoretical interest or has some bearing on clinical matters. While Laplanche and Green argue that clinical material cannot in any way be adduced in support of the existence of a death drive, Segal maintains that theory cannot be dissociated from clinical practice in such a manner.

In order to give the reader some idea of the arguments put forward, I shall summarize the point of view of Laplanche (1986) and that of Green (1986). In the preceding sections of this chapter, I have summarized the paper that Segal herself read before the Symposium (Segal 1993).

Jean Laplanche: the death drive is necessarily sexual

Laplanche's point of view is based on the following basic premise: the concept of drive is fundamental in psychoanalysis, only one sort of drive exists and it is sexual in nature. "Only sexuality has the right to call itself a drive", writes Laplanche. "The unconscious is purely sexual in content" (1986: 19). It follows from this that the death drive must therefore be sexual in nature. For Laplanche, sexuality ultimately derives from what he calls "primal seduction". This is not some kind of sexual manipulation by an adult, but the fact that the immature child is faced with messages filled with meaning and desire – they are, so to speak, "enigmatic signifiers", the key to which he or she does not possess. Thereupon, the sexual content of these enigmatic signifiers is repressed into the unconscious, where they become the source of the drives – which, as I have said, Laplanche considers to be exclusively sexual in nature. "The effort to bind the trauma that accompanies primal seduction leads to the repression of these original signifiers or their metonymical derivatives. These unconscious objects or unconscious representations are the source of the drive" (ibid.: 18).

For Laplanche, what was fundamentally innovative in Freud's theory was not the introduction of the concept of the death drive in *Beyond the Pleasure Principle* (1920g) but the observation, developed in "On Narcissism: An Introduction" (1914c), that the sexual drive can follow two possible directions, such that it can be cathected both in the object and in the ego.

> This is an entirely new exploration – the ego as a love object – and there is the idea that external objects are reflections of or at least related to that initial cathexis of the ego, since we love another person either in our own image or thanks to a potential for love which initially is the potential to love ourselves. Sexuality therefore tends to be absorbed by that aspect of love. (Laplanche 1986: 19)

That observation led Freud to reaffirm in 1920 that sexuality had a strong tendency to fulfil its desires and never ceases to strive for complete satisfaction (Laplanche 1986: 20). That aspect is the "diabolical" dimension of the drive in the service of the primary process and the compulsion to repeat. Laplanche goes on to argue that sexuality thus finds itself torn between these two contradictory tendencies that Freud called life instinct and death instinct. The pleasure principle itself is also torn apart, by being pulled either towards zero (what was later to be called the *Nirvana principle*) or towards a constant level (the *principle of constancy*). "When the 'pleasure principle' means an absolute decrease in tension, it is said to be 'in the service of the death drive'. When the tendency towards absolute zero is designated by the term 'Nirvana principle', the pleasure principle is distinct from that and merges with the principle of constancy: it then represents the demands of the life drives with their tendency towards homeostasis and synthesis" (ibid.: 20).

Laplanche claims that his theory of primal seduction is very close to at least some aspects of the ideas of both Freud and Klein, in the sense that they are in agreement as regards the part played by self-destructiveness – the "internal attack of the drives" or the "id's hatred of the ego". It is true that, in Laplanche's theory of primal seduction, the death drive is quite simply an internal attack by objects – the adult seducing the immature child – which are both stimulating and dangerous for the ego.

How does Laplanche resolve the contradictions which his theory implies? On the one hand, there is a dualism of the drives – the conflict between the life and death drives – while, on the other, there is an energizing monism, represented by the libido, which is based solely on the sexual drive. Laplanche argues that, basically, there is a common source of energy which can only be sexual, while at the same time there is a fundamental dissymmetry between the life and death drives, the dissymmetry that Freud described in terms of the binding and unbinding of the drives (*Mischung* and *Entmischung*): "A fundamental dissymmetry exists: the life drive tends towards union between itself and the principle of disunion, the death drive tends towards the disunion both of its union with the life drive and of the life drive itself" (ibid.: 24).

André Green: the objectalizing and de-objectalizing functions of the drives

Like Laplanche, Green bases his own hypotheses concerning the drives on Freud's theory, but takes a different direction. Comparing the respective properties of the two drives, Green says that it is impossible to see in the death drive a function which corresponds to that of sexuality in the life drive. The sexual function is the representative of the life drive (Eros), whereas the only function representative of the death drive is that of self-destruction.

> The real issue lies in attempting to get some kind of answer to the enigma that Freud left unresolved: what function could play the corresponding role as representative of the death drive? It will be recalled that, for Freud, self-destruction is the essential hallmark of the death drive, allo-destruction being simply an attempt to relieve internal tensions. That point of view is challenged by many post-Freudian theories. (Green 1986: 52)

According to Green, the role of the self-destructive function in the death drive does indeed correspond to that played by the sexual function in the life drive (Eros). However, unlike Freud, Green does not think that this self-destructive function operates in a primitive, automatic and spontaneous manner.

In Green's hypothesis, object relations play a crucial role, more so than in Laplanche's thinking. Given that drives can be identified only through their psychic representatives, Green argues that it is the object which bears witness to the drive. By integrating object and object relations with the way in which drives function, Green is able to shed new light on the "binding" and "unbinding" of the drives, the two principal mechanisms described by Freud as characteristic of the life and death drives. Green goes on to postulate an objectalizing function, which he associates with the life drive, and a de-objectalizing function, linked to the death drive.

Green defines the objectalizing function of the life drive not simply as relating to the creation of internal and external object relations; he emphasizes the fact that cathexis itself becomes objectalized. Conversely, the aim of the death drive is to fulfil as far as possible its de-objectalizing function through unbinding. "Such a definition makes it clear that it is not only object relations that are attacked but also any substitutes for them that may exist – the ego, for example, and cathexis itself insofar as it has undergone objectalization" (ibid.: 55). In other words, the characteristic feature of the destructiveness of the death drive is de-cathexis (withdrawal of cathexis).

Green goes on to say that a parallel can be drawn between, on the one hand, the objectalizing and de-objectalizing functions and, on the other, the phenomena of binding/unbinding between the life and death drives as postulated by Freud.

> The closer we get to repression in the true sense of the word, the more the binding/unbinding polarity is backed up by a re-binding in the unconscious thanks to other mechanisms (displacement, condensation, double reversal, etc.). The further away we are from repression, the greater the extent to which other kinds of primary defences (splitting, repudiation) operate; unbinding thus tends to gain the upper hand, with the result that re-binding is thwarted or at the very least restricted. (ibid.: 56)

In his conclusion, Green states that the objectalizing aim of the life drive has the effect of supporting symbolization – essential for mental functioning – through the mediation of the sexual function.

Do we really need a concept such as the death drive?

During that Symposium, Eero Rechardt argued that the compulsion to repeat has both a destructive and a constructive dimension. He went on to claim that, if need be, he could do without the concept of the death drive. Clifford Yorke, for his part, felt that many of the ideas discussed by the panellists had little to do with the death drive; he claimed to be representative of those psychoanalysts who do not accept the concept.

My own impression at the end of the Symposium was that, compared to the various theoretical debates, Segal's clinical examples shed a more helpful light on my daily work with my patients. Also, I could better understand why Freud said of the death drive that it is "mute but powerful" (1923b: 59).

Current opinions among psychoanalysts as regards the conflict between the life and death drives

More than twenty years have elapsed since the Marseilles Symposium, yet Freud's hypothesis concerning the death drive remains controversial. Jorge Luis Maldonado is a psychoanalyst who has made a detailed study of what he calls the "analyst's iatrogenic interventions" – interpretations which, insofar as they are a partial re-enactment of some traumatic experience to which the patient had been subjected, amount to a re-traumatization. Maldonado argues that the destructiveness which psychoanalysts can observe in their clinical work – this, after all, is what the idea of the death drive tries to account for – has in fact many component features.

JMQ: What do psychoanalysts in Latin America think today of Hanna Segal's ideas about the death drive?

Jorge Luis Maldonado: Well, I would start off by saying that Hanna Segal's work is very widely known among psychoanalysts in Argentina and in the rest of Latin America. Her ideas on different aspects of psychoanalysis are adopted even by analysts whose conceptual approach is quite different from hers. The concept of the death drive is accepted in Argentina by those psychoanalysts – and there are many of them – who follow Melanie Klein's theories and the developments that Hanna Segal has brought to these. That said, the concept is challenged by other psychoanalysts; in my view, their disagreements (which are sometimes justified) arise from several misunderstandings that are implicit in Freud's writings.

JMQ: What are the main points of controversy?

I shall mention a few aspects that seem to me to be well worth discussing because of certain distortions in the *use* of theory that would later turn out to be distortions *of* the theory itself.

The usefulness of the concept of the death drive for understanding pathological states is important when we see it as highlighting the notion of intra-psychic conflict, as the ultimate agency of the implicit destructiveness of human beings. In my opinion, however, the use of this concept may make it more difficult to look for other factors that contribute to pathology, such as damage that affects one's sense of identity and which comes from the object.

On another level, there is another misunderstanding, which comes from the use of the same term – "repetition" – to describe processes that are quite different from one another. At first, repetition was conceptualized as being the opposite of remembering; as such it could account for clinical phenomena based on the pleasure principle. These are different from what is included in the death drive, which is beyond the pleasure principle. Lagache's (1953) aphorism "need for repetition" and "repetition of needs" defines the necessary coexistence between the two ideas. Other writers have highlighted other differences in the concept of repetition. Lacan, for example, locates repetition in the "Tyké" (the "Real" dimension), the *locus* in which there is no capacity for representation, simply the immanent tendency to repeat. This concept is different from the "compulsion to repeat" which arises from the insistence on going back to the pleasure principle. The factors that integrate the death drive (repetition and destructiveness) are, in Freud's writings, inherent in human nature. However, Hanna Segal's development (1993) focuses mainly on destructiveness, whereas Lacan deals above all with repetition.

JMQ: How can that be identified in clinical terms?

In those repetitive dreams we find in cases of traumatic neurosis, the experience that triggers them, given that it becomes the subject of a dream, is included in the sphere of representations, hence the possibility of transforming it. The presence of representation differentiates it from other forms of repetition. In psychotic processes, however, the representational system is gradually eroded in parallel with the slow loss of life forces – the end point being a catatonic state, the paradigm of being inanimate. Repetition tends towards fusion in traumatic dreams and towards a gradual defusion in other contexts such as that of the psychoses.

JMQ: How would you understand the concept of trauma in this context?

The concept of trauma has always been marked by injustice in a certain sense, because it was erroneously associated with concrete thinking and mechanical processes considered as being based simply on reality. The concept found itself associated with non-integration of phantasies as well as the specific characteristics of the individual. It would be helpful were we to go back to the original notion of trauma, linked not only to an "event" supposed to have actually occurred in the past but also to what has been lost since that event. The psychoanalytic value of the concept of trauma lies in this idea of "what has been lost" – especially in the structure of lost ideals.

Patients who have lived through traumatic experiences tend to implicate their objects, and in particular the analyst in the transference – they reproduce the trauma by stimulating in their analyst his or her own hostility, which is then expressed through the formulation of accusatory interpretations (Maldonado 2006). That kind of repetition leads to defusion and has to do with the death drive. The problem is a highly complex one, given that not all trauma is brought about by the tendency to repeat which is implicit in that drive. I would agree that it is quite possible to attribute to that drive the capacity to generate and reproduce traumatic experiences, but at the same time, doing so can be controversial if we consider the drive to have so much importance that other determinants are excluded, such as significant trauma, that are the work of factors external to the individual (Maldonado 2006). Failure to differentiate trauma brought about by the individual's own destructiveness from those which are due to exogenous factors – by "exogenous", I mean also the complex relationship between reality and fantasy – may lead to disagreements with respect to Freud's second theory of the instinctual drives.

JMQ: Are there other factors that hinder the investigation of these aspects?

If the transference is seen as focussed only on envy as a determinant of anxiety, this is another factor that may give rise to obstacles in exploring and evaluating the various elements that go to make up human suffering. I shall mention some of these without exploring whether or not they are, for example, failures in what Winnicott called the "facilitating environment", or failures in the maternal function of containing and transforming beta-elements in Bion's sense, or, again, in the essential value of the paternal prohibition in the Oedipal organization as defined by Lacan.

In narcissistic rivalry (which is similar to but not identical with envy), the need that the self feels for the object awakens the wish to destroy it, because the object's presence casts a shadow over the self's feelings of grandiosity based on the illusion of experiencing oneself as unique and superior to the object world. Perhaps that form of rivalry is one expression of destructiveness in which the drive remains unmediated and requires a direct interpretation in terms of destructiveness. Oedipal rivalry (which is different from narcissistic rivalry and from jealousy) is something else again. It is linked to some other person (brother or sister, father or mother) insofar as he or she represents an obstacle to possessing the libidinal object; love for the object precedes and determines Oedipal rivalry. Aggressiveness, implicit in patricidal and fratricidal wishes, derives from the libidinal link to another object. If the analyst incorrectly evaluates what can be attributed to primary destructiveness and what to the aggressiveness derived from the libidinal element, this may give rise to contradictory reactions in the patient such that any conceptualization will be far removed from actual clinical experience.

JMQ: What role, in your opinion, does destructiveness play in depression?

As for pathology, depression depends on ambivalence towards the object, which reaches its highest point in melancholia. Ambivalence in turn depends not only on the self's destructiveness but also on factors that involve the actions of the object that triggers them. Projective identification – not simply that which the self sends out towards the object but also that which the self receives from the object – hidden behind secondary feelings of guilt also has to be taken into account. There are other forms of depression which depend not only on ambivalence but also on the loss of an ideal. As for perverse structures, destructiveness is here the major factor, hidden behind sexuality and by that component of envy which, in my opinion, is significant for the prevalence of perversion. Nonetheless, there are other elements implied in perversion, such as the nature of the infant's primary relationship with the parents, early losses, the alliances each parent may set up to oppose the other, etc.

I would like to conclude by highlighting the value of Hanna Segal's thinking as regards the concept of the death drive. Our appreciation of any given writer increases with the possibility we have to express not only our agreements but also our disagreements with what he or she proposes. What Segal says may not coincide with our criteria, but what is indisputable is that her ideas have dialectical value, and that in itself is highly supportive of the development of psychoanalysis, the growth of which has, from the outset, been rooted in dialectics.

(Interview, October 2006)

Jorge Luis Maldonado (Buenos Aires) is a training analyst and supervisor with the Buenos Aires Psychoanalytic Association.

Chapter 6

PRESENTING THE KLEINIAN APPROACH TO PSYCHOANALYSIS

I really think she [Dr Segal] is by far the best person both to explain my work succinctly and also not to be provocative [. . .]
(Letter from Melanie Klein to Marcelle Spira, 8 May 1956)

Explain, give clinical illustrations, avoid polemics

Hanna Segal soon became well known in the psychoanalytic world and beyond thanks to the talent with which she explained and illustrated Kleinian concepts and to her capacity for establishing constructive dialogue without needlessly stirring up controversy.

Her ability to do this was explicitly underlined by Melanie Klein herself in one of her letters to Marcelle Spira, the Geneva-based psychoanalyst (see Chapter 1). In the extract which I quote above, Klein emphasizes both Segal's talent for explaining the Kleinian approach and her non-provocative style, i.e. her ability to avoid needless controversy. What did Klein mean by that? In my view, the need to explain Kleinian concepts arises from their sheer complexity, which in turn is due to the primitive nature of the infantile anxieties and phantasies described by Melanie Klein, which emerge much earlier than Freud had thought. In addition, it must be said that Klein's style of writing is not always very clear; her ideas are sometimes difficult to understand, given the somewhat austere not to say abrupt and blunt manner in which she expresses her thinking. This is particularly the case when she reports some of her interpretations without saying much about the groundwork that led up to them.

Similarly, it should be remembered that Klein herself never wrote a short guide to her work. Like other pioneering spirits, she wrote her various papers as she went along, in parallel with her findings as they developed over a period of some forty years. Segal's work in drawing up a synthesis of all this was therefore all the more commendable; it made Klein's findings more accessible and meant that those of her principal followers, including Segal herself, became more widely known.

As to the avoidance of unnecessary controversy, Segal's contribution was particularly valuable, because a mere explanation of Klein's ideas and those of her followers does not mean that they will be understood. It was essential to create a climate of scientific discussion over and above the intolerance and hostility with which Kleinian hypotheses have often been greeted.

It is not difficult, therefore, to understand why Segal, with her diverse qualities, soon came to be seen as an ambassador of the Kleinian approach in psychoanalysis and as such has been invited as a guest speaker in many different countries throughout the world.

Differentiate Klein's ideas from those that rightly belong to Segal

Before going any further, I would like to make one brief comment. When Hanna Segal puts forward Klein's ideas, her discretion and modesty mean that she herself usually stays very much in the background. As a result, it is often difficult for the reader to know which ideas are Klein's and which arise from developments that Hanna Segal herself has made. Nonetheless, Segal's own thinking permeates all her writings on Melanie Klein and the Kleinian approach – as any attentive reader will have noticed. First of all, I would say that the most visible aspect of Segal's own contribution lies in the many clinical examples drawn from her own psychoanalytic work which are there to illustrate the theoretical points made by Klein and her followers, including, of course, Segal herself. Secondly, it seems to me that we can hear Segal's voice in the choice she makes of Klein's concepts – she describes them in her own way, and goes on to discuss them in the light of her own hypotheses, both from a theoretical and from a technical perspective.

The need to differentiate Segal's own ideas from those of Klein seems to me to be particularly important for the present chapter, in which I examine that part of Segal's work which presents the Kleinian approach. The reader will thus see that, beyond the presentation of Melanie Klein's technique as such, Segal's comments show that she has developed her own technique, which does all the same lie within the general framework of Kleinian theory.

Four major texts

It is of course possible to see all of Segal's writings as a presentation of the Kleinian approach. Four of her texts are nonetheless worth highlighting because of their specifically didactic character. Firstly, two of her books: *Introduction to the Work of Melanie Klein* (1964) and *Klein* (1979a), a book which is both a biography of Melanie Klein and a history of the development of her ideas. I shall then go on to study two papers that Segal wrote on technique, "Melanie Klein's technique" and "Melanie Klein's technique of child analysis"; these two papers were published in 1967 as chapters in a book to which several authors contributed, the aim of which was to present different kinds of psychoanalytic technique. I shall not summarize the above-mentioned two books, since each is itself a synopsis; I shall simply give a brief presentation of each of them. I shall, however, go into more detail as regards Segal's two papers on Klein's technique, since any reader who is not particularly familiar with the Kleinian approach may well find them all the more interesting.

Introduction to the Work of Melanie Klein *(1964)*

Segal, H. (1964) *Introduction to the Work of Melanie Klein*, London: William Heinemann Ltd.

This *Introduction to the Work of Melanie Klein* was originally meant for students and is based on a series of lectures Segal gave at the Institute of Psychoanalysis in London as part of the third-year curriculum for trainees. Segal notes that a thorough knowledge of Freud's writings is a prerequisite for anyone who wishes to learn about Melanie Klein's work: "*The lectures are meant as an introduction and not as a substitute for the study of Melanie Klein's own writings. They can be used as a guide to reading*" (1964: 1). In order not to overburden the text, Segal decided not to append a complete bibliography, preferring to indicate at the end of each chapter the essential references to Melanie Klein's work, as well as to papers by her principal followers – W. R. Bion, P. Heimann, S. Isaacs, B. Joseph, J. Riviere, H. Rosenfeld and H. Segal.

As regards the order of the chapters, Segal opted to take as her roadmap the psychological growth of the individual, beginning with early infancy. From a didactic point of view, it is more useful to proceed in that manner rather than to follow the chronological order in which Klein and her followers made their discoveries. Just as Freud's findings proceeded retroactively – his observations of adult patients led him to discover the child behind the adult – so did Klein's: her observations of her child patients led her to discover the baby behind the child. The other reason that led Segal to abandon the chronological order of Klein's discoveries in favour of following the psychological development of the individual was that, in her view, the Kleinian school of thought had by then done enough solid groundwork to make an overall presentation an entirely plausible undertaking. "*We have accumulated sufficient knowledge, and our theory is sufficiently comprehensive to warrant an attempt to present it as a whole*" (1964: 2).

The initial chapters define some general notions such as unconscious phantasy, the paranoid-schizoid position and the depressive position. Segal then goes on to examine some major Kleinian concepts with these as a backdrop – in particular envy, manic defences, reparation and the early stages of the Oedipus complex. All chapters contain examples taken from Segal's own practice as a psychoanalyst. "*In a limited number of lectures it is possible only to give a rather simplified and schematic description of Melanie Klein's theoretical contributions, but as psycho-analytical theories are derived from clinical experience and meant to throw light on clinical material I rely on my clinical illustrations to convey them more fully*" (1964: 1).

An Introduction that is essential reading

JMQ: In 1964, you wrote your Introduction to the Work of Melanie Klein, *a book that has been translated into many languages and which has been highly successful . . .*

Hanna Segal: And which was quite a worry to me! Klein knew I was writing the book and she expected it to appear in her lifetime. However, it took me a long time to write it – at least four years! I think the reason was that I did not have a contract – I'm a very punctual person as a rule. If I sign a contract which states that I have to have the manuscript ready in eighteen months' time, then I do the necessary. If I do not have a deadline – a knife at your throat – then it takes me much longer. So the book wasn't published until after Klein's death.

JMQ: I wonder whether, when you wrote your Introduction to the Work of Melanie Klein, *your motives had to do with the kind of creative impulse that you describe in your papers on aesthetics: did you feel the need to re-create a new world out of one that was threatened with destruction? Perhaps one can understand Klein's work only after doing the necessary bringing-together of all the scattered pieces? What do you think?*

That is true, but not of all of Klein's written work. It is indeed the case for *The Psychoanalysis of Children*, which is a very badly-written book. I think her writing ability improved enormously over the years – look at *Envy and Gratitude*, for example, which is the best written of all. I think she was so involved in what she was doing that it took her a long time before she could formulate it properly. Take, for example, her papers on the depressive position then, later, on the paranoid-schizoid position – that article is only about seventeen pages long, if I remember correctly, yet the whole of present-day psychoanalysis derives from it. She had so much to choose from! She discovered a world which was so complex that she needed time to sort it all out . . .

JMQ: You played an important role in explaining Klein's conceptions – for example, in demonstrating the relationship between the depressive position and the paranoid-schizoid position thanks to your clinical illustrations . . . Klein never wrote a synopsis of her theory as Freud did with An Outline of Psycho-Analysis (*1940a [1938]*).

I think that she did synthesize her ideas through the way she formulated the depressive position and the paranoid-schizoid position with respect to the Oedipus complex. I think she made that very clear.

Later, she added other elements that made it all much more complex – the concept of envy and that of projective identification. She did not develop the latter concept at all. In her paper "On identification" (Klein 1955), she says that projective identification comes long after the depressive position; it has to do with whole objects, not with primitive levels at all . . . The development of psychoanalysis after Klein is more than anything else an extension of the pathology of projective identification, but she herself did not go into any of that. She could not, of course, do everything – a bit like Freud, who discovered so many things that some questions had to be left unanswered. I don't think Klein realized just how revolutionary her discovery of projective identification was. Just a few lines in a short paper . . .

JMQ: Klein, the second book you wrote about Melanie Klein, was published in 1979. It's as much a biography as a history of her ideas, isn't it?

My first book, *Introduction to the Work of Melanie Klein*, was meant as a guide for students; it did not have a proper bibliography, with references to the scientific literature, etc. The second book, *Klein*, was a commissioned work: it was due to be part of the Fontana and Collins "Modern Writers" series. The requirements were very strict: the length of the book, i.e. the number of pages, as well as other features that were very precisely defined – for example, as regards the relationship between Klein's life and her psychoanalytic work. It was much more of an academic work than any of my other books.

JMQ: When Phyllis Grosskurth wrote her biography of Klein, did she interview you?

She did, yes, but there are some errors in what she wrote – particularly as regards a patient who had been in analysis with Mrs Klein for several years and who later came to me. I gave Mrs Grosskurth my version of what had really happened, and she took that into account in the second edition. [. . .].

(Interview (in French), 15 August 2006)

Klein *(1979)*

Segal, H. (1979) *Klein*, Glasgow: Fontana/Collins. Reprinted London: Karnac (1989, 1991).

In this book, Segal looks back on the major stages of Melanie Klein's life, from her birth in Vienna in 1882 until her death in London in 1960. She succeeds in the quite daunting task of both giving an account of Klein's often eventful personal life and describing the story of her revolutionary discoveries, which met with as much hostility as enthusiasm. The leading characteristic of that pioneer's life was undoubtedly her commitment to psychoanalysis.

Klein is a book that is impossible to summarize, and in that sense resembles Segal's *Introduction to the Work of Melanie Klein*; indeed, *Klein* is to a considerable extent a development and an expansion of that earlier work. Here, Segal paints a brief portrait of Melanie Klein, and I shall use that as a basis for my presentation of the book as a whole. This is, indeed, one of the rare occasions on which Segal talks of Klein as a person and as she knew her. Klein's personality is not easy to describe; she was many-faceted, and accounts of her differ. She was described by some as warm-hearted, tolerant and good-tempered; by others as intolerant, aggressive and demanding. She once described herself as primarily a very passionate person. According to Segal, it is that aspect of Klein that was most striking. "*When she discovered psychoanalysis she became wholly committed to it, and this passion for and devotion to her work was certainly her leading characteristic*" (Segal 1979: 170). She was an ambitious woman, particularly in her wish for the future of psychoanalysis, not for herself. This goes some way to explaining why she was felt to be intransigent, a character trait that some resented. "*Although she was tolerant, and could accept with an open mind the criticisms of her friends and ex-pupils, whom she often consulted, this was so only so long as one accepted the fundamental tenets of her work. If she felt this to be under attack, she could become very fierce in its defence*" (1979: 170).

Klein expected a very high standard of work from herself and from others. She could become quite scathing in her criticism, which made it difficult for some people to show much sympathy for her. Considering herself to be the main successor to Freud and Abraham, she found it very difficult to accept not only Freud's coolness towards her and her work but also the support he gave his daughter Anna. According to Segal, what was most striking about Melanie Klein as a private person was her warmth and her quite extraordinary vitality, which remained with her to the end of her life. "*She was a person who aroused strong emotions. She received a great deal of love and affection from her friends and close colleagues, and often inspired passionate devotion. Her uncompromising attitude about her work made her many enemies, but she was a powerful personality and commanded almost universal respect*" (1979: 174).

Hanna Segal looks back on Melanie Klein's work
Innovations in technique, the Oedipus complex, present and past

JMQ: You were in analysis with Klein shortly before she published her seminal paper "Notes on some schizoid mechanisms" in 1946. What consequences did that major discovery have on technique?

Hanna Segal: Well I think that up until now – sixty years on – we haven't quite fathomed all the changes that took place in this area because every year, as it were, some new aspects are still being discovered. In my opinion, Klein always knew that there was something before the depressive position – a concept she had introduced a few years before, in 1934 and 1940 – but she couldn't quite put it all together. I think at the time she analysed me and Rosenfeld she was learning those things and already using them technically before she wrote the paper. I know for a fact that she had a conflict with Rosenfeld, because Rosenfeld wanted to write a paper on schizoid mechanisms and she said, "Hold on. The paper you're writing is *my* paper!" And she stopped him. [. . .] I remember that she had already worked with me a bit on that level.

But the real changes in technique came over the years. We interpreted a lot more phantasy and related a lot more to actual childhood, paying less attention to the interplay occurring at any particular moment. Also, we had at that point no way of interpreting the different levels of communication – that appeared over the years, and quite gradually. I speak about that in quite an early paper about dreams (1981a), in which I say that you don't analyse the dream, you analyse the dreamer; the dream that the patient tells you may be a discharge – if you like, he leaves the dream with you and there you are, analysing the dream, but he's already far away. You have to take that up in the session – it's not just the *content* but the *function* of the dream – in other words, how the patient gets rid of things into your mind and disassociates himself from it, or wants to affect your mind by some striking dream. Those were very very gradual changes.

JMQ: That seems different from the classical approach to dream analysis.

Very different. When Freud analysed dreams it was day by day and, usually, he interpreted only the content. Nowadays we have come to realize that the simple fact of reporting a dream and talking about it may be used as a form of concrete projection. And that's true not only of dreams but also of many other things that occur in a session. As I say, all these changes came about very gradually.

(Tape 4, end side A, 1 February 2004)

JMQ: What were the other changes?

Technique evolves, but some things remain unchanged, especially some of Freud's ideas. The primary importance of psychic reality and reality testing, the life and death instincts and the Oedipus complex – all of that remains largely the same as it was in Freud's day. Except, perhaps, that nowadays the Oedipus complex is put under a microscope, as it were. It's not just the genital form . . . And our idea about the resolution of Oedipal anxiety – we have a very different view on that.

Freud's view, I would say, was predominantly paranoid: the resolution of the Oedipus complex had to do with the threat of castration and, to some extent, the loss of the object. Nowadays we tend to say that there is no final resolution and that the important thing is the ability to experience Oedipal anxiety, to admit one's neediness, one's smallness, one's desires, one's conflicts, one's hates and so on. That's the sort of resolution we think of now – being able to face up to the Oedipal complex and work with it, not getting rid of it.

JMQ: So in that sense we no longer speak of "extinction" but rather of evolution because we have to work with an Oedipus complex which is present all through life, would that be right?

Everyone has an Oedipus complex. "Tell me your Oedipus complex and I'll tell you who you are!" Some are very deeply schizoid for instance. What looks like a normal Oedipus complex, loving mother/hating father (or the other way round), is not a real Oedipus complex at all – it's a splitting. Good object and bad object. The real Oedipus complex is the desire for both, the hatred of both, feeling guilty about all that and – an essential element in the depressive position – the restoration of the parental couple as a creative aspect of the inner world.

JMQ: Freud thought that depressive patients could not be analysed because they had what he called a "narcissistic neurosis". Did the idea of a transition between the paranoid-schizoid and depressive positions change the way we treat this kind of patient?

Yes indeed, because a depressive patient is not in a real depressive position. Real depression is a defence *against* the depressive position. It's still very omnipotent: we think we've killed the parents and therefore we carry inside ourselves a dead parent – depression and mania are inextricably linked. The depressive patient, real depression, has a lot of manic mechanisms: keeping the object inside, controlling it, feeling omnipotent and feeling omnipotently controlled. In fact, to analyse a depressed patient you have nowadays to think less in terms of depressive and schizoid and more as to how psychotic the underlying pathology is.

JMQ: That would mean getting some idea about the extent of splitting, of omnipotence, of denial and of idealization with respect to manic defences, is that it?

That's right. All manic defences bring about a regression to paranoid-schizoid positions.

JMQ: So perhaps we could say that there are various levels within the depressive position?

Yes, indeed, there are degrees. There's the early depressive position, with a very persecuting superego, which you find in profoundly melancholic patients who are very psychotic; and there is a normal depression – after all, you've got cause to be depressed if you lose a loved object or all your plans fall apart. The normal depressive position, however, leads to reparation and reconstruction and is a great positive motivation. This is particularly the case with artists who, I think, are basically all depressed deep down. Britton describes these different stages very well. It's not that we develop in a straight line, if you like, from the paranoid-schizoid to the depressive; we constantly waver between the two because with each working through of the paranoid-schizoid level you reach a higher level of the depressive position. It's a much more fluid thing.

JMQ: Francisco Palacio-Espasa (2003) also describes different stages in the depressive position . . .

It's continuously developing.

(Tape 4, side B, 1 February 2004)

JMQ: Betty Joseph has developed a technique in which she makes a detailed study of the here-and-now of the interaction between patient and analyst. In order to find the "words that touch", as Danielle Quinodoz (2002) puts it, I have the impression that you, on the other hand, do pay more attention to childhood events and underlying phantasies. Would that be correct?

Your supervision with me was a long time ago and was very very classical Kleinian. It was before we learned to pay much more attention to the acting-in and the constant attempts to manipulate the analyst into a certain role. It is true that old-fashioned Kleinians analysed phantasy material and paid hardly any attention to the interaction.

Since then it has changed a bit towards the Betty way – but not completely. I think it becomes a bit too arid, all this here-and-now "you and me" and "what you have done" thing. At some point I would interpret both [the transference] phantasy and [the link to the patient's] childhood much more. I would say that, as far as theory is concerned, Betty and I have the same standards – one has to speak of the transference and follow the immediate here-and-now of the session. But at some point I would want to link this with the underlying phantasy and childhood. Where we differ is when this point comes. I'll interpret more phantasy once I've analysed what the patient is doing in the session – if there's a clear underlying phantasy to this here-and-now, I would interpret that, and I think I do make more links to the past.

(Tape 5, side A, 1 February 2005)

People tend to use certain differences between Betty and me to make a split, particularly in America where there are many who think that psychoanalysis is all a matter of "here and now" and "you and me" – for them, old-fashioned Kleinians analysed phantasies but didn't see the interaction. I'm sort of midway between the two. Klein's work on projective identification helped us to understand much better the very concreteness of it, in other words that it's always acting-in. That step forward started with Klein but it actually involves a lot of work done by others, with

Klein's agreement. It enabled us to see just how much projective identification is constantly acted-in, pushing the analyst to collude with the system.

In fact, Klein always started with the interaction and the here-and-now of the session, with the immediate feelings, if you like – and always with reference to the transference. The question is how much to link this with unconscious phantasy and with the past – if you link too much with unconscious phantasy and the past you can sometimes get too far away from the immediate reaction, but on the other hand if you stay with the immediate reaction and don't relate it in any way with phantasies, then you lose one of Klein's most important discoveries – that both mechanisms are linked to phantasies. Then we lose the link. Some people just interpret a mechanism and don't actually interpret the phantasy involved in that mechanism.

JMQ: Let's stay for a moment with this idea of a link between present and past.

I think that when something is overwhelmingly enacted – and there we would immediately think that there must be a link with the past – I would tend to relate it to the patient's childhood much more than Betty Joseph seems to do. More specifically, much more than the extremists do – it is a well-known fact that disciples go much further than . . .

I remember once an analyst presenting something of that kind. He had a woman patient and kept interpreting that he was in touch with her, then out of touch, this and that, and so on – interpreting only the here-and-now interaction with his patient. I had a vivid picture of a very small child confronted with a pregnant mother and not being able to get through to her. The analyst didn't give any background history. I always think that is an important element. During a break, I asked him how old she was when her next sibling was born. He replied: "Oh, I don't remember but I think the patient was about a year old." So I said something along the lines of a little child whose mother's belly is filled by another child, the patient gets inside, gets confused and doesn't know whether she's the baby or whether she is the mother . . . She's full of anxiety and hatred about penetrating into this situation. I would say – even if you don't actually make an interpretation relating to this baby experience – that you have to have it in your mind: it's not just that she's trying to get into your mind or that she won't let you into hers. I suggested an interpretation linking the here-and-now interaction with the patient's childhood phantasy, bringing things together in the psyche . . .

I don't think that there's any fundamental disagreement between Betty and me, it's more a quantitative thing. It's my way of keeping a balance between different aspects.

(Tape 4, side B, 1 February 2004)

(For the second part of this interview, see page 104.)

Psychoanalytic technique in the Kleinian approach
"Melanie Klein's technique" (1967a)

Segal, H. (1967a) "Melanie Klein's technique", in B.B. Wolman (ed.) *Psychoanalytic Techniques*, New York and London: Basic Books; reprinted (1981) in *The Work of Hanna Segal*, New York: Jason Aronson, pp. 3–24.

An extension of Freud's classical technique

Segal begins by pointing out that the technique introduced by Klein and her school is strictly based on Freudian psychoanalytic concepts. The formal setting is the same as in classical Freudian analysis, with the patient being offered five or six sessions per week; the patient lies on the couch with the analyst sitting behind him or her. In all essentials, the psychoanalytic principles as laid down by Freud are adhered to. The role of the analyst is confined to interpreting the patient's material, and all advice, criticism or reassurance is avoided. Interpretations focus essentially on the transference situation, both positive and negative. The transference is not only the "here and now" relationship with the analyst; it includes any references to past relationships and current problems that have to do with the analytical situation. "*In these respects, the Kleinian analyst may be considered to be following the classical Freudian technique with the greatest exactitude, more so indeed than most other Freudian analysts, who find that they have had to alter their analytical technique in some of its essential aspects when dealing with prepsychotic, psychotic, or psychopathic patients*" (Segal 1967a [1981: 3–4]).

This approach is based on a certain number of new concepts, discovered in the analysis of young children, which gave rise to new kinds of interpretation as compared to the classical approach. Examples of these are unconscious phantasy, the paranoid-schizoid and depressive positions, manic defences, the early Oedipus complex and envy. Segal has a particular gift for explaining very clearly these concepts, which can be difficult to understand if one has not experienced them oneself in the course of a personal psychoanalysis.

Segal argues that the Kleinian technique is a development and an extension of Freud's classical technique, based on a certain number of new elements that have broadened its domain. "*She [Klein] saw aspects of material not seen before, and interpreting those aspects, she revealed further material which might not have been reached otherwise and which, in turn, dictated new interpretations seldom, if ever, used in the classical technique*" (1981: 4).

An approach based on the analysis of young children

To appreciate Klein's innovative contribution, it is best to place it in its historical context. When she began her work with children in the 1920s, Klein thought that Freud's method could be applied more or less directly to children. However, since children do not verbalize as easily as adults, and since play is their preferred means of expression, she provided each child patient with a drawer of toys. In her view, these modifications did not alter the essence of the psychoanalytic relationship or the interpretative process. "*She interpreted their play, behaviour, and verbal communications in the way in which she would have interpreted an adult's free associations*" (Segal 1981: 4). Klein observed also that children develop a transference, both positive and negative, and that this transference sets in rapidly and often intensely. She discovered that, through various activities in the session, children reveal their unconscious conflicts with a clarity identical to or even greater than that of the adult's free associations.

Certain new facts emerged. For example, in young children, the Oedipus complex and the superego seemed to be in evidence at an earlier age than one would have expected; this enabled pregenital and genital forms of mental organization to be identified. Klein was impressed also by the prevalence of the mechanisms of projection and introjection leading to the building of a complex inner world, and by the intensity of projections which colour much of the child's perceptions of reality. She observed also that splitting preceded the mechanism of repression, and that the child's development appeared to be a constant struggle towards integration and the overcoming of powerful splitting mechanisms.

Once these mechanisms were seen in the child, they could be identified, understood and interpreted in the material of adult patients.

Unconscious phantasy

Working at the primitive level of the child's world led Melanie Klein to widen the concept of unconscious phantasy. In her 1948 article, Susan Isaacs defined unconscious phantasy as "the mental correlate of the instincts" or "the psychic representative of the instincts". In the infant's omnipotent world, drives are expressed as the phantasy of their fulfilment. "*To the desire to love and eat corresponds the phantasy of an ideal love-, life- and food-giving breast; to the desire to destroy, equally vivid phantasies of an object shattered, destroyed and attacking*" (Segal 1981: 5). From a Kleinian point of view, phantasies are of a crude and primitive nature, and are experienced in a somatic as well as a mental way. As development proceeds, later phantasies evolve through contact with reality and conflicts in the course of maturational growth. These derivatives can be displaced, symbolized and elaborated and can even penetrate into consciousness as day-dreams, imagination, etc. These later derivatives – the dreams or images – are what Freud considered to be phantasies.

In classical psychoanalysis we are familiar with the use of phantasy as a defensive function. It is a flight from reality and a defence against frustration. As mental life becomes more complicated, phantasy, says Segal, is called upon as a defence in various situations of stress. For example, manic phantasies act as a defence against underlying depression. Similarly, a patient may represent repression by means of a phantasy of a dam holding back floods; denial may be represented by a phantasy in which objects are actually annihilated; and the mechanisms of introjection and projection may be represented by phantasies of incorporation and ejection. According to Isaacs, what we call mechanisms of defence is an abstract description from an observer's point of view of what is in fact the functioning of unconscious phantasy. That conception, according to Segal, has decisive consequences for psychoanalytic technique. *"Clinically, if the analysis is to be an alive experience to the patient, we do not interpret to him mechanisms, we interpret and help him to relive the phantasies contained in the mechanisms"* (1981: 7).

Adopting the point of view according to which psychic mechanisms such as resistance and defences are an aspect of phantasy life enables Segal to answer an objection that is often raised. Kleinian analysts are often criticized for interpreting the content of unconscious phantasies while ignoring the analysis of defences. *"This criticism is, I think, based on a misunderstanding of our way of handling defences"* (1981: 7). Segal notes that in the early days of psychoanalysis it was considered dangerous to analyse prepsychotics in case the analysis of their defences would expose the weak ego to a psychotic breakdown; this is no longer thought to be the case. *"It is far safer to analyse prepsychotics now, when we do not analyse predominantly resistance or defences, leaving the ego defenceless, but have some understanding of the psychotic phantasies and anxieties that necessitate these defences and can modify these anxieties by interpretations, which are directed at the content as well as at the defences against it"* (1981: 7). The concept of mental mechanisms as an aspect of phantasy life, argues Segal, implies also that there is less of a divergence between interpretations of defence and those of content; this means that interpretations can deal more readily with the patient's total experience.

In a similar vein, Segal extended the idea of unconscious phantasy, connecting it with the ego, id and superego structure. Susan Isaacs had begun to establish a relationship between the instinctual drives, mental mechanisms – resistance and defence – and unconscious phantasy. Segal extended that hypothesis when she showed that the structure of the personality – which, as we know, depends on the relationship between ego, id and superego – is the end result of complex phantasies which involve the introjection of parental figures, as Freud had argued. Segal points out that this way of understanding the mind has important technical consequences. *"The fact that structure is partly determined by unconscious phantasy is of paramount importance from the therapeutic point of view, since we have access to these phantasies in the analytic situation and, through mobilizing them and helping the patient to relive and remodel them in the process of analytic treatment, we can affect the structure of the patient's personality"* (1981: 8).

Interpretations are made as early as the first session

This view of unconscious phantasy means that the patient's material can be looked at differently from that of the classical approach. From the outset, a Kleinian analyst will try to make contact with the patient's unconscious phantasy as it is expressed through the transference. All the patient's communications in the session are looked at as containing an element of unconscious phantasy, even though they may seem to concern events that take place in the external world. Furthermore, in the phantasy world of the analysand, the most important figure would appear to be the person of the analyst. It follows, therefore, that all the patient's communications contain something of relevance to the transference situation. That is why the interpretation of the transference is often more central in Kleinian technique than in the classical technique.

That conception of unconscious phantasy in close relationship to the transference affects the course of the analysis from the very first session.

> *The question is often asked by students, Should transference be interpreted in the first session? If we follow the principle that the interpretation should be given at the level of the greatest unconscious anxiety and that what we want to establish contact with is the patient's unconscious phantasy, then it is obvious that, in the vast majority of cases, a transference interpretation will impose itself. In my own experience I have not had a case in which I did not have to interpret the transference from the start.* (1981: 8–9)

Should interpretations be deep or superficial? According to Segal, this again is dictated by the level at which anxiety is active. *"For instance, to establish contact with a schizophrenic, it is usually necessary from the start to interpret the most primitive forms of projective identification if one is to get in touch with him at all*" (1981: 9). She illustrates this point with reference to a schizophrenic adolescent. Even with a relatively healthy individual, oral or anal anxieties may be clearly present in the transference situation in the very first session, and therefore should be interpreted. That said, no interpretation is given before some later material enables the analyst to understand the underlying phantasy more fully. A full interpretation of an unconscious phantasy involves all of its aspects. "*It has to be traced to its original instinctual source, so that the impulses underlying the phantasy are laid bare. At the same time, the defensive aspects of the phantasy have to be taken into account, and the relation has to be traced between phantasy and external reality in the past and the present*" (1981: 10).

Identifying infantile phantasies as the transference unfolds

JMQ: For something like ten years, along with Danielle and myself, you attended Hanna Segal's seminars in Geneva and in addition you had individual supervision with her. What impresses you particularly about her technique?

Francisco Palacio-Espasa: What seems to me to be particularly original in Segal's work is her understanding of the theory that underpins her technique, based on the way in which she identifies the transference phantasies – that is, those aspects of infantile phantasies that are part of what the patient is actually expressing. Segal is more subtle than Klein in her approach to this. Nowadays, Antonino Ferro is one of those who try to bring back – to re-create would be a better word – an attitude of close attentiveness towards the "here and now" of that interpersonal relationship. That attitude tries to make the analyst's particular attentiveness into the patient's own creation.

Segal's idea, on the other hand, aims at rediscovering the patient's past, either real or in phantasy. In other words, she attempts to reconstruct the past on the basis of what is actually transpiring in the patient's transference. That seems to me to be the most interesting feature. For example, to my knowledge, few people are able to highlight oral phantasies in what the patient communicates through the psychoanalytic relationship as well as Segal does; the same is true of anal phantasies. Oedipal phantasies are much easier to identify. I think, too, that Segal really understands the containing aspects of the maternal object in the transference. That, for me, is the most significant feature of what she has given us. In my view, people like Ferro, who are neo-constructivists, if you like, do not pay sufficient attention to infantile phantasies in the transference relationship; their ideas are close to those of Betty Joseph's followers, who speak of the "total transference situation".

Segal, then, is the person who helped me most to identify very infantile and regressive phantasies in the transference. There may well be, of course, other factors, such as trauma, that have to be taken into consideration. Trauma, however, is not a concept that particularly appeals to Segal, although of course she does take real-life events, illness, etc. into account when they come into the transference relationship via the patient's free associations.

(Interview (in French), 12 August 2006)

Francisco Palacio-Espasa is a training analyst and supervisor with the Swiss Psychoanalytical Society.

The paranoid-schizoid position

In psychoanalysis, as in most sciences, changes in technique end up by revealing new material which in turn leads to new theoretical formulations; these new concepts then give rise to modifications in technique. Melanie Klein described two kinds of structure which she called the paranoid-schizoid and depressive positions. To each of these positions corresponds a particular type of ego and object-relation organization.

This is Segal's concise but nonetheless very graphic presentation of how she would define the paranoid-schizoid position.

In the paranoid-schizoid position, the infant has no concept of a whole person. He is related to part objects, primarily the breast. He also experiences no ambivalence. His object is split into an ideal and a persecutory one, and the prevalent anxiety at that stage is of a persecutory nature, the fear that the persecutors may invade and destroy the self and the ideal object. The aim of the infant is to acquire, possess, and identify with the ideal object and to project and keep at bay both the bad objects and his own destructive impulses. Splitting, introjection, and projection are very active as mechanisms of defence. (1981: 11)

The analysis of these persecutory anxieties and of the corresponding defences plays an important part in Kleinian technique. *"For instance, if the analyst is very idealized, he will be particularly watchful for the appearance of bad figures in the patient's extra-analytical life and take every opportunity of interpreting them as split-off bad aspects of himself. He will also be watchful for the projection of the patient's own destructive impulses into these bad figures"* (1981: 11).

The clinical distinction between projection and projective identification

In the paranoid-schizoid position, we find another important mechanism: projective identification. *"In projective identification, a part of the patient's ego is in phantasy projected into the object, controlling it, using it, and projecting into it his own characteristics"* (1981: 11). It is a phantasy that is usually very elaborate and detailed. Projective identification is, from this perspective, an expression of the drives in that the patient's libidinal and aggressive desires are felt to be omnipotently satisfied by the phantasy; in addition, like projection, projective identification is a defence mechanism to the extent that it rids the self of unwanted parts.

Segal gives two clinical examples in order to illustrate the difference between these concepts. The first is taken from a supervision case.

A student reported a case in which his woman patient, preceding a holiday break, was describing how her children bickered and were jealous of one another in relation to her. The student interpreted that the children represented herself, jealous about him in relation to the holiday break, an interpretation that she accepted without being much moved. He did not interpret that she felt that she had put a jealous and angry part of herself into the children, and that that part of her was changing and controlling them. The second interpretation, for which there was plenty of material in preceding and subsequent sessions, was of very great importance, in that it could be shown to the patient how, by subtle manipulations, she was in fact forcing the children to carry those parts of herself. (1981: 11–12)

Segal adds that often a transference situation can only be understood in terms of projective identification: *"a situation, for instance, in which the patient is silent and withdrawn, inducing in the analyst a feeling of helplessness, rejection, and lack of understanding, because the patient has projected into the analyst the child part of himself with all its feelings"* (1981: 12).

The second example is taken from the analysis of a schizophrenic patient, again a case which Segal supervised. She shows that it is not sufficient for the analyst to use his or her countertransference feelings to interpret what the patient seems to be projecting. Sometimes the patient can experience that as the analyst forcibly and perhaps vengefully pushing these feelings back, without having transformed them. In the example given by Segal, the patient was reversing the earlier situation between his mother and himself, reproduced in the transference – he identified with a rejecting mother, while putting into the analyst the rejected child part of himself. Segal points out that it was not enough simply to show the patient that he was reversing the situation. *"One has to interpret in detail his introjective identification with the rejecting mother and the projective identification of the rejected child part of himself, identifying and describing its feelings and interpreting the detail of the phantasy of how this part is projected"* (1981: 12).

Segal goes on to say that when projective identification predominates the patient may well feel depleted (since a part of the self is felt to be missing), persecuted by the analyst filled with the patient's projections, and confused with the analyst. Schizophrenic patients, who immediately form a psychotic transference, may well feel relieved by interpretations of projective identification. Segal points out, all the same, that the analysis of paranoid-schizoid object relations and defences is not confined to psychotic and prepsychotic patients only; in all patients, schizoid defences are repeatedly regressed to and revived as a defence against feelings aroused in the depressive position.

The depressive position

Having presented the paranoid-schizoid position, Segal goes on to describe the concept of the depressive position as simply as possible.

The depressive position starts when the infant begins to recognize his mother. Throughout the paranoid-schizoid position, normal processes of maturation are helped by, and help in turn, the psychological drive to integration, and eventually, sufficient integration is achieved for the infant to recognize his mother as a whole object. The concept of the whole object contrasts both with that of the part object and that of the object split into good and bad. The infant begins to recognize his mother not as a collection of anatomical parts, breasts that feed him, hands that tend him, eyes that smile or frighten, but as a whole person with an independent existence of her own, who is the source of both his good and his bad experiences. This integration in his perception of his object goes pari passu with the integration in his own self. He gradually realizes that it is the same infant, himself, who both loves and hates the same person, his mother. He experiences ambivalence. (1981: 13)

This fundamental change in the infant's object relations brings with it a change in the content of anxiety.

While he was previously afraid that he would be destroyed by his persecutors, now he dreads that his own aggression will destroy his ambivalently loved object. His anxiety has changed from a paranoid to a depressive one. Since at that stage the infant's phantasies are felt as omnipotent, he is exposed to the experience that his aggression has destroyed his mother, leaving in its wake feelings of guilt, irretrievable loss, and mourning. (1981: 13)

The mother's absence is often experienced in terms of her being dead.

As the depressive position starts in the oral stage of development, where the infant's love and hatred are linked with phantasies of incorporation, this ambivalence is felt also in relation to the mother as an internal object. And in states of depressive anxiety and mourning, the infant feels that he has lost not only his mother in the external world, but that his internal object is destroyed as well. Melanie Klein viewed these depressive anxieties as part of normal development and an unavoidable corollary to the process of integration. They become reawakened up to a point in any subsequent situation of loss. (1981: 13–14)

The introduction of the notion of the depressive position highlights the difference that exists between the Kleinian view and the classical conception of mourning, both normal and patho-logical. In the classical conception, normal mourning involves only the loss of an external object; depressive illness (or melancholia, as it was called in Freud's day) implies ambivalence in rela-tion to an internal object and regression to an oral fixation (Abraham 1912, Freud 1917e [1915]). In the Kleinian conception, ambivalence towards an internal object and the depressive anxieties associated with it are a normal stage of development and are reawakened in the normal mourning process. That is why working through the mourning process is a major aspect of Kleinian technique.

It is often contended by classical Freudian analysts that when a patient is actually mourning it is usually an unproductive period in his analysis. Kleinian analysts, in contrast, find that analysis of mourning situations and tracing them to their early roots often helps the patient greatly in working through the mourning and coming out of it enriched by the experience. (Segal 1981: 14)

Segal illustrates what she means by the depressive position with the example of a dream that one of her patients reported soon after his mother's death. Considerations of space prevent me from quoting that extract *in extenso* here; suffice it to say that in this case the mourning situation was analysed both in relation to its early roots in the patient's childhood and with respect to the transference situation.

Manic defences

The pain and anxiety linked to the depressive position mobilize new and powerful defences, the system of manic defences. *"The manic defences involve a regression to splitting, denial, idealization, and projection, basically schizoid mechanisms, but organized into a system to protect the ego from the experience of depressive anxiety"* (1981: 14). Depressive anxiety arises out of the infant's recognition of the mother as a whole object on whom he or she depends and of the fear of losing her because of his or her ambivalence and ensuing guilt. *"Because of this, the whole relation has to be denied. Denial of the importance of his object and triumph over it, control, contempt, and devaluation take the place of depressive feelings"* (1981: 15).

Segal then goes on to show how manic defences can lead to a vicious circle. *"The depression results from the original attack on the object; the manic defences keep the experience of depression from the ego, but they also preclude a working through of the depressive position and necessitate a further attack on the object by denial, triumph, and contempt, thereby increasing the underlying depression"* (1981: 15). It is well known that behind manic phenomena there is an underlying depression. It is less well known, says Segal, that behind depression there are manic aspects that have to be identified because they impede the working-through of depressive feelings and perpetuate the situation of depression.

Reparation: the key to working through the depressive position

The working-through of the depressive position in normal development depends on the capacity to make reparation. *"When the infant feels that in his hatred he has destroyed his good external and internal object, he experiences not only an intense feeling of guilt and loss but also pining and a longing to restore the lost loved object externally and internally, and to re-create the lost harmony and well-being. He mobilizes all his love and creativity to that end"* (1981: 15–16). Segal gives the example of a woman patient who dreamt that she was putting together a jigsaw puzzle; her associations showed that the analytic process was experienced by her as a way of restoring and of re-creating her very shattered internal world. In addition, her wish to write a book represented the need to produce a whole picture of her life out of shattered fragments.

Repeated experiences of loss and recovery of the object enable the infant to acquire increasing confidence in the strength of the good object and in his or her own love and creativity. In the depressive position, the reality principle develops and the external object is gradually felt to have an independent and separate existence. In the process of working through, the ego becomes integrated, and is enriched by the introjection and assimilation of good objects. At the same time, omnipotence diminishes as well as the infant's feelings of guilt and fear of loss. *"A successful working through of the depressive position is fundamental to mental health"* (1981: 16).

The paranoid-schizoid and depressive positions are not only stages of development, they are two types of ego integration and organization. It follows that the ego has a constant struggle to maintain a state of integration. Segal points out that all through life, our internal organization oscillates between paranoid-schizoid and depressive forms. These oscillations vary in intensity with each individual's psychopathology. At one end of the spectrum there is the schizophrenic patient who may rarely reach a depressive integration, while at the other end there is the fully mature individual whose inner world is well integrated.

The Oedipus complex

It was by analysing young children that Melanie Klein discovered that the Oedipus complex has very early roots, earlier than Freud had thought, and that these lay in the oral phase. Later, when she developed the concept of the depressive position, it became clear that the Oedipus complex begins at the same time.

> *If the infant becomes aware of his mother as a whole person, a whole separate person leading a life of her own, having other relationships of her own, he is immediately exposed to the experience of sexual jealousy. The fact that his world is still coloured by his omnipotent projections increases his jealousy, for when he senses the emotional tie between his parents, he phantasies them as giving one another precisely those satisfactions he desires for himself. Thus he*

will experience jealousy first of all in oral terms, but the triangular situation will have the configuration and the intensity of the Oedipus complex described by Freud. (Segal 1981: 18)

The child's experience of the Oedipal situation will therefore be dictated by the stage in libidinal development that he or she has reached, and will be expressed, to begin with, in oral terms. "*Also, the earlier the stage of the Oedipus complex, the more it will be dominated by the infant's omnipotent projections*" (1981: 18). This is very important technically, because the analysis of the early roots of the Oedipal conflict liberates it from the dominance of omnipotent mechanisms and phantasies. "*Tracing the Oedipus complex to its early roots enables one also to analyse the complex interplay between the early relationship to the breast and the Oedipus complex; for instance, how anxieties experienced in relation to the breast make the infant turn to the penis or, conversely, how the Oedipal jealousy may affect the feeding relationship to the breast*" (1981: 18).

To illustrate her presentation of the Oedipus complex, Segal gives two clinical examples which show in detail how the Oedipal situation is processed in her work with her patients.

Mourning and working through

According to Segal, the oscillations between paranoid-schizoid and depressive feelings underlie the process of working-through. In the analytical situation, the patient relives his or her relation to the original objects. Attachment to them has to be lived through again and given up again. It is for this reason that the mourning process lies at the heart of working through.

In Freud's view, no object can be given up without being introjected into the ego. In the Kleinian view, this introjection is part of the depressive process. No object can be given up successfully without a complete process of mourning, as in the depressive position, ending in the introjection of a good internal object, strengthening the ego. Any new insight of any importance necessitates this process. The pain of the mourning situation mobilizes new manic and schizoid defences, but with each repeated experience the ego is strengthened, the good object is more securely established, and the need to have recourse to new defences is lessened. The process of working through is completed when some aspect of the object has been given up in this way. (1981: 20–21)

The role of envy

In the Kleinian approach, special attention is paid to envy, a notion which Melanie Klein distinguished from jealousy. Envy is more primitive than jealousy and has its early roots in the infant's relation to the breast. Envy is a two-part relationship in which the envious subject attempts to take possession of an object or a quality of the object; no other live object need enter into it. Jealousy, on the other hand, pertains to a triangular relationship. It is a more developed affect, based on love, and its aim is to possess the love of the loved object and the removal of the rival. Jealousy is a whole-object relationship, while envy is essentially experienced in terms of part-objects.

From a clinical point of view, it is important to identify the role played by envy in order to interpret it, for it interferes with the normal operation of the schizoid mechanisms. "*Splitting into an ideal and a bad object cannot be established since it is the ideal object that is the object of envy, and therefore hostility. Thus, the introjection of an ideal object, which could become the core of the ego, is disturbed at its very roots*" (Segal 1981: 21–22). Also, the analysis of patients suffering from a harsh superego often reveals that it is the envious aspect of the superego that is most destructive. This may manifest itself by a negative therapeutic reaction, with feelings of hopelessness. As soon as the analysis and the analyst are felt to be good, the superego attacks any creativity on the part of the ego and tries to do away with it entirely.

Segal points out that the analysis of envy is extremely painful and disturbing but it gradually reintroduces hope through the introjection of a good desirable object. "*Latent appreciation can be mobilized and the battle can be fought again between love and gratitude and envy*" (1981: 22). The discovery of the part played by envy gave significant impetus to new techniques in psychoanalysis; in particular it led to the analysis of psychotic patients and of other intractable cases, as not only Segal herself has shown, but also Rosenfeld and Bion.

Termination of analysis

Segal ends with the question: has the Kleinian approach modified the criteria for the termination of an analysis and the therapeutic aim? She says that, in certain basic ways, the criteria remain the same – the lifting of repression, insight, freeing the patient from early inhibitions, enabling the patient to form full and satisfactory personal relationships. Given all that, she nonetheless feels that Kleinian analysts will be guided more by their assessment of the patient's internal world. Agreeing with the criteria that Melanie Klein herself laid out in her 1950 paper, Segal adds that the Kleinian analyst *"will try to evaluate the state of integration in the patient's ego and his internal objects, and his capacity to maintain the state of integration in situations of stress"* (1981: 23). She would later come back to the question of the criteria for termination of an analysis, in particular in her 1988 paper, "Sweating it out", in which she insists on the need for evaluating the patient's capacity to cope with anxiety and to deal with the depressive position, given of course that one never achieves a complete resolution of that situation.

Hanna Segal looks back on Melanie Klein's work
Integration, counter-transference, the analytic setting, intuition

JMQ: You lay considerable emphasis on the need for balance between different elements when making an interpretation. What exactly do you mean by that?

Hanna Segal: When people speak of balance they think it means that when you interpret something bad you must also interpret something good. One example is that of a very nice child analyst whom I saw on television discussing his work. When a little boy broke some small toys, the analyst interpreted that the patient wanted to kill his little brother – immediately adding: "But you love him too, of course!" That wasn't in the material – it's an example of automatic balancing-out: if you say bad you must also say good. I always say that my main experience of my analysis with Klein was one of balance: nothing exaggerated, never too much bad or too much good. Klein doesn't actually use the word "balance", but John Steiner and I thought that it was the idea behind much of her work.

Some people feel that Klein over-interpreted the negative. That's not my experience at all. When I look at Klein's early writings, I can see just how balanced they were. Elizabeth Spillius has the same impression – giving the whole picture, not just one side of it. For John and I, that was the real balance in her work, even though Klein herself doesn't describe it that way – seeing the emotions behind the other emotions. To see love behind hatred and to see hatred behind love. And never to take only the conscious manifestations. She always spoke of deep-down integration.

JMQ: In the television example you spoke of, the little boy's love for his brother is unconscious . . .

Well, his hatred also is unconscious. He symbolizes it and expresses it, but at that precise moment the love is just not available. It could turn up in another session, the next day perhaps, when he comes and brings all the toys together.

I'm thinking also of the paranoid-schizoid and depressive positions. If the patient is really very split, the analyst may spend quite a long time interpreting mainly on the negative or mainly on the positive level. Sometimes you can bring them together – but sometimes you can't. You have to work for a long time on the persecution and the idealization that lie behind it. The idealization covers the persecution. When you can bring them together at the same time in the session, that's already an integration. That's what's meant by balance.

JMQ: That is an important suggestion for technique, one which is often misunderstood.

Klein speaks of anxiety quite a bit, and she always says you must go for the deepest anxiety. Well, that isn't quite true. You interpret the anxiety that is active at the moment.

JMQ: But that could in fact be deep anxiety, couldn't it?

It could be. For example, if somebody arrives for his or her session in a state of acute projective identification the classical idea would have you start at the top and gradually – but only gradually – work down to the bottom. Our idea is different: you start with what is presented at that particular moment. If the patient comes with a completely paranoid delusion about the analyst you interpret that. If somebody comes presenting things on a different level, let's say depressive anxiety, you interpret that.

JMQ: So the idea is not to interpret systematically at the deepest level?

Nor systematically the superficial, just what is going on at that particular moment.

JMQ: What are your views nowadays on the counter-transference?

Our ideas on counter-transference have slowly evolved over time, and that's one of the changes I spoke about. Although Klein was not very hot on it, I think that, in fact, she took it into account a lot . . .

JMQ: . . . In her practice but not in her theory?

That's right, not in her theory. We seem to have forgotten that the counter-transference, like the transference, is unconscious. We have to look for the unconscious roots of it because it can often be very misleading. That's one of the difficulties. If you find yourself very irritated with a particular patient, you have to discover not only what the patient uses to irritate you but also what your own weak points are, the ones that are being provoked. Patients know these very well – it's not done by magic. This is especially true of psychotic patients – they have an extraordinary, almost telepathic intuition about what you're up to.

I think it is particularly important for analysands, during their training analysis, to be able to come up against their counter-transference.

I would make a distinction between the counter-transference disposition inside yourself – the unconscious part – and the actual counter-transference manifestations in this or that session with this or that patient. I think that the basic counter-transference is ideally one in which we can recognize both what the patient projects and where it does or doesn't touch us – so we have to be in touch both with our infantile self and our parental self. In my view, this is based on the introjection of a good analytic experience and all that goes with it – a good experience of the creative parental couple.

That, if you like, is the basic positive counter-transference: being able to identify with a parent who tolerates projections well. That would put us in a sort of ideal position of always being able to understand the patient and never showing any reaction, a position that is never achieved. Then there's the counter-transference feeling that we have when we become too fond of the patient or when we are given material of a certain kind – this has to do with the basic counter-transference models that we have, and we have constantly to examine these in ourselves.

I think, too, that there is a basic bad counter-transference situation. A bad feeling, unconsciously, about analysis – that is when you start colluding with the patient and his or her anxieties. It's complicated. I speak about that in one of my counter-transference papers (Segal 1997a), where I formulate it much better than I'm doing right now!

JMQ: Would the basic positive counter-transference be something like empathy?

Well, empathy is a word that's so much abused. What I call positive counter-transference does not mean loving the patient, but being able to be open-minded in a tolerant way. Have feelings, but recognize them. Some people speak of counter-transference as though those feelings were as strong as the patient's feelings. They are not. If they are, then there is something very wrong. If you have intense counter-transference feelings, whether positive or negative, then there is something wrong.

JMQ: So the intensity of feelings could be an indication . . .

. . . Or the opposite – a complete lack of feelings, which also is bad.

JMQ: In what you say about psychoanalytic technique, you never fail to stress the importance of the setting.

Very important. As far as the setting is concerned, you can't get any more Freudian than we are! The way I formulate it is that the setting represents the analyst's state of mind. It should have no intrusions.

Acting-in is very important – just as acting-out is. In the end, all acting-out is also an acting-in. In a way, the patient acts out partly to protect the analyst – doing it "outside" (hence the term acting-out). At the same time, the patient partly forces the analyst to listen to all the bad (or wonderful) things he did. When patients act-in, it's aimed at the analyst's state of mind. I'm thinking here of a patient, a woman, who had intercourse with five men in a single weekend; that was not simply defensive – the point of the acting-in was to be able to come to her session and wave penises in front of the analyst! The idea being to stimulate jealousy or envy or anger or whatever.

JMQ: Nowadays we treat many different kinds of patient, with a whole range of pathologies from neurotic to psychotic. Do you make any modifications to your technical approach according to whether you have a neurotic, borderline or psychotic patient on the couch?

No, not really. Except that the interpretations are different – and maybe I pay even more attention to the setting with a psychotic patient, because everything is so concrete.

JMQ: Do you sometimes take patients sitting face to face?

Well, if the patient wants to sit up – that's something you have to analyse. With some patients, psychotics, sometimes too with adolescents and borderline cases, I wouldn't push them to lie down on the couch because they are so afraid of disintegrating. Of course, you do take it up in interpretations – why they can't use the couch, I mean – but you don't make them feel guilty over the fact that they won't lie down.

(Tape 1, side A, 28 January 2005)

JMQ: For you, interpreting seems much more important than remaining silent – the kind of approach in which the analyst waits for the patient to do his or her own processing.

I knew Jean and Evelyne Kestemberg very well, they were friends of mine for a very long time but of course we disagreed completely on theory. They wrote a beautiful book on anorexia, and they had very good results thanks to group psychodrama, as you call it – but then they say that such patients are not suitable for analysis. I said to Jean: "Look, Jean, the difference is that when you've got a patient on the couch, you don't say a word. Yet when you're in psychodrama, as I understand the description, you interpret all the time! Maybe if you tried interpreting to your patients on the couch, it wouldn't take five of you to make up a psychodrama group, you could perhaps get through to them." I found the difference really amazing – they had so much clinical intuition and understanding but it just didn't seem to come into their analytic work. For instance, they described beautifully the basic narcissism of the anorexic and I think they were the very first to see that in every anorexic there is a definite delusion, a delusional system about their body and so on – yet they never used it to interpret to their patients on the couch. You see, if a patient is silent or doesn't communicate or talks nonsense and the analyst says nothing, well, nothing happens.

(Tape 3, side B, 31 January 2004)

JMQ: How do you treat borderline patients? Is the setting still five sessions a week, and on the couch?

Oh yes, absolutely. I don't myself put the patient face to face. It depends on the patient. Some know already about lying down on the couch. When somebody undertakes an analysis, if you say something about the setting, you say at that point that the usual thing is for the patient to lie down on the couch.

JMQ: And if the patient becomes anxious and asks to sit?

Well, you interpret that – but not systematically as a naughty thing to do. Sometimes in terms of anxiety or perhaps defiance. Sometimes the patient is quite ready for the couch but just won't lie down. It must be said, all the same, that I've actually had little experience with face to face. Even my most psychotic patients – there are only two I can think of – always used the couch. Edward, the very first psychotic patient, wasn't on the couch in the hospital nor at home; but he knew that analysis means on the couch. As soon as I had him home – it lasted a few months – he lay down on the couch even though he was terrified to begin with. It meant losing sight, losing control. I've had patients who sit up. You must never push the patient into anything. When it's a case of not lying down on the couch, you can sometimes interpret it as a resistance, sometimes as an anxiety.

The less ill they are, the more I think it is all about attack and defiance and keeping control. The more ill they are, the more they're right not to want to lie down because they're afraid of terrible aggressions. But that I know more through supervision, because I've never had this particular problem very much.

JMQ: Your intuition has always impressed me, whether in individual supervision with you or in groups. For example, you were able to describe very early infantile phantasies that I would manage to get hold of only several weeks later.

Well, there you're bringing up a very important concept: psychoanalytic intuition. Mediocre analysts know the theory by heart, their setting is perfect – but they don't necessarily have any psychoanalytic intuition. They know something and so they apply it, but in sessions in which there are three different ways of looking at the material, when you don't have time to think and have to choose which interpretation you give, that all depends on psychoanalytic intuition. It's the kind of person you are which decides that. I had a supervisee who was devoted to his supervisions and everything – but he was totally lacking in intuition. I think that psychoanalytic intuition is a bit like what I said about counter-transference: it's a state of mind in which the thoughts that come into your head are the most appropriate ones to share with your patient.

JMQ: Do you have any tips for learning about intuition?

Sorry, no – except having analysis! Analysis helps us to be more comfortable with our unconscious. And, of course, the more experienced you are, the more faith you can have in your intuition!

(Tape 1, side A, 28 January 2005)

The perspectives opened up by Segal's work – and the questions it raises

JMQ: You are familiar with Hanna Segal and her work. Over the years, she opened up several new perspectives and raised many theoretical and technical questions. What are your thoughts on that?

Juan Manzano: Just as with Freud himself, the concepts Segal introduced over the years have opened up new ways of understanding and exploring our theoretical postulates and have raised many stimulating questions. I would like to give a few examples of what I mean.

Nowadays it is impossible not to have some sort of debate going on between psychoanalysis and the neurosciences, which could well provide the opportunity for both of these scientific fields to progress even more – independently of each other, perhaps, but in a mutually rewarding manner. For example: Segal's developmental theory of symbol formation and the function of symbols, born of her experience as a psychoanalyst, makes for a fascinating comparison with what we now know thanks to the contribution of cognitive neurophysiology. I am thinking here particularly of what we have learned from the discovery of the mirror neuron system (Rizzolatti *et al.* 2001). These neurons, which are activated whenever we accomplish a specific motor activity, are activated also when we observe someone else doing that particular activity. Recent research on the brain mechanisms involved has enabled further progress to be made in our understanding of phenomena such as imitation and identification, thereby highlighting more and more the foundations of the infant's communication and language. So it is no longer simply a matter of mechanisms involving motor activity – here we are talking about the organization of affects and pre-verbal mental activity which includes representations and coded concepts (Stern 2006).

JMQ: But isn't there sometimes a problem with some of the ideas Segal has put forward?

Among the questions raised by Segal in her work there is one issue that to my mind goes right to the heart of the Kleinian conception of psychoanalysis: the relationship between the theory of the "positions" and Freud's theory of psychosexual development. These questions have to do also with the link between Freud's formulation in terms of the life and death drives and his earlier drive theory. For example, when Segal makes use of the concept of sublimation in her explanation of the aesthetic experience (the artist's as well as that of the audience), that sublimation, as far as she is concerned, has to do with the drive to possess the object. As regards the aesthetic experience, that may well be related to what Freud calls the pregenital drives; it would then follow that these pregenital drives play a role also in the pleasure that one feels when contemplating a work of art.

In the same vein, the question arises as to the significance of Segal's developmental theorizations in the context of the theory of narcissism – so conspicuous by its absence in Kleinian thinking (Manzano and Palacio-Espasa 2006). It is of course clear that formulations in terms of manic and schizoid defences necessarily imply narcissistic object relations, but this is seldom stated explicitly. The reason for this absence seems to me to lie in the exclusive or at any rate predominant use of the theory of the life and death drives. Adopting that stance does make for an in-depth understanding of clinical phenomena, but it does not give sufficient weight to narcissistic libidinal satisfaction.

JMQ: Segal, it would seem, gives little weight to narcissistic attitudes in her papers on the danger of nuclear warfare. Would you agree?

Yes, indeed. The extraordinarily perceptive insight that Segal has brought to individual and group attitudes as regards the nuclear danger focuses exclusively, I think, on defensive reactions against the threat of destruction coming from one's own death drive and of the guilt which that generates. Here, too, we could argue that she does not give enough weight to the pleasure obtained via the individual and group narcissistic-grandiose structures that have arisen as a consequence of that phenomenon. That, to my mind, means that we are left without certain interpretative tools that could contribute to the kind of awareness that Segal herself is trying to develop.

Segal's hypotheses are a major contribution to Kleinian theory, but – inevitably, one is tempted to say – they do at times differ significantly from that approach. For instance, both Klein and Rosenfeld argue that the distinction between self and object exists from birth and is only later blurred by the operation of defensive phantasies of a symbiotic kind; in Segal's theory, however, particularly when we think of the "symbolic equation", the distinction between self and object is less obvious.

In addition, I would say that, as regards guilt feelings, Segal seems to hesitate between seeing these as a direct expression of the death drive and Klein's more structural definition which sees guilt as the outcome of a positive integration of the depressive position.

(Interview (in French), February 2007)

Juan Manzano (Geneva) is a training analyst with the Swiss Psychoanalytical Society.

The Kleinian approach in child analysis

Segal, H. (1967b) "Melanie Klein's technique of child analysis", in B. B. Wolman (ed.) *Psycho-analytic Techniques*, New York: Basic Books; reprinted (1981) in *The Work of Hanna Segal*, New York and London: Jason Aronson, pp. 25–37.

Segal, H. (1979b) "The play technique", in *Klein*, Glasgow: Fontana/Collins, pp. 35–44

Segal, H. (1979c) "Psychoanalysis of children", in *Klein*, Glasgow: Fontana/Collins, pp. 45–62

Segal, H. (1979d) "The 'Controversial Discussions'", in *Klein*, Glasgow: Fontana/Collins, pp. 91–111.

Hanna Segal's contribution to the psychoanalysis of children is contained in several papers, some of which are aimed at a more general readership, while others are more for the specialist. For example, in the chapter she wrote in 1967 on "Melanie Klein's technique of child analysis", accessible to those who are not particularly familiar with child analysis, she points out the innovative features of the Kleinian approach. For those who do have a good knowledge of the subject, Segal gave a detailed presentation of Klein's conception of child analysis in her 1979 book, *Klein*, to which I refer those who are interested in the topic. In that book, Segal devotes three chapters to child analysis: "The play technique", "Psychoanalysis of children" and "The 'Controversial Discussions'". As part of Segal's biography of Melanie Klein, these chapters shed light on the historical circumstances in which Klein was developing her technique and on the controversy between her and Anna Freud in the 1940s. Since then, of course, the points of view of those two schools of thought, with their different theoretical backgrounds, have drawn closer together. For that reason, in her 1967 paper – which I shall discuss later in this chapter – Segal makes no mention of the controversies that opposed Melanie Klein and Anna Freud.

The specific issues involved in child analysis

JMQ: What experience do you yourself have of child analysis?

Hanna Segal: One day, my friend Evelyne Kestemberg said to me: "A child analyst is someone who, twenty years ago, once analysed a child . . . ." I have indeed analysed a child patient, but that was when I was still in training. My first supervision was with Mrs Klein – the analysis of the little girl I often talk about in my articles. She was the youngest patient of all, I think – Klein's youngest patient was 3 years old, but that little girl was only 2½. She was adorable, but the analysis was not particularly successful. I have analysed adolescents too.

I would say that once I had children of my own, it became very difficult to find a proper place in which to do child analysis. My consulting room has always been in my home. It's one thing when your Mummy is locked away working with adults, but quite another when she's not available for you because she's playing with another child! I never treated child patients in my own home. I used to rent from Sydney Klein a room that I used as a consulting room. It can be quite time-consuming when you work quite far away from home. Then I had neighbours who didn't use their kitchen at all, so they leased it to me – just next door to where I lived. There was running water and everything – it was great to work in an old kitchen, with children in analysis.

The other thing is that I did not want to specialize in child analysis; I preferred working with adults.

JMQ: You worked with adolescents too, didn't you? Isn't it sometimes difficult to keep them in analysis for any length of time?

With some adolescents, I managed that quite well. And young adults of around 20 or so, well they're still close to their adolescence.

I did, however, supervise many child analyses. You asked me what changes in technique have occurred over the years. I have an idea about that. I think things have become more rigorous than in Melanie Klein's day. Nowadays, I think that analysts do not play as much with their child patients, they tend to interpret more. You could ask other people, Betty Joseph, for example, who have specialized in child analysis. Six or seven years ago she analysed a young psychotic boy, and the analysis was a success. I used to do a lot of supervision work – less, nowadays, because there are fewer child analysts interested in that.

I always wanted to avoid being labelled a "specialist" in one field or another – child analysis, psychotic and borderline patients, elderly patients, etc. – I wanted to be a kind of general practitioner.

JMQ: Has the technique changed a lot?

Nowadays, more attention is paid to acting-in. That's Betty Joseph's influence. There's more of the "here and now" technique. No reference to the real parents, not too much interpretation of unconscious phantasies, more focus on interpreting acting-in and using the analyst's counter-transference.

(Interview (in French) 15 August 2006)

"Melanie Klein's technique of child analysis" (1967b)

Segal, H. (1967b) "Melanie Klein's technique of child analysis", in B. B. Wolman (ed.) *Psycho-analytic Techniques*, New York: Basic Books; reprinted (1981) in *The Work of Hanna Segal*, New York and London: Jason Aronson, pp. 25–37.

Transference in child analysis

For her presentation of the Kleinian technique in child analysis, Segal goes back to Melanie Klein's first papers on the subject. That is where one finds a clear description of the basic principles of her technique, a technique which has remained essentially unaltered since then. There are three basic points to the Kleinian approach: transference, the analytical situation, and the play technique.

According to Melanie Klein, children, like adults, develop a real transference with respect to the analyst. It had been thought that children could not develop a proper transference because of their attachment, in reality, to their real parents; nevertheless it could be seen that a transference did develop on the basis of the child's projection on to the analyst of internal parental figures. *"Since the child's object relation already had a long history in which parental figures were both internalized and distorted, it is those figures, pertaining to the internal world and to the past, which form the basis of the transference"* (Segal 1967b [1981: 25–26]). It is not the current parental figures that are projected on to the analyst, but the internal ones, just as in the case of adults. Melanie Klein observed that splitting is an important mechanism, particularly in small children, and that they tend to split the internal parents into ideal figures and extremely bad ones. Splitting enables young children to defend themselves against their ambivalence with respect to their parents; both the ideal aspect and the persecutory aspect can be transferred on to the analyst.

The analytical situation

Melanie Klein's aim was to establish with children as strict an analytical situation as was possible. Contrary to the theories current in her time, she discovered that such an analytical situation could be established and maintained with children, no matter how young, if one relied on interpretative work and gave up any attempt at a moral, educative, or reassuring attitude. *"These two aspects of the situation were, according to [Melanie Klein], interdependent: one could not observe the transference if one did not establish a proper analytical situation, and a proper analytical situation could not be established if one did not analyse the transference"* (1981: 26). In Klein's view, reassurance comes from the analytical situation itself, i.e. from the analyst's uncritical understanding and from his or her reliability and capacity to relieve anxiety. In other words, reassurance results from the psycho-analytic process itself, which takes place in depth and brings about real changes in the child's inner world, not from a reassuring attitude.

The play technique and setting

Melanie Klein very quickly understood that children's play was a symbolic expression of their conflicts and anxieties, hence her use of it as an analytical tool. She treated their play, together with their verbal communications, as the equivalent of the adult's free associations, and used the symbolic content of both as a basis for her interpretations.

Over the years since she first introduced the play technique, the use of toys for child analysis and for other forms of treatment derived from it has become commonplace. Given that the setting and the toys used, however, vary enormously depending on the analyst's approach, it may be worthwhile looking again at Melanie Klein's original recommendations. It is important, she noted, that every child has his or her own individual drawer or box, so that the toys that particular child uses quickly become his or her own. The kind of toys that are available are: small bricks, fences, a few small cars or trains, balls, small containers, some animals of various sizes and human figures also of different sizes, etc. In addition, the child is provided with paper, pencils, glue and modelling clay; if possible, running water should be provided, as well as some towels and soap. *"The aim of this material is to provide the child with toys which leave maximum scope for his imagination"* (1981: 27).

The room should not contain anything easily breakable, the walls should be washable and the floor covering robust. *"The room should be so organized that the child is free to express aggression without danger to himself or actual damage to the surroundings"* (1981: 27). There should be a table and a couple of chairs, as well as a couch on which the child can lie down if he or she feels like free associating. Within this setting, the analyst should maintain a strictly psychoanalytic role; unlike the situation with adult patients, however, the analyst is also an adult in charge of the child and must therefore take responsibility for the child's safety. *"He must be able to stop an action of the child that is dangerous to the child himself as well as put a brake on any physical aggression against the analyst. He may also have to restrain the child from destructive behaviour in the room which would lead to lasting damage and prevent the room being used by other patients"* (1981: 27).

Segal notes that children are quick to grasp the difference between the toys in their individual drawer, which are for their use only, and the therapy room, which represents the setting and the analyst's other child patients. *"While they are free to do what they please with their own equipment, and what they do with it is an object of interpretation, what they do to the room has quite a different character and sometimes has to be restrained as well as interpreted"* (1981: 28). Depending on the child's age and degree of illness, it may be necessary to alter the setting somewhat. One may, for instance, have to remove toys which could be used as weapons by psychotic children or by abnormally aggressive children in latency or at puberty.

The technique of interpretation

Establish from the outset a contact with the unconscious

Through the child's play and other communications, the analyst aims from the start to establish contact with the child's unconscious. *"From the first contact, the analyst tries to understand the child's communication and relies on the fact that his interpretation relieves unconscious anxiety to maintain the child's interest and co-operation"* (1981: 28). There is no attempt to get the child used to the situation or to cater to his wishes by providing the kind of toys that might interest him.

To show how she makes contact with children, Segal gives as an example the first session with a little girl of 2 years 9 months. When she went to collect the patient from the waiting room, the little girl clung to her mother and refused to go into the playroom. Segal observed the little girl's attitude, and suggested some interpretations as to what seemed meaningful to her; these helped the child to let go of her mother and go into the playroom. At the second session, before going into the playroom, the little girl again hesitated. When she heard the interpretation that Segal suggested, the little girl laughed and followed the analyst into the room, showing that henceforth she felt able to trust her analyst. In the course of the session, the little girl responded to the analyst's interpretations by showing both her astonishment at what the analyst said and her wish to learn more. She said to Segal: *"You talk very funny, but go on talking"* and, later: *"Go on talking . . . tell me"* (1981: 29).

Different ways of beginning

There are as many ways of beginning as there are children. Sometimes the first contact will be made with anxiety, as in the preceding example, sometimes with hope, which makes the beginning much easier. Segal gives the example of a latency boy who, after having expressed his hopes and expectations at the beginning of the first session, suddenly became anxious. The analyst was able to interpret both the boy's hopes and expectations of the wonderful things the treatment would give him and his anxiety linked to the rivalry and jealousy that the other children in therapy might feel at the gifts he would be receiving.

Segal gives the example of another first session which was handled well by a candidate in training. In this very vivid report, the analyst describes in some detail the way in which she followed the development of the patient's unconscious phantasies and transference, and how she adjusted her interpretations by taking into account the young adolescent's responses as the session progressed.

Adjusting the approach to the child's age

Child analysts have to accept all the modes of communication that are presented by child patients, and whenever possible, to communicate back to the child through their interpretations. Modes of communication vary with the age of the child. Young children communicate primarily by move-ment and play. Latency children can alternate between communication through speech and some-times free association, and communication through play and behaviour. Adolescents are capable of free association, but are more inclined than the average adult to express themselves through their behaviour: acting-in and acting-out.

Unlike the analyst of adults, child analysts must up to a point also co-operate in the child's play. They have to do things that the child cannot do him- or herself, such as sharpening a broken pencil or participating in a game that requires two players. To what extent the analyst should participate in the child's play is a very tricky question, the answer to which demands a lot of experience. "*The main principle should be that the analyst should participate as little as possible in action and co-operate only to the extent to which his co-operation is necessary for the child to express himself or herself fully*" (1981: 32). In other words, from the point of view of the analyst, the child's play is a communication that has to be understood and interpreted, and all the analyst's actions should be directed at furthering this communication. Segal goes on to describe a session with a little girl of 6 who wanted to play at being a teacher, with the analyst in the role of the child. In her role as the child, the analyst had to be stupid and ignorant, while the little patient playing the teacher was cruel, mocking the child and humiliating her. The little patient began by resisting the analyst's interpretations, screaming and shouting the analyst down. Her attitude changed, how-ever, once it was interpreted to her. "*It could be interpreted to her how she needed to put herself in the role of the teacher because she felt it so unbearable to be little and not to know, but also how in doing that she stopped herself from learning (this being one of her important symptoms)*" (1981: 33). After that interpretation, the little girl changed the game; the analyst was henceforth the teacher, and the little girl the pupil, showing that the young patient had given up her initial reversal of the situation.

The compulsion to repeat

Quite often, latency children will insist on going on and on with the game; this may correspond to a feeling of gratification derived from the position of control over the analyst. Here the game is no longer a communication but a repetitive "acting-in", an expression of the compulsion to repeat. In such situations, the analyst may have to stop acting the role demanded by the child and simply offer interpretations. Segal emphasizes that interpreting the compulsion to repeat is technically more difficult with children than with adults. The analyst has to participate in the child's game in order to understand the pattern of repetition, but at the same time there is the risk of colluding in the repetition compulsion. "*Any situation in which the analyst participates can be easily used for purposes of repetition compulsion and/or direct gratification of instincts*" (1981: 33).

It is for that reason, observes Segal, that child analysts have to be active to a far greater extent and must therefore examine the child's response very carefully in order to take it into account. "*We always have to watch the patient's response, not only to our interpretations but also to our behaviour. A cough, a squeaking of the chair – all actions are experienced by the patient as communications. [. . .] The apparently most innocent actions become imbued with meaning*" (1981: 33).

Using simple language

How well can young children really understand verbal interpretations, particularly complex ones? That question is often raised, and this is how Segal answers it. *"It has invariably been my experi-ence, both in analyses and in supervisions, that, provided the interpretations are put in simple lan-guage, and provided they are correct and close to the child's experience, the child can follow the interpretations, on the whole more easily than a sophisticated adult, who tends to mobilize intellectual defences much more readily"* (1981: 34).

Segal gives a clinical illustration of the way in which she managed to make herself understood by a little 4-year-old girl patient; the case was supervised by Melanie Klein. Segal had given such a condensed summary of the material that Klein looked at her with a really shocked expression and then said, very quietly, "I think I would rather like to see this session: I do not quite see how you interpreted all that to a child under 4." Segal then told Klein in much more detail what had gone on between her and her little patient: the girl had had the phantasy that her analyst was pregnant. From the girl's responses to Segal's interpretations, it could be deduced that she had understood them quite correctly.

> At no time in the session did I have the feeling that my interpretations were too complicated for her or that she could not follow them. And though she verbalized little in this session, in the next she spoke quite freely of her anxieties that either I or her mother would go on producing new babies, and of her envy and wish to be a "mummy full of babies" herself. One can well see, however, that in summarizing one's interpretation one may sound as though one were talking a language which would be complete gibberish to the child. (1981: 35)

Melanie Klein agreed with the line of interpretation chosen by Segal.

The problem of language can sometimes present difficulties with adolescents who use a vocabulary more appropriate to their own age group. To what extent should the analyst adopt the patient's language, with the risk of being in collusion with the adolescent's opposition to the adult world, or stay with his or her customary language, with the risk of being experienced as a superego figure, unable to understand? Segal's general rule of thumb is as follows: *"I have always used the patient's own language – 'groovy' or 'high' or whatever the current 'in' word is – when referring to what the patient has said himself. When interpreting, however, I use the current ordinary English"* (1981: 35–36).

The patient's language itself may also become an object of analysis. Often those slang expres-sions that adolescents use prove to be rich in unconscious phantasy content. *"If one can analyse the patient's language itself, one can make him experience that one does indeed understand his language and does not reject it, but that one is not oneself involved and identified with the patient's unconscious processes as expressed by his language"* (1981: 36).

The relationship with the child's parents

The relationship with the child's parents is a problem specific to child analysis, one which is not encountered in the analysis of adult patients. The child's external environment is largely deter-mined by the parents. For example, as the child's analysis progresses, his or her parents may modify their attitudes. Some parents respond to their child's improvement by having a better relationship with him or her; on the other hand, it can happen that the parents react adversely to their child's improvement if, for example, the child's illness was necessary to the family equilibrium.

Analysis cannot alter the environment itself, but, by strengthening the good internal figures and the ego, the analyst can enable the child to deal better with whatever situation he or she has to face. It is often a great temptation to try to influence or educate the parents, but this does not lead to favourable results and is liable to interfere with the relationship between analyst and child. Generally speaking, if the parents are looking for help and advice, it is always better to refer them to somebody other than the child's own analyst.

With respect to the question of contacts between analyst and parents, their frequency, etc., Segal points out that there is no general rule because each situation is different. The answer, in other words, varies with the personality of the analyst and the needs of the parents. *"I do not think that in all my experience of analysis and supervision there have been two situations in which I would deal with the parents in the same way"* (1981: 36).

The aim of child analysis

A question which is often raised is "What is the aim of child analysis, and in what way does it differ from the analysis of an adult?" In Segal's view, the aim of psychoanalysis is fundamentally the same whatever the age of the patient: "*it is always to get the patient in touch with his psychic realities. The analysis of defences and of object relations, in phantasy and reality, should help him to differentiate between external and internal realities, and to foster the process of psychic growth*" (1981: 36).

Linking Klein's approach with that of Bion in child analysis

Child analysis in Sao Paulo

Teresa Rocha-Leite Haudenschild is the present Head of the training programme for child and adolescent psychoanalysts in Sao Paulo. Her work bears witness to her own specific synthesis of Kleinian and post-Kleinian developments, in particular those of Segal and of Bion. In her 1997 paper, "Retaking the first steps towards symbolization", she describes her work with a 6-year-old girl who, after emerging from adhesive identification, manages to acquire a capacity for symbol formation.

> When I embarked on the work of analysis with Amanda, I felt that here was a child who did not yet have the capacity to contain her own emotions and anxieties. Their containment by an internal object capable of understanding is the beginning of mental stability (Segal 1975). I therefore took it that the main function of the analysis would be to enable her to introject a comprehensive object that would make her emotional experiences meaningful to her and allow her to "think" them (Bion 1961). (Rocha-Leite Haudenschild 1997: 735)

JMQ: Psychoanalysts who begin by working with children generally tend to move on and work exclusively with adults, leaving child analysis behind them. You seem to be something of an exception . . .

Teresa Rocha-Leite Haudenschild: Well, I was 36 when I first had a child patient in analysis; now I'm 64, and I still treat child patients. For example, at present, I have two children in analysis with three sessions per week and another with two sessions per week – I'm hoping we will soon be able to have at least three sessions per week.

JMQ: Do trainees and newly qualified psychoanalysts still take on child patients in Sao Paulo and in Brazil as a whole?

Yes. In the training programme, the Psychoanalytical Society requires the supervision cases for trainee child analysts to be four-sessions-per-week analyses. It is, all the same, becoming more and more difficult to find child patients able to come four times a week. The main obstacle at present is the distance they have to travel and the traffic jams that are so endemic in Sao Paulo. It's too difficult for parents to accompany their child four or even three times a week.

JMQ: To what extent is the Kleinian technique employed in child analysis by you and your colleagues?

Our Society has a solid Kleinian basis. Virginia Bicudo, one of its founder members, had supervision in London with Kleinian psychoanalysts and even with Klein herself, I think. Overall, our evolution has paralleled that of the Kleinian movement as a whole. Hanna Segal, Betty Joseph, Edna O'Shaughnessy, Martha Harris and Donald Meltzer came here to offer supervision. Bion, as you know, used to spend his holidays here and he agreed to supervise child and adolescent analyses. We have learned a lot also from Esther Bick, Winnicott, Tustin and Anne Alvarez, particularly as regards children whose mental apparatus, at least at the beginning of their analysis, is underdeveloped. Fundamentally, though, the Kleinian approach remains our reference.

JMQ: What influence did Hanna Segal have on the training of child analysts in Brazil and more particularly in Sao Paulo?

A tremendous influence. All the more so for me, in fact, because she links Klein's theories with those of Bion in a very clear and simple manner. In my opinion, that helps us a great deal in our clinical understanding of certain situations.

JMQ: You have worked with Hanna Segal and with Betty Joseph. Are their ways of looking at certain situations very different?

I would say that Segal has a deeper understanding of certain phenomena that emerge in psychoanalytic treatment than Betty Joseph has. I feel she gets closer to the patient, that she is more "with" the patient, as Bion put it. Betty Joseph, to me, seems to be much more "analyst here – patient there", if you like – her interpretations are very accurate, but they come from her.

(Interview (in French) October 2006)

Teresa Rocha-Leite Haudenschild (Sao Paulo) is a training analyst and supervisor with the Brazilian Psychoanalytic Society of Sao Paulo.

Child analysis in Los Angeles

Yvonne Hansen has spent many years practising child analysis and training future child analysts. She has thus been very much involved in how psychoanalytic technique has developed as a result of various post-Kleinian developments.

JMQ: What changes in psychoanalytic technique have you noticed since you began practising as a child psychoanalyst?

Yvonne Hansen: My exposure to Melanie Klein came through the treatment of very young children in Geneva and the discovery of Klein's book *The Psychoanalysis of Children*, at the time a revelation for my work. This exposure was followed by visits of several British Kleinian analysts to our small "Kleinian" study group, among them Don Meltzer and Herbert Rosenfeld. With that input, the fundamental components of Klein's approach were established in my work-setting.

Within that structure, changes have occurred in my work with children (and adults) as new influences have modified my approach and understanding. Input of Bion's theory and for me the experience of my analysis with him have had a significant impact. The influence of Bion has also penetrated the analytic community of the Psychoanalytic Center of California (PCC). Other British analysts also influenced that way of working, such as Segal, Betty Joseph, Tustin, Meltzer or Winnicott. Infant Observation, which is taught in the first year of classes to all candidates, opens an "in vivo" emotional experience of primitive expressions and interactions, as it resonates in the candidate's infantile experience and helps to develop the equipment of analysis. Several members of our Institute, mostly adult candidates and analysts, have had supervision with Segal, and of course her ideas are passed on and respected in LA.

The Institute offers a two-year child analytic programme following the completion of the adult programme. However, few candidates are involved in training. They seem to experience that, after the relatively demanding programme of adult analysis, an investment in additional training is too heavy. In addition, difficulty in finding child control cases able to be seen four or five times a week keeps them away from the programme. In consequence, there are few candidates that avail themselves of that training.

(Interview, October 2006)

Yvonne Hansen (Los Angeles) is a training analyst and supervisor with the Psychoanalytic Center of California.

Chapter 7

INTERPRETING THE FUNCTION OF DREAMS ALONG WITH THEIR CONTENT

Reciprocal feedback between clinical practice and theory

Her expertise in clinical matters means that Hanna Segal relies heavily on dream interpretation in her work. This can be seen in the many clinical examples we find in her writings – such an approach really does make her work with her patients come alive. These examples, however, are not simply clinical illustrations; Segal uses them to shed new light on clinical matters through her use of theory and on theoretical issues through her use of clinical examples.

This constant to and fro movement between clinical practice and theory is typical not only of her lectures and articles but also of her book *Dream, Phantasy and Art* (Segal 1991), which to a large extent focusses on the psychoanalytic theory of dreams and on the technique of dream interpretation. The chapters of that book which deal with dreams will be the focus of this chapter; those sections of the book devoted to art have to a considerable extent already been discussed in my earlier chapter on the aesthetic experience.

The first chapter of *Dream, Phantasy and Art* opens with an in-depth discussion of Freud's ideas seen from two angles. Given that Freud made few modifications to his theory of dreams after 1900, Segal takes a fresh look at it in the light of concepts that Freud himself subsequently introduced – for example, the conflict between the life and death drives (Freud 1920g) and the concepts of ego and superego (Freud 1923b). Her study of these issues is all the more interesting in that few psychoanalysts have dared re-examine Freud's ideas on dreams in the light of the subsequent theoretical developments that he himself introduced. Secondly, Segal takes another look at Freud's theory of dreams with respect to more recent post-Freudian developments and her own ideas on the subject. In the chapters that follow, she deals with the relationship between dreams and unconscious phantasies and with the process of symbol formation.

With respect to the analysis of dreams, perhaps the most innovative of Segal's ideas springs from the distinction she draws in Chapter 5 of *Dream, Phantasy and Art* between the *content* of the dream as such and the *function* it has in the patient–analyst relationship. She observes, for example, that with certain patients her interpretations seemed to have no effect whatsoever when she interpreted the content of their dreams in the classical manner. Her attention was thus drawn to the way in which these patients used their dreams when they reported them in the session: they seemed more to want to be rid of them rather than to try to understand their meaning with the help of the analyst's interpretations. In other words, for these patients, reporting a dream was a way of unconsciously *doing* something to the analyst – an acting-in; this could be, for example, an attempt at seduction, making the analyst confused, attacking the analyst, and so forth. In such cases, argues Segal, the *function* of the dream must be interpreted in order to be able to interpret its actual *content*.

Dreams as communication and/or as a means of action in the psychoanalytic relationship

JMQ: You make a distinction between the content of dreams and their function in the analyst–patient relationship. In cases where the patient uses dreams to act upon the analyst rather than in an attempt to understand what they might mean, it is therefore useful to interpret the function of any given dream before dealing with its actual content . . .

Hanna Segal: Well, I would say rather that its function should be interpreted *along with* its content. It depends a great deal on the actual circumstances, which tend to vary over time. There are dreams that can be interpreted in the way Klein would have done, i.e. in a wholly classical manner – but that kind of patient is much more in touch with the depressive position. In these more approachable cases, you can distinguish dreams that are used in the analyst–patient relationship for communicating something from those that have acting-in as their aim. In this latter case, positive actings-in – the infant's earliest means of communication is, after all, through acting-in – are to be distinguished from their destructive counterparts. I wrote about that a long time ago in an article, but at the time I don't think I sufficiently analysed the way in which that obsessional patient was using his dreams to act on me. He would write his dreams down in his diary and report them whenever he felt like doing so – sometimes he would report a dream that he had had six months previously, sometimes it would be from the night before. Very often it would be a complete acting-in as far as the session was concerned. I think I have described the mechanism underlying this kind of dream in several of my papers but, for reasons of discretion, I have never given any clinical examples. There will be a chapter on this in the third volume of my collected papers, to be published in 2007 under the general editorship of Nicola Abel-Hirsch.

(Interview (in French), 15 August 2006)

Dream, Phantasy and Art *(1991)*

Segal, H. (1991) *Dream, Phantasy and Art*, London and New York: Routledge.

Freud's theory of dreams re-examined by Segal

The royal road

In *The Interpretation of Dreams* (Freud 1900a), Freud's study of dreams goes far beyond an attempt to understand nocturnal dreams as such, for he came to see the analysis of dreams as the royal road to a knowledge of the unconscious. Hence the famous aphorism that is often quoted: "The interpretation of dreams is the royal road to a knowledge of the unconscious activities of the mind" (1900a: 608). Unfortunately, as Segal points out, that sentence is often quoted in a much less complete version: "dreams are the royal road to the unconscious". Doing away with the idea that it is the *interpretation* of dreams – and not dreams as such – that leads to a *knowledge* of the unconscious – and not directly "to the unconscious" – is tantamount to eliminating the role of the "psychic work" of both patient and analyst which Freud emphasizes.

Freud thought that dreams were predominantly sexual in nature, but, contrary to common belief, not exclusively so, as Segal points out. In her view, Freud probably underestimated the importance of repressed aggressiveness, equal to that of sexuality. At that time Freud had not yet introduced the concept of the superego; he calls the agency that forbids the fulfilment of wishes unacceptable to consciousness the "censor" or "dream censorship". Freud saw dreams as being the result of a compromise between the repressed and the repressing forces, which is a way of bypassing the dream censorship – it follows that, for Freud, the dreamer's ego does not disappear while he or she is sleeping.

Dream-work and dream language

A dream is the product of what Freud calls "dream-work", which converts the dream thoughts unacceptable to the ego even in the state of sleep into the apparently innocuous manifest dream content. According to Segal, the idea of dream-work foreshadows that of a wider form of mental activity, that of "psychic work" (Freud 1900a), which, to my mind, implies a kind of working-through that is similar to the mourning process. *"The dream-work is Freud's first description of a wider concept which is, I think, fundamental to the understanding of psychoanalysis, that is, psychic work"* (Segal 1991: 5). Psychic dream-work uses a particular mode of expression – the "dream language" – which aims at fulfilling the unacceptable wishes by disguising them. In order to do this, the dream language uses such classic mechanisms as displacement, condensation, indirect representation, and symbolism. Segal then goes on to describe each of these mechanisms in more detail and illustrates their functioning by means of examples taken from her own clinical practice.

Displacement

Segal begins by pointing out that displacement can be of two kinds: one concerns psychic values, the other feelings or phantasies belonging to one situation that are displaced on to another. When displacement involves psychic values, the dream appears to emphasize a dramatic situation, to which it apparently gives some importance – but some insignificant detail in fact contains the most important latent dream thought. Segal gives an example of this. One of her patients dreamt that he was walking with a girl in a place which reminded him of Venice. This, at first sight, was a pleasant dream, and had to do with the analyst's forthcoming holiday. But there was a detail in the dream which had no apparent emotional significance: a concrete structure on the Lido beach, which reminded the dreamer of a bunker built during the Second World War. That dream fragment, says Segal, had to do with the patient's most significant thought at that point in the analysis, that is, his unconscious wish that she should perish in a concentration camp.

Condensation

Condensation is an invariable feature of dreams. However short the dream, many contradictory thoughts and wishes are contained in the dream as a whole and in its various elements. The work of decondensation often brings in its wake a whole series of meanings, giving the impression that the analysis of a dream could go on for ever. *"That is one of the reasons why it is difficult to report fully on the analysis of a dream, and indeed a dream can never be analysed fully in one session. In the next session the patient brings new associations and new dreams long before the analysis of the first one can be exhausted – if indeed it can ever be"* (1991: 6). Segal illustrates the idea of condensation with a dream from a patient who suffered from a gastric ulcer. In his dream he was completely tied to a chair in a half-lying position. From all sides he was threatened by some elongated animals with crocodile mouths. When the dream was analysed, it became apparent that condensation was operating on several different levels. There was a very primitive and concretely psychosomatic level, referring to when, up to the age of 3 or 4 months, the patient had been completely swaddled; this included the anxiety of being devoured by the babies contained inside his mother, etc. In addition, the dream referred to much later levels involving punishment for masturbation and castration anxiety. That patient had another dream in which a number of different people were condensed into a single character; in that case, the condensation involved the many possible rivals the dreamer felt he had – another analysand, the analyst's husband, and her son.

According to Segal, what Freud so beautifully called the "dream thought" is of much wider and more complex significance than he allowed. *"I think Freud originally had in mind simply the repressed wish, disguised in the dream. But wishes are contradictory and complex and I think the dream thought is more than a simple wish. It is itself a complex organization of wishes and defences. [. . .] The dream thought, as I see it, is an expression of unconscious phantasy and our dream world is always with us"* (1991: 8–9).

Segal does not completely share Freud's point of view on condensation; in her opinion, condensation is much more extensive than Freud thought. Freud saw it more as various strands arising from different impulses and trends of thought, converging together and being expressed in one condensed element, whereas, for Segal, condensation is a connected "story".

Indirect representation

Segal illustrates indirect representation with examples of dreams of a patient with a manic character structure. She goes into quite some detail in her analysis of his dreams, and shows that every element in them is reversed in order to disguise the true meaning: the lucky number is the bad number; benevolence and generosity replace rage and meanness. "*In this dream I think we can see how complex dream language is. One could say that in the dream everything is represented by its opposite, by the reverse, but at the same time that way of representing it changes a deeply traumatic situation into a wish-fulfilling one*" (1991: 11).

Symbolism

As far as symbolism is concerned, Segal challenges some ideas that Freud put forward. She reminds us that Freud excluded symbols from dream-work, because he considered symbols to be universal and derived from the ancient past. In support of her argument, Segal quotes the following extract from Freud's *The Interpretation of Dreams*:

> *Things that are symbolically connected today were probably united in prehistoric times by conceptual and linguistic identity. They are, one could say, given, not achieved by psychic work implied in other methods of indirect representation.* (Freud 1900a: 352)

That point of view was later challenged, firstly by Melanie Klein's work on symbolism and then by Segal's own research, as we have seen.

In her discussion of symbol formation in the light of Bion's developments, Segal notes that the alpha-function is closely linked to the symbolic function. Alpha-elements are the elements that go to make up thoughts, dreams, myths and symbolism. Since they are "unsaturated" – in Bion's sense of the term – alpha-elements are available for various "realizations" and reality-testing, in other words for all sorts of transformation such as those we observe in dream-work.

Associations are not the latent content

The process of analysing a dream consists in doing the dream-work in reverse, based on the associations to the dream which expand what had been condensed, rectify the displacement, and decipher the indirect representation. Segal points out, all the same, that analysing dreams is not an easy task, because it proceeds against the general trend of resistance. Part of the dreamer's associations will lead to the latent meaning, but other trends of association break off and acquire a defensive character. This implies that the patient resists seeing the significance of the dream because repression continues to operate in the form of resistance. That is why it is important, warns Segal, to distinguish between associations to the dream and the latent content as such. "*But the associations to the dream are not, as some therapists think, in themselves the latent content. They are only a path leading towards latent content, because repression continues to operate and to manifest itself as resistance*" (1991: 12). This is the point at which the interpretation of the analyst will seek to demonstrate the resistance and indicate the latent content. "*Where the patient's own work falters, the analyst's interpretation provides the missing link. The psychic work of deciphering the dream-work is essential in the analysis of dreams. This is done jointly by the patient and the analyst*" (1991: 12).

Secondary elaboration

Secondary elaboration is a further factor which aims to conceal dream thoughts. After waking, as we remember the dream, so we distort and transform it. The process that leads to distortion in the actual remembering of the dream is called "secondary elaboration". This, says Segal, rather tends to call into question the value of the memory that we have of our dreams. In the final analysis, the memory of a dream is rooted in unconscious phantasy. "*What is remembered may be altered as the dream reveals new aspects and deeper levels. The remembered dream has its roots, in my view, in an unconscious phantasy the full depth and extent of which can never be remembered*" (1991: 13).

Dreams and the conflict between the life and death drives

Segal notes that, after the publication of *The Interpretation of Dreams* in 1900, Freud never much altered his theory of dreams; in particular, he made no attempt to bring it into line with later developments of his theory, particularly after 1920, when he wrote *Beyond the Pleasure Principle*. If we take into account the conflict between the life and death drives, as Segal suggests, the work of the dream is not only to reconcile the forbidden wish and the superego or the ego, as Freud thought, but also to find a compromise or resolution for the unconscious wishes contained in the basic conflict between the life and death drives.

Segal concludes her discussion of Freud's thinking on these issues with three comments. She observes that, although Freud did develop the concept of working-through, he did not explicitly apply it to the dream-work as one of the ways of working through a conflict in her sense of the term. Her second remark concerns psychosis. Freud spoke of dreams as being similar to psychosis but happening entirely in sleep. Segal cannot agree with that. "*This seems to me in some way questionable, since the kind of psychic work elaborating a conflict, akin, I think, to a working through, which happens in the dream, is precisely what is lacking in psychosis*" (1991: 14). In her third and final comment, Segal wonders what happens when the ego is too damaged to carry out the psychic work involved in dream-work. Freud left the question open, she says, because he was more concerned with describing the formidable task that the ego accomplishes in creating a dream. In doing that work, it has to carry out repression adequately, but not excessively. The post-Freudians would subsequently shed new light on the development of the ego and its pathology.

Unconscious phantasy and dreams

Phantasy, for Freud, is much the same as day-dreaming

Segal begins by examining the differences between Freud's concept of "phantasy" and that of "unconscious phantasy" in the writings of Melanie Klein and those of Susan Isaacs. In her view, the Kleinian concept of unconscious phantasy is one of the most significant post-Freudian contributions to the psychoanalytic theory of dreams.

The idea of unconscious phantasy plays in many ways an important part in Freud's work, says Segal, despite the fact that he never worked out in full a theory of the concept. The idea was already present in his work on hysteria. "*Freud's discovery of unconscious thoughts underlying hysterical symptoms can be seen as equivalent to the discovery of unconscious phantasy*" (1991: 16). Later, Freud abandoned his original seduction theory in favour of the view that seduction scenes – which were apparently remembered – were most frequently a child's wish-fulfilment phantasy, rather than actual facts. "*Hysterical symptoms are not attached to actual memories but to phantasies erected on the basis of memories*" (Freud 1900a: 491). As early as 1914, Freud sometimes spoke of phantasy as being *the* psychic reality, observes Segal. However, he never devoted a book, or even a paper, wholly to that subject, despite the importance of the concept in his work.

One could say that for Freud, phantasy is fairly close to day-dreaming. Phantasy activity comes into play when an unconscious wish is frustrated. Phantasy is then worked on by the capacity for logical thought so as to give rise to an imaginary fulfilment of the drive-related wish. In a case like this, the phantasy is known not to be true. When the wish-fulfilling phantasy is unacceptable to consciousness it is repressed and becomes unconscious phantasy. Segal reminds us that "*in the System Unconscious phantasies 'proliferate in the dark', as [Freud] put it*" (1991: 17).

Phantasies and drives in Freud's theory

Freud intuitively sensed that there was some kind of relationship between drives and phantasies, but he did not take the question any further. According to Segal, he saw phantasies as highly organized and referring mainly to whole objects. Given that, for him, phantasy was similar to day-dreaming, more primitive phantasies do not enter much into his description. "*More primitive functioning on a pre-verbal, even pre-visual, psychosomatic level is not included in his concept of phantasy*" (1991: 18). Segal adds that mostly Freud referred to unconscious phantasy as connected with pathology, but he was also very aware that there was only a "short step" to be taken for phantasy to result in a symptom or in artistic creativity. "*It is as though Freud had opened a door to a fascinating, rich, mysterious world, but did not quite take the full measure of his own discovery and the connections between that and his other major discoveries, such as the dream-work and the dream language"* (1991: 18).

Unconscious phantasy in Klein's theory

Segal then goes on to discuss the idea of unconscious phantasy as introduced by Klein and Isaacs, pointing out that it was the psychoanalysis of children which revealed the ubiquity and the dynamic power of unconscious phantasy. From that perspective, unconscious phantasies are active from the very start, contrary to what Freud thought. That difference of opinion comes from the fact that Freud and Klein did not share the same conception of the early ego. In Klein's view, from the beginning of life there is sufficient ego to experience anxiety, to form some object relationships in reality and phantasy, and to use primitive defences. Unlike Freud, she did not hold the view that phantasies can only be formed when the infant or child has developed a capacity for logical thought.

In order to bring out the difference between Freud's conception of unconscious phantasy and that of Klein, Segal makes a highly evocative comparison. *"Most of Freud's statements give the impression that he thought of unconscious phantasies as if they were like islands in the sea of mental life. Reading Klein's work with children, one gets a glimpse of an internal phantasy world like a vast continent under the sea, the islands being its conscious, external, observable manifestations"* (1991: 19).

The view that phantasy is operative from the beginning, at the most primitive stages of development, implies that this phantasy is to begin with physical. Segal again has an apt way of putting it: *"the hallucinated breast is not to begin with a visual experience, but a bodily one. Early experiences, such as hunger or satisfaction, are experienced and interpreted by the infant in terms of object-relationship phantasies"* (1919: 20). With maturation and increasing experience, the phantasies become more complex with more differentiated sensory components and motives, and elaborated in various ways. It follows that unconscious phantasies underlie dreams, symptoms, perception, thought and creativity. *"They do not intrude into a dream; they are 'such stuff that dreams are made on'"* (1991: 30).

Symbolism and dreams

In the third chapter of *Dream, Phantasy and Art*, Segal examines the relationship between symbolism, dreams and unconscious phantasy. She reminds us of her own ideas on symbolism, in particular of the distinction she draws between concrete symbolization – the symbolic equation – and symbolic representation, and of the conclusion she came to that these two modes of symbolism pertain respectively to the paranoid-schizoid and the depressive position. In her discussion of symbolism in dreams, Segal argues that here too different levels of functioning can be observed. *"It is arguable that for the imagery of dreams to be formed at all a depressive level of functioning must have been achieved. Nevertheless, in some dreams, or some elements in some dreams, a regression occurs to concrete symbolization with all its consequences for the nature and function of the dream"* (1991: 48). Where there is a failure of symbolization, patients tend to use their dreams as a way of producing some effect on the analyst's mind – acting-in – instead of putting their transference phantasies into words.

In the fourth chapter, "Mental space and elements of symbolism", Segal explores the significance for mental processes of concepts such as projective identification and containment, in the light of Bion's analysis of them. She mention dreams only *passim*; I shall therefore go directly to the following chapter of *Dream, Phantasy and Art*, more in line with the topic I am at present discussing.

Interpreting the function of dreams along with their content

Dreams can have several functions

In Chapter 5, "The dream and the ego", Segal develops the highly original idea she introduced in 1981 according to which dreams may function not as symbolic communication but at a more primitive level of communication. Dreaming means that the ego has to take on an arduous task in order to accomplish the dream-work, i.e. to express and process the unconscious phantasy. At times, the ego may be temporarily or permanently unable to carry out the tasks involved in producing a neurotic or a normal dream. The dream then functions as a symbolic equation and is used to evacuate certain elements in the manner that Segal goes on to describe. For example, in borderline cases, we find patients whose dreams occasionally or habitually do not fulfil the dream function as described by Freud. "*The dreams of these patients serve the function not of elaborating and symbolizing latent dream thoughts, but the function of getting rid of psychic content (Bion 1958)*" (Segal 1991: 64–65).

Dreams and the function of evacuation

The process of evacuating something from the mind can take various forms. "*Dreaming is thus felt as an expulsion and is sometimes equated with actual urination or defecation*" (1991: 65). Writing one's dreams down in a notebook may be a way of getting rid of dream content. Sometimes it is dreaming and telling the dream to the analyst that accomplishes the evacuation. The aim here is twofold: one, to split off and get rid of certain unwanted psychic contents; and two, to affect the object, in other words to produce some effect on the analyst in the analytical situation. Segal illustrates this twofold function in one of her patients who used to flood her with his dreams. She gradually came to realize that the patient's main objective was not so much to get rid of his dreams as to make the analyst feel moved by the emotional content of the dreams he was evacuating.

When people experience dreams as concrete events or objects – a stream of urine, a stool, or anal gas – which are expelled into an object, their reality perceptions are unavoidably affected. For example, one of Segal's patients would complain that the analyst's room smelled of gas; it was only later that the patient remembered that she had a dream in which a gas balloon exploded. When she had a quarrel in a dream, the analyst was perceived as a quarrelsome person.

In these evacuation dreams, the dream-work has partially or completely failed. One of their characteristics is a certain crudity in symbolization. "*It is as though the barest minimum of effort went into symbolization*" (1991: 70).

"Predictive" dreams

Evacuation dreams are more often than not acted out, either in the actual session or in the outside world. Sometimes the dream content is evacuated by means of a very precise and detailed enactment. Segal gives the example of one patient who had numerous dreams in which he would be late for a meal or a meeting by a precise number of minutes – and who then would come late to his session by exactly the same number of minutes. "*I have called this kind of dream a 'predictive dream', because it seems to predict future happenings as they are almost automatically acted out*" (1991: 69). Of course all dreams are to a certain extent enacted, either in the session or outside of it. This is what Rosenfeld (1964) described as "normal acting-out". However, the dreams Segal is speaking about in this chapter, especially predictive dreams, are exceptionally compulsive, particularly in the session.

Dreams as part of the whole situation

The analysis of evacuation dreams encouraged Segal to devise a technical approach that takes into account the function that the dream serves in the session. In the case of dreams in which the dream-work is defective, it is useless, she says, to try to interpret only the content of the dreams, since analysing the content in a classical way has no therapeutic effect. What must first of all be done is to analyse the function of the dream, and only then its actual content. "*Generally, in these dreams, which are primarily used for acting out in the analytic session it is this function of the dreams that has to be interpreted first of all. Only gradually, and where it connects with this function, can one address the actual content of the dream*" (1991: 72).

In her concluding paragraph, Segal observes that if the interpretation of dreams is the royal road to the understanding of the unconscious, as Freud thought, it is not always sufficient to limit oneself to the interpretation of the content of a dream.

As I suggested, following only the content of the dream has its limitations. If we analyse not the dream but the dreamer, and take into account the form of the dream, the way it is recounted, and the function it performs in the session, our understanding is very much enriched and we can see how the dream's function throws an important light on the functioning of the ego. (1991: 73)

This fifth chapter brings to an end the part of *Dream, Phantasy and Art* that Segal devotes to the study of dreams. The final three chapters of the book deal with the relationship between art and psychoanalysis, a topic that I have discussed in Chapter 2, "Psychoanalysis and the aesthetic experience".

"The Interpretation of Dreams *one hundred years on*" *(2001, 2003)*

Segal, H. (2003a) "Le rêve et le moi" [The dream and the ego], in A. Nakov *et al. Le rêve dans la pratique psychanalytique* [Dreams in psychoanalytic practice], Paris: Dunod.
Segal, H. (2007) "*The Interpretation of Dreams*: 100 years on", in N. Abel-Hirsch (ed.) *Yesterday, Today and Tomorrow*, London and New York: Routledge.

This short paper, several versions of which have already appeared in print, summarizes, with her customary clarity of style, Segal's main ideas on dreams.

Chapter 8

THE ANALYSIS OF ELDERLY PATIENTS

An Area that Psychoanalysis Had Left Largely Untouched

Hanna Segal analysed a patient who was a little over 73 years of age when the analysis began. The short paper she wrote about it had important repercussions, because at that time most psychoanalysts were reluctant to take on patients who were already over 50 years old. Freud, of course, had said that 50 years of age was something of a watershed as far as psychoanalysis was concerned: "*on the one hand, near or above the age of fifty the elasticity of the mental processes, on which the treatment depends, is as a rule lacking – old people are no longer educable – and, on the other hand, the mass of material to be dealt with would prolong the duration of the treatment indefinitely*" (Freud 1905a: 264). Many psychoanalysts, of course, have not followed Freud to the letter as regards this issue; people in their fifties and sixties have had classical psychoanalytic treatment. Not much was said about this, all the same – in fact it was hardly ever mentioned, and psychoanalytic literature as a whole tended to echo that silence.

Given that state of affairs, Segal's 1958 paper was quite definitely ground-breaking – all the more so, indeed, since the patient she treated was not suffering from neurotic problems but from a psychotic illness with delusional ideas of persecution: the kind of symptom that many psychoanalysts tended to see as incompatible with a classical psychoanalytic approach.

Segal's paper encouraged several psychoanalysts to take elderly patients into analysis – with, it must be said, some success. A new domain for the exploration and treatment of the internal world thus opened up; the many papers that are published nowadays on this theme often quote Segal's pioneering article.

"Now death is really present!"

JMQ: In 1958, when you wrote an account of the analysis of an elderly man, that was the first time anything like that had been done in psychoanalysis. Since then, have you taken other elderly patients into analysis?

Hanna Segal: Oh yes, especially elderly colleagues. But I would like to say firstly that the patient I describe in that paper was almost 74 years of age, and nowadays that's not really so very old. I think people no longer consider age to be such an absolute criterion as regards beginning analysis: it all depends on the circumstances. I learned one thing too: my patient and I were lucky, because not many people as old as he manage to have analysis. That patient's son brought his father to London. The patient's wife was with him every day, she accompanied him to his sessions and waited for him in the waiting-room. She developed a positive alliance with me. In the postscript I wrote to the paper, I mention how he died. His wife was looking after him, and he said he was feeling hungry; she gave him a sandwich and a glass of milk. For him, dying always meant dying of hunger – as a child, he was very over-weight. His wife was by his side, and she gave him a glass of milk, whereupon he fell asleep.

How lucky he was, at his age, to have had such a caring environment. The only patient I envy – the only one of all my patients – is that man! Now that I no longer have my husband with me, when I wake up in the middle of the night, lonely and afraid, what am I to do?

Nowadays, analysing elderly patients is quite common.

The Tavistock Clinic published a good collection of papers on the issue of growing old – there is a paper by me in it as well as others. Also, there is a department at the Tavistock called the "Workshop for old age psychotherapy".

JMQ: Your 1958 paper opened the way for the psychoanalytic treatment of elderly people.

It has now become quite a common practice in Britain – and in the US too, I think – because 70 nowadays is not looked upon as being particularly old.

You were asking if I had other elderly patients in analysis. I had for example – several years ago now – a woman who came for a second analysis with me, when we were both over 70. She is still very active; that analysis gave her a new lease of life, and she was very grateful to me for that. [. . .]

JMQ: Is there any difference, in your view, between the analysis of elderly people and that of younger patients?

Yes. The great difference has to do with the fear of dying, which of course is a much more acute issue. Also, difficulties about becoming dependent, because it is really very humiliating when people become so infantile. Fear of death is always present – it existed before, of course, perhaps in the form of infantile anxiety. But now, death as such is really present! Even when your health is still excellent, there are often complications of one kind or another – for example, physical disorders linked to growing old and the constraints that they entail.

I would just like to remind you that Karl Abraham had older people in analysis. Abraham was a pioneer in so many ways. He was really very gifted, perhaps the most gifted of all of the people in Freud's circle. Unfortunately, Freud had a great liking for people who were charismatic; I don't think he liked Abraham as much as he did some others – Ferenczi and Jung, for example. At the very beginning, indeed, Freud didn't have much taste when it came to choosing his friends. In 1920, Abraham wrote a paper on the psychotherapy of an elderly male patient, so he did not hold with the idea that older people are unsuitable for psychoanalysis.

(Interview (in French), 15 August 2006)

"Fear of death: Notes on the analysis of an old man" (1958)

Segal, H. (1958) "Fear of death: Notes on the analysis of an old man", *International Journal of Psycho-Analysis*, **39**, 178–181; reprinted (1981) in *The Work of Hanna Segal*, New York and London: Jason Aronson.

A psychotic breakdown

This patient consulted Segal after suffering an acute psychotic breakdown two years previously in Rhodesia, where he lived. He had had the usual psychiatric treatment (electroconvulsive therapy, medication). He settled into a chronic psychotic state characterized by depression, hypochondria, paranoid delusions and attacks of rage. Given that he had shown no improvement, his son, who lived in London, brought him for psychoanalytic treatment. This lasted eighteen months, with five sessions per week, and was not a completed analysis. It did, however, enable the patient to resume normal life and activity, and to achieve for the first time in his life a feeling of stability and maturity. Eighteen months later, the patient was back in Rhodesia, enjoying good health. "*In his analysis I came to the conclusion that the unconscious fear of death, increasing with old age, had led to his psychotic breakdown. I believe that the same problem underlies many breakdowns in old age*" (1958: 178).

Born in the Ukraine, the patient came from a very poor Jewish family and had seven siblings. His father died when the patient was 17. He emigrated to Rhodesia, became a salesman, and married. Several factors precipitated his illness, writes Segal, all of which were related to his fear of death. The first occurred when he was visiting his son in London: he learned that all the members of his orthodox Jewish family had perished in Nazi death camps during the war. Back in Rhodesia, he learned that various dubious financial transactions entered into by one of his associates had been discovered; he was terrified at the idea that his own financial misdeeds might also be brought to light. Within a matter of hours he was in a state of acute psychosis with delusions of persecution – he believed that he was being talked about in the press and on radio. According to Segal, this breakdown had to do with the patient's fear of death. *"I suggest that my patient was unconsciously terrified of old age and death, which he perceived as a persecution and punishment; that his main defences against this fear were splitting, idealization, and denial. [. . .] When he returned to Rhodesia he was faced with the fear of punishment, which to him at that point represented death"* (1958: 178).

From the point of view of the patient's anxiety about death, Segal divides the analysis into three phases.

First phase: complete denial of ageing and fear of death

The patient described himself, before falling ill, as working and looking like a young man. This, it soon became clear, was a complete denial of growing old and of his fear of death. He felt his illness had robbed him of his youth, and he unconsciously expected that his treatment would give him back his youthfulness. This denial was reinforced by the patient's idealization of his son, who represented for him another self, young and ideal, into whom he had projected all his own unfulfilled hopes and ambitions. In addition, this relationship to his son was partly a repetition of the one he had had with his own father: he was his father's favourite, and he felt that so long as he had his father's love, he would be protected from starvation and death. In his relationship with his son, he identified with his father and projected himself, the favourite son, into his own son. Accompanying this idealization was a splitting thanks to which any unconscious feelings of persecution linked to the idealized object were immediately split off and projected into another object, which then became the persecutor. He could therefore idealize his father completely, because any negative aspects were immediately split off and projected into his mother, whom he experienced as unloving and cold, or into his brothers.

During this initial phase, the analyst represented mainly the patient's ideal father and son, occasionally an ideal feeding mother. His bad feelings and figures were projected into remote persecutors, either geographically remote – in Rhodesia – or belonging to the distant past.

Second phase: splitting between idealized object and persecutory object diminishes

After an interruption in the analysis due to the first holiday, the split between consciously idealized objects and unconsciously dreaded ones lessened, so that persecutory feelings came nearer to the transference. Instead of being projected into remote persecutors, his persecutory feelings centred on the very cold English winter which was going to kill him. Death was no longer denied. *"Gradually it was possible to point out to him how much [. . .] the cold climate and country that was going to kill him was the other aspect of the analytical treatment and of myself"* (1958: 179). At that point, the patient was able to acknowledge his disappointment in his son, whom he no longer unconditionally admired as he had done before. Although his son was devoted to him, he had his own life to live; this was felt by the patient as losing his greatest hope, namely that his son would give him a new lease of life.

> *At this point it became clear to the patient that his ideal and his persecutory object were one and the same person. In the past he had split off his fear of his father on to his brothers. Now he saw clearly that it was his father's retaliation that he was afraid of. He feared that his son would leave him to his persecutors and to death and disown him, as he had left and disowned his family.* (1958: 179)

In the transference, the patient had either to placate or to control the analyst in order to prevent her from becoming a persecutor. He felt that his idealization of the analyst was his only protection against death. She was the source of food, love and warmth – but she was also the one who could kill him by withdrawing all that. "*Idealization and placation of me alternated with only thinly veiled persecutory fears*" (1958: 180).

Third phase: acknowledgement of ambivalence and depressive anxiety

Changes in his perception of the object, in particular of the analyst, meant that gradually the patient was able to become aware of his aggressiveness towards her.

> *Slowly he was beginning to realize that if his symptoms now appeared only during breaks and weekends it was not simply because I, the ideal object, abandoned him to his persecutors; he was beginning to realize that everything I had given him – interpretations representing the good breast and food or the good penis – turned in my absence to bad burning, poisonous, and persecutory substances, because when he was away from me, hatred welled up in him and turned everything bad.* (1958: 180)

At the same time, he began to admit how greedy he was for the analyst, and how impatient and angry he felt when away from her.

Then memories of his early childhood came back to him, especially of when he was about 2 years old – he recalled his fury at being weaned when his baby brother was born. The memories were relived by him with so much intensity that, when he expressed the fury he had felt towards his younger brother, the fine tremor that for years had affected his hands disappeared immediately – it had been diagnosed as a senile form of Parkinson's disease.

The analysis made it possible to trace the beginning of the patient's secret drinking to the outbreak of the war, in 1939. He admitted that, had he thought about it, he could have brought his family over to Rhodesia and thereby save them from extermination. Unable to bear his depression and guilt because of this, he split these feelings off and denied them, and turned to drink. He gradually became aware of the contempt in which he had held his mother and of the hard struggle she had had to keep the family alive. He had turned away from her and from his own depression towards an idealized, homosexual relationship with his father, thereby robbing her both of his father's affection and of his own.

With this changed relationship to his mother and his family came a very different relationship to his own death. The end of the analysis had by then already been fixed, and symbolized for him his approaching death, of which he now spoke freely. For the first time he could mourn the loss of his mother and of the breast. This was no longer experienced as retaliation and persecution, but as a reason for sorrow and mourning for the loss of something that he had deeply appreciated. This mourning and sadness, however, did not amount to clinical depression, and seemed not to interfere with his enjoyment of life.

At this point in the analysis, he began to feel hopeful. "*He felt that his life was worth living and that, however old he was, his internal objects were rejuvenated and worth preserving. It was also clear that his children and grandchildren were no longer felt by him as projections of himself, but as his objects that he loved, and he could enjoy the thought of their living on and growing after his own death*" (1958: 181).

A major contribution to the analysis of elderly patients

According to Segal, the patient had been unable, from his early childhood on, to face up to his ambivalence and the depressive anxiety that resulted from his fear of losing his objects. Consequently, he could not face the prospect of his own death, and defended himself against those anxieties by denial of depression, splitting and projective identification. Idealization and denial were defences against both depression and persecution. In old age, when he had to face up to the prospect of approaching death, the loss of his life appeared to him to be a situation of persecution and retaliation. That was when he had his acute psychotic breakdown. The analysis of his anxiety and defence mechanisms in the transference enabled him to work through the infantile depressive position, so that he could then face up to old age and death in a more mature way.

In the postscript she added in 1980, Segal informs us of the fact that after his analysis the patient returned to Rhodesia and had a very active life. He suffered from time to time from mild depression, but did not have to take anti-depressive medication. He remained in excellent health until he died suddenly in his sleep, in his 85th year. "*This analysis has illuminated for me the problems of old age. Certainly it has altered my views on the prognosis of analysis at an advanced age"* (Segal 1981: 182). I would add that Segal's account of that analysis also changed the way in which many psychoanalysts thought of the prognosis of analyses that begin when the patient is already an elderly person.

What does the future hold for the analysis of elderly patients?

Gabriele Junkers has brought to our attention the new possibilities opened up by the psycho-analytic treatment of older people. This field of study, which represents a new challenge for psychoanalysis, nevertheless remains relatively unexplored (Junkers *et al.* 2006).

JMQ: In 1958 Segal was one of the first analysts to write a paper on the psychoanalytic treatment of an elderly man. What impact did that article have?

Gabriele Junkers: Hanna Segal's paper was really the first to have such an impact on the psychoanalytic world. It shows very clearly that Freud was wrong when he advised against beginning analysis with elderly patients. Segal shows that older people have a very rich emotional life and that neither the "mass of material" nor the lack of "elasticity" of which Freud wrote should be thought of as obstacles to their treatment. Segal writes of her elderly patient's transference and describes how it developed. She argues that it is above all the unconscious anxiety about death that lies at the root of mental problems in older people.

JMQ: Do psychoanalysts nowadays take more elderly patients into analysis, or are they still reluctant to consider this form of treatment?

Nowadays, population growth is quite alarming: elderly people make up an ever-increasing proportion of the population and, in 20 years from now, half the population will be over 50 years of age. From that point of view, there will be an increasing demand for therapeutic help for older people, but more often than not they are treated by medication rather than by psychotherapy. Many psychoanalysts are reluctant when it comes to working with older people: there seems to be a tendency for people in general to turn away from those who are getting old . . .

JMQ: At what age nowadays do analysts feel that someone would be too old to begin analysis, given that, for Freud, the upper limit was 50 years of age?

I would say that it is not one's chronological age that should determine the limit. What is important is the patient's motivation – is he or she distressed, is there some interest in his or her mental world and past history? Elderly patients must also have adequate hearing and not have too many lapses of memory. The oldest patient of whom I have heard – in analysis with four sessions per week – was 84 when he began.

JMQ: Have you noticed any differences between the analysis of an elderly person and that of adults in general?

When you present clinical material from the analysis of an elderly patient, the audience is usually surprised by the fact that the material does not appear to be in the slightest bit different from that of younger patients. In my view, all the same, the analyst's position is more difficult, and this is for the following reasons:

- older patients tend to bring to mind a parental figure towards whom one would tend to be submissive;
- the analyst is faced with material of which the main themes are loss, madness and limited time – those aspects attack the analyst's narcissism and trigger unpleasant feelings;
- the analyst has to be careful that his or her wish not to hurt the patient does not get in the way of the duty to give proper interpretations.

JMQ: What personal experience do you have of analysing elderly people?

I have had only two elderly people in analysis. The first was 68 years of age when she began, and the other, 62. My other elderly patients decided to choose psychotherapy rather than psychoanalysis. The first patient had a cardiac problem and her husband had just left her. She had had some consultations with a psychiatrist, who referred her to me for psychotherapy. I found her very motivated and willing to go much deeper into herself, so I suggested psycho-analysis. In the German health service, up to 300 psychoanalytic sessions can be reimbursed. We began analysis, four sessions per week, and it lasted for about three years.

JMQ: The analysis was interrupted at that point?

Yes, because she couldn't afford to pay out of her own pocket.

JMQ: Stopping like that after 300 sessions – wasn't that a problem?

Hardly at all, surprisingly enough. What was specific about that patient was that she had gone through hard times, especially with her daughter – for years they had not got on well at all. During the analysis, her daughter fell ill with a serious neurological condition; the patient was able to make peace with her daughter and take care of her. After the analysis, the patient wrote to me saying that the main benefit she had drawn from the work we did together was the opportunity to talk to her daughter again; she no longer felt rejected by her daughter, who accepted her mother's offer of help. I could then understand that the patient had made some reparation, and that in itself had given her much relief. It also made me think that, as we grow old, that time of life is all the more difficult because reparation can no longer be projected into the future. In that patient's case, it was fate that made reparation possible.

JMQ: And your other elderly patient?

She was referred to me by a member of her family who had had analysis. She had problems which had to do with certain events that had taken place during the Second World War, in particular reliving nights when the bombs prevented her from sleeping. Her husband too was ill. In my opinion, he was suffering from mental deterioration consequent on a neurological condition. The patient, however, saw this not as an illness but as a means whereby her husband put pressure on her. We began analysis, with three sessions per week; she made use of several kinds of defence linked to music. Gradually, she began to see her husband in a more realistic light. She realized that he wasn't being aggressive towards her, nor wicked – he was ill, and there was nothing he could do about it.

JMQ: Is that also a kind of reparation?

Yes, because the patient was able to go through a mourning process and say how sad she felt about his being unwell. The analysis helped her to put less pressure on him; as a result, she was able to approach her own distress at growing old, and thereby process her feelings of loss as old age drew near.

JMQ: According to Hanna Segal, it is the fear of death that is the major issue in analyses of elderly people. Do you share that point of view?

There could well be some misunderstanding about that. If somebody who knew very little about these issues read what Segal has to say, he or she might well think: "Well, *I'm* not afraid of death!" But that would mean forgetting that what Segal is talking about is the *unconscious* anxiety about death, not its *conscious* equivalent. But there is more to it than that. Linked to unconscious anxiety about death, there are primitive phantasies such as feelings of distress, the inability to move about, to see, etc. – Mary Chadwick pointed all this out in a paper she wrote (1929) about fear of death in children.

To get back to your question about whether or not I agree with Segal. In my opinion, when she says that the fear of death is the most important issue you have to deal with in the analysis of elderly people, that is perhaps putting it too concisely. I do agree with her when – this is my reading – she says that the fear of death corresponds implicitly to an unconscious anxiety linked to a feeling of distress, the inability to move about, to see, and all the losses with which you have to deal as you grow old.

JMQ: What are the counter-transference issues an analyst has to deal with in treating older patients?

As you know, Segal was the very first psychoanalyst who described the transference/counter-transference process in the analysis of elderly people. That aspect did not strike many chords among analysts when she wrote about it in 1958. It took twenty years – until the IPA Congress in New York – before Pearl King, in her keynote address on the counter-transference at different ages in life, mentioned that counter-transference issues do occur with elderly patients too (King 1980).

JMQ: How would you explain that gap?

When Segal wrote her paper, the London Kleinians were not all that well known, at least in Germany. Anyway, it often happens in psychoanalysis or in psychology that new discoveries with adult patients are put into practice much later with elderly people, sometimes ten or twenty years later.

JMQ: Does the counter-transference with elderly patients have any particular features?

It often happens that analysts do not like working with older people because of the counter-transference. It is sometimes unpleasant: older people are in their declining years, they may have various disabilities, they are getting towards the end of their life . . . Some therapists prefer to have a series of consultations with elderly people rather than psychoanalysis or psychotherapy as such. They know then that they will not feel too emotionally involved as regards disability or other experiences of loss that are linked to growing old. Outward appearances also play an important part. I have tried to find out if anything has been written about the influence outward appearances can have on the counter-transference, but without success. For the moment, all scientific interest as regards the counter-transference focuses on internal processes, not on the reaction one may have to outward appearances – you know, things like wrinkles, white hair, perhaps a particular smell, and so forth. The kind of thing that clearly shows the patient is an elderly person . . .

(Interview, October 2006)

Gabriele Junkers (Bremen) is a training analyst and supervisor with the *Deutsche Psychoanalytische Vereinigung* (DPV).

Chapter 9

SEMINARS AND SUPERVISIONS

Hanna Segal became a member of the British Psychoanalytical Society in 1947, at the remarkably young age of 29. She soon extended her teaching activity beyond Great Britain; as more and more invitations were addressed to her, she began teaching in other European countries, in Latin America and in the United States. From the 1950s until the present day, she has participated on countless occasions as supervisor, seminar leader and keynote speaker in round tables and in various symposia with audiences ranging from specialists to the general public; she has been interviewed by journalists from newspapers, radio and television — and much more besides. In 2006, in her 88th year, Hanna Segal had the signal honour of being the guest on BBC Radio 4's iconic programme *Desert Island Discs* as part of the celebrations for the 150th anniversary of Freud's birth.

Why do so many people want to hear what Segal has to say? Firstly, because her articles and papers have been so widely read. In addition, in my opinion, they appreciate her talent as a speaker — in other words, the clarity of her presentations — as well as her open-mindedness and her willingness to take what other people think into account.

Creating a climate of freedom

Seminars and group phenomena

JMQ: What can you tell us about your experience of teaching seminars?

Hanna Segal: Well, I have certain views about seminars. I think that the most important thing in a seminar is to create an atmosphere in which people feel really free to bring their problems without being put down or criticized. Yet at the same time, I never wear gloves. What I mean is, I say what I think . . . although I do not put down people's contributions. People are at the seminar to engage the whole group.

I learned that lesson during a seminar in Geneva in the 1980s, perhaps you remember it. At the first seminar somebody presented material and one of the participants started very aggressively, telling him "It's all to do with your homosexual counter-transference" etc. With an atmosphere like that people are afraid of presenting. I immediately put a stop to it. I said, "What you think of your colleague's counter-transference, you tell your analyst. But we're not going to have that kind of fight in the seminar." I didn't say that in an authoritarian way as seminar leader, but in order to make relationships easier in the group. The participants were really quite aggressive with one another – with that kind of atmosphere, people are reluctant to present anything. Later, some of them explained to me that it wasn't that they were frightened because the seminars were very aggressive, but because that particular participant would often be sarcastic and attack the other students. So it was a sort of competition, a battle on his part. Criticism yes, everyone should be open to criticism – but I don't allow any sort of hostile comments that are meant to undermine other people.

I think that I made it very clear at that point, when I said that the counter-transference was his business and his analyst's business. I wasn't trying to exclude discussion of the counter-transference, because now, of course, we do pay a lot of attention to it. I am, however, very much against people speaking for half an hour about what they feel, etc. It's all right if some-body says, "I've got a problem – this patient really irritates me . . . ." If the presenter then talks about what he or she felt in reaction to the patient's transference, with the idea that it would be worthwhile discussing it, that's fine. Sometimes I would simply say: "Well, that perhaps has to do with your analysis, but here we're more interested in the actual material." Counter-transference is a very good guide but a very bad master!

In a seminar, the relevant material is not only what happened between patient and analyst but also what the whole group feels about it. And, remember, quite a lot of people choose not to present what they did best but the problems they come up against.

Then there's the problem of the relationship between technique and theory. I think it's not good to put in too much theory, but you do need a theoretical framework in order to do things. So sometimes one has to put in a bit of theory on some particular point or other, like projective identification for example, or the transference, because from time to time people can't quite get hold of it.

Nowadays I do some supervisions over the phone – it works quite well – but in that case it is very much better if you occasionally see people; otherwise, it's not quite the same . . .

JMQ: Are phone supervisions very different from live seminars? You have spoken about non-verbal communication – is that what's lacking?

Yes, you do miss that a bit. Now I wear headphones for the phone so I hear better, but my voice doesn't carry as well as it used to.

JMQ: You have given seminars in countries all over the world, so you must have encountered many different ways of thinking about psychoanalysis. How did you react to these various thought patterns in your seminar participants?

Actually, nowadays Kleinians are popular in unexpected places. Also, there's a difference between small postgraduate groups made up solely of Kleinians, and the mixed groups, where there are candidates from various groups, plus foreign seminars. These are not necessarily Kleinians. [. . .] If you have a small group you've been working with for years, you don't have to go back to basics. But if you have a seminar with people from various groups and orientations, sometimes you have to be very tactful – and not say to them, for example: "That's rubbish", but rather something like: "Well, from my angle, I would do this . . ." I always try to show how things come from the actual material; I don't start with theory . . . I look at what's happening in the material and show them from that why such and such . . .

[. . .]

(Tape 1, side A, 28 January 2005)

JMQ: In your seminars, on what technical points did you feel there was divergence?

Sometimes I was dealing with colleagues who were analysing really very superficially. I would say that they think an analysis is going well if nothing nasty happens in the transference, so that they are always sort of stroking their patients. In the seminars, some are very good and get the idea very quickly, but I do have tremendous difficulty with others and sometimes it takes years to correct that.

For example, I heard that at a recent meeting of training analysts, one of them [. . .] said that a supervisor should always be positive and encouraging and never critical towards the student's presentation. I'm absolutely against that. Some analysts are very soft with their patients, I think – it's almost as though they feel that the session was a good one because the patient didn't get angry. They're always trying to pacify and collude in idealization. I'm not saying that those analysts are more sadistic than we are – we're all the same – but very often there's a combination: they're so goody-goody that it becomes an unconscious cruelty.

I think that we are there to teach and the best way of teaching is always to show from the material what is upsetting, or damaged, or wrong, and why another approach would be better. But you have to teach; that's what you're there for. And also, once again, never humiliate a supervisee. They are often just beginners.

I can give you another example to show how some colleagues deal only with the positive transference and don't take into account the negative aspect of it. There was a very interesting symposium some years ago. We were two psychoanalysts, each presenting a case. The two patients were depressed women, very similar, but my colleague's technical approach was very different. For example, the patient he presented always complained that, during her childhood, her mother never paid any real attention to her. There was plenty of material about how she resented the analyst's silence from the outset – but none of this was ever taken up and interpreted in the transference. She was always complaining about it, but it was never taken up. Even negative interpretations were communicated with gloves: "Of course you might be angry with me today." The patient kept on complaining about her husband's analyst, saying that her husband was not doing well at all. For me, this was the split-off negative transference that just wasn't being addressed. She kept on complaining that her analyst had sent her husband to the wrong analyst; she went on and on about it, but the colleague just kept telling her: "But I didn't recommend that analyst. No-one told him to go to that analyst." She never once took it up that she was putting on to the husband's analyst her feelings about her own analyst.

Some people you meet immediately take that kind of thing up. Their analytical approach changes and they do very good work. But with people who for years are used to turning a blind eye to real transference, you just have to wait for the right angle to come up. It takes years and some never manage it. It's a very different perspective. I've got examples and examples – it can take years to get them to shift their perspective.

One last example. A patient said at some point that his father had given him some money. "Oh, how wonderful", said the analyst, to which the patient responded: "Nonsense. That was nothing for him. He's so rich that it only amounted to a few pence." So I took the analyst up on that, saying that, next time, your patient will expect you to say how awful it is. "What are you?" I continued, "A Greek chorus just repeating what he says in an exaggerated way?" Three weeks later the father fell ill and the analyst I was supervising said: "Oh, how awful for you." The patient replied: "Awful for me? You know I hate my father. Anyway, he's not as ill as all that." I showed him how the patient uses what he says to completely devalue him as a psychoanalyst, implying that he's not strong. But that colleague repeats and repeats, not in any way changing his approach.

JMQ: Have you met supervisees who use "self-disclosure" and communicate their counter-transference directly to the patient?

I am absolutely against that, because it's an acting-in and it only increases the patient's omnipotence.

JMQ: Your papers show that you have an extensive knowledge of art and literature – Proust, Apollinaire, for example. Do you make use of that with your patients?

I think I use it in my thinking, but I wouldn't quote anything to a patient. Then again, it depends. You could say: "You're behaving like Hamlet." If you use it again it's giving some of your experience, imposing something; and also, if the patient doesn't know the painting or the book you're referring to, that could be very humiliating. And if the patient does know – "Hooray, we can talk about something else!" I used literature in relation to one girl because she knew Shakespeare by heart and in one session she was turning round and round, dancing and doing this and that. I said, "You're being Ophelia." I knew she was completely familiar with it and it turned out to be one of the best sessions we had; it was all about the death of her father and the dispersal of her feelings about it. But I use that kind of thing very very rarely.

JMQ: In any given seminar, I imagine that not all the participants necessarily adopt a Kleinian approach.

You want to know how I managed the seminars abroad and the mixed seminars? Of course, it's even more important to be able to get the right atmosphere when there are so many different points of view. Also in some seminars participants can be very hostile to the Kleinian approach, so again the point is to try to remain courteous. I think courtesy is very important. You don't have to be courteous with your patients, but in my opinion we have to be courteous within the Society. We have to try to defuse the hostility by saying: "Well, that is one point of

view, but what I would like to share with you is how I personally would look at this material."
In my interventions, I try to encourage the Kleinians – who may be very enthusiastic and
very hostile to the others – to behave themselves: to listen carefully, to see what points of
agreement there are, and what makes for disagreement. Sometimes it's quite difficult.

JMQ: And you stress the importance also of being tactful with people.

Not to say certain things, even if you think them! But you mustn't convey that. Just emphasize
that you're simply presenting a point of view. Even if you can see in the material that
the presenter is a very anti-Kleinian person, just point out how *you* would look at the
material.

*JMQ: Have you learned anything through your contacts with colleagues who have a
different approach to and experience of psychoanalysis?*

Oh yes! Well, yes and no. I have learned an enormous amount about how they see things, etc.
I can't say that I learned an awful lot that would make me change my own technique. But some
things resonate with me. I remember that one of the younger Kleinians presented a paper – a
very good paper in some ways – about thinking and interferences with thinking, how some
things get divided from one another, how links are attacked, etc. At the meeting, one colleague
asked him: "In your world, does anything ever happen below the waist? Do people ever
actually fuck?" I thought that remark hit the weak point of some developments that go too far
into things which, of course, are tremendously important and new – but sometimes they forget
the body and the ego. You have to remember that part too.

*JMQ: You have chaired seminars in many psychoanalytic Societies – you came regularly to
Geneva, for example, between 1980 and 1990. When did you start to travel for teaching
purposes?*

The first such trip abroad I made was to Uruguay. I think I was the first Kleinian to travel that far.
They wanted me to be a training analyst in their Society, but I turned the invitation down. I have
taught in Argentina and in Brazil. Invited by the Americans, I have twice taken part in meetings
in the US on various different topics. I have been in Los Angeles, and very recently in San
Francisco. The first time I was officially invited to the US was by Roy Schafer – he was at
Harvard University – but I don't remember now which Society it was. I have something very
important to say about Roy Schafer. He was a complete ego psychologist. In 1968, he wrote a
book about internalization that is a thousand pages long and in it he mentions Klein just once,
and then only to dismiss her. But despite that, he was the first to invite me to America to give a
series of seminars on clinical work. They asked me to present a case, over several weeks, if
I remember correctly. Much later, I went to Los Angeles several times. I've been to Baltimore
and New York, but that was more occasional. I've never been to Boston. Boston never officially
invited me but I did attend a major symposium on the war situation. In Europe, I was recently in
Stuttgart and Heidelberg.

JMQ: Have you been to Italy too?

Oh yes, a long time ago. Also, I had a seminar in Geneva and in the University of Bordeaux
too, with Pierre and Claudine Geissmann; Pierre was Professor there. At one time, I travelled
to Barcelona a lot. I don't remember all of it, I must say. And now I have two German groups
that come to me.
      For many years now, I have had a seminar group of psychiatrists who are also psycho-
analysts and who work in a mental hospital. They had a seminar with me three times a year on
the analysis of psychotics. That seminar ran for several years in Vienna. [. . .]

(Tape 1, side B, 29 January 2005)

JMQ: And California?

Some years ago, there was a group who were very keen to bring in Kleinians. I was the first to
go there, and they very much wanted me to stay on, but I wouldn't. Then Rosenfeld came, so

he was second. He did some work there, but he wouldn't stay either. Then Bion went and they asked him and he did stay.

JMQ: Why did Bion stay?

The version they like to put out is that he wasn't respected enough here in Britain, particularly by the Kleinians, which isn't true. He was the first Kleinian to be made President of the British Society. He was respected by all the groups. He was very much respected by the Kleinians. He had a little seminar for a few years to which all the senior Kleinian analysts came – well, no, not a seminar really, but sort of conversations. There were seminars too, I think. So we all learned from him.

I think there were two or three reasons why Bion left. One is that he was getting very old, and very concerned about money for realistic reasons. He had a very young family, because he married very late – that was one reason. The other reason, a bit strange perhaps, was that he felt flattered that they invited him. He came back saying, with a catch in his voice – "and do you know what? They invited me to stay!" I said, "Wilfred, they invited me to stay, they invited Rosenfeld to stay. Have a good think about whether you really want to go." The other thing is – Bion's relation to death was very strange. For me, the most beautiful book he wrote is not psychoanalytic but the book in which he describes his experience in the army – *The Long Weekend* – he was very traumatized. He had, I think, a pathological fear of death – which he was aware of. [. . .]

He really was adored and deified and became a kind of guru. He still had flashes of extraordinary insight [. . .]. He later started cutting sessions, telling the people: "It's not analysis, we have analytic conversations." But they all treated it as analysis. He became very much a sort of prophet, and to my mind a bit mystical. I asked him: "Wilfred, what do you mean by O?" He replied: "Oh, I don't know. It may be God or it may be Gracia Belle!" There was something of the prophet about him.

(Tape 8, side B, 31 March 2004)

"What she says always has a solid clinical basis"

What do French-speaking psychoanalysts think of Hanna Segal's ideas? That was the question I asked Colette Chiland, from Paris.

JMQ: You have often met Hanna Segal, what is your impression of her?

Colette Chiland: I have heard her speak on many occasions, sometimes in Paris — we invited her because she speaks French and some of us are not particularly well-versed in English. We appreciate what she has to tell us because every theoretical point she makes has a solid clinical background. She never just tacks Kleinian formulae on to things — one day I jokingly said to her: "When I hear you speak, I think I'd like to be a Kleinian too!" What strikes me most of all about Segal is that the extracts she gives show that her analyses are very lively. There are many transference interpretations and her interpretations are easy to follow. All this seems to me to give rise to analyses that are more enthusiastic and more lively than the way we do things in France — you could say that our technique is more silent. Even if a certain number of French analysts do make quite a lot of comments, we do not always make transference interpretations as, it seems to me, she does. With Segal, I have never had the impression that her use of Kleinian theory is in any way artificial. It really is an instrument that helps her to think and she communicates very clearly what that means.

JMQ: Do you find Segal different from other Kleinians you know?

I used to travel to London on a regular basis, for example to the Weekend Conferences organized by the British Society — that was where, for instance, I heard Rosenfeld: do you remember his manner of speaking? Not at all as energetic as Hanna!

JMQ: What do they think of Segal in Paris?

She was always invited to meetings involving child psychoanalysis because they were organized by the Alfred Binet Centre. Our discussions, however, extended well beyond child analysis. She herself would often allude to a child patient she had had, supervised by Melanie Klein, but she was never really a child analyst, she no longer took child patients. She would talk about psychoanalysis in general and of psychoanalysis with psychotic patients. René Diatkine, who was very familiar with Kleinian concepts, did not reject them. I surprised Danielle, your wife, one day during a discussion about projective identification when I said to her that René Diatkine was perfectly familiar with the concept and that he made use of it.

JMQ: That surprises me too because when he came to Geneva, René Diatkine was somewhat critical of the Kleinian approach . . .

Let me give you another example. In the book that Diatkine wrote with Janine Simon on the analysis of a little girl, *La Psychanalyse Précoce* (Diatkine and Simon 1973), he refers really quite often to Melanie Klein as far as theory is concerned. We were not sectarian by any means. On the other hand, I was very surprised at the Hampstead Clinic (now the Anna Freud Centre), where some of us used to go. Anna Freud was unquestionably an intelligent woman and at over 80 years of age her intellectual ability was still outstanding. Whenever she made a summary of discussions it was always very much to the point. But, for example, she would never use the word "projection", what she said was "externalization": anything remotely Kleinian was banned. In 1978, I heard her give a talk at a meeting of the Association for Child Analysis on the topic "Various trends in child psychoanalysis". At the end of her talk, I asked my colleagues: "Did I hear that correctly? Anna Freud spoke about child psychoanalysis and didn't once mention Melanie Klein or any other Kleinian for that matter! And Winnicott got just one mention!" Over here, at the Alfred Binet Centre, it wasn't like that at all. We were not, by any means, "devout Kleinians", but we did read Klein's articles and those of other Kleinians. For instance, in 1972 we organized an international symposium on the long-term treatment of psychotic states. I was the scientific secretary and I edited the report on the proceedings. Naturally enough, we invited Herbert Rosenfeld.

JMQ: Since then, there has been something of a reconciliation between the two groups . . .

People have since become more open-minded and they have a good relationship now with their colleagues from the Tavistock Clinic — the Tavistock used to be thought of as Kleinian in outlook. For a long time Anna Freud argued that children do not establish a transference, so that child analysis was simply not possible. Melanie Klein, on the other hand, built up quite a significant part of her theory on child analysis. I think that these controversies have calmed down; some people are even talking of doing away with the groups in the British Society.
    I have always felt particularly close to Winnicott. I met him, listened to him and read a great deal of his writings. What I like about reading Winnicott is the fact that it is not an intellectual discourse; he always says something that helps you associate to your own patients, to yourself, to your own analysis. There are so many psychoanalysts nowadays with whom you have the impression that you are reading some kind of philosophical treatise. Although I find Anna Freud's written work pretty boring, I did enjoy listening to her because she could at times be quite amusing — that side of her does not come through at all in her writing.
    I remember one day asking Hanna Segal why, when she arrived in England, she chose Melanie Klein. She told me that she found Melanie Klein's written work very lively and interesting, whereas Anna Freud was so boring . . . I like Hanna a lot, she sometimes has a sharp tongue, she is not always easy to get along with and she can be uncompromising at times. But overall, she is a very warm-hearted person.

(Interview, 23 August 2006)

Colette Chiland (Paris) is a training analyst and supervisor with the Paris Psychoanalytical Society.

Hanna Segal in New York

Not long before he invited Hanna Segal to New York for the first time, Roy Schafer wrote a book on internalization. Segal tells us in the above interview how surprised she was to find that Klein's work on that topic was hardly mentioned. Since then, Schafer's interest in the Kleinian approach to psychoanalysis has grown steadily, and he and Hanna Segal have become close friends.

JMQ: When you first invited Hanna Segal to New York, what did North American psychoanalysts think of the ideas developed by Melanie Klein? To what extent were they accepted or rejected, and for what reasons?

Roy Schafer: During the 1950s, 1960s, and 1970s the large influx of European refugee analysts, most of them clearly loyal to Anna Freud, and the virtual absence of Kleinians in the US, except for the Los Angeles area (Bion, Mason, etc.), assured exclusion of Klein from serious consideration. Kleinian thought was left vulnerable to unchallenged and consistent misrepresentation and derogation, some of which continues today. Reference to it focusses on early Klein. Sympathetic mention of Klein was professionally risky back then, as I believe it was for Elizabeth Zetzel of Boston who returned from London and wrote positively on what she understood of the depressive position. In Los Angeles, Fenichel showed Klein's influence, I would say clearly but not with strong emphasis. In New York, Edith Jacobson, a strong and independent thinker about the self, the object world and internalization processes, made some acknowledged use of Kleinian thought in her important writing, but her influence was pretty limited by the writings, teaching, and politics of the dominant group of "ego psychologists" organized around Hartmann, Kris and Loewenstein in New York.

My careful reading of that New York triad and their numerous followers, especially of Kris who championed studies of child development, found that the ego psychologists' otherwise extensive scholarly references seemed carefully to exclude mention of Klein while their texts seemed to offer Anna Freud-compatible, subdued, substitute versions of Klein's emphasis – for example, on early aggression, the signs of superego-like functioning, and in general pre-Oedipal psychic life. I saw this as a mix of actual debate and censorship by otherwise worthy contributors to analysis. My own primary teacher for many years, David Rapaport, also an active contributor to ego theory, dismissed Kleinian thought as a "demonology".

As a student I was for some time obediently blind and biased, but in the 1960s, as I began my studies and writings on internalization, I began to break free and read a lot of Klein, Riviere, and others. My second analysis helped me pay more respect to my own observations and subjective experience, especially in working with borderline patients and doing analysis myself. Sometime around 1970, I began teaching an elective course on British analytical thought in my relatively open-minded Institute (the Western New England Institute), adding that teaching on to my role as a major teacher there of the received versions of metapsychology and ego psychology – still doing so ambivalently, however, as one can tell from my references to the Kleinians in my 1968 book on internalization. I was, however, learning as I went along. With all my differences from Jacobson on internalization, I was taking a careful or compromised stand alongside Jacobson.

JMQ: What gave you the idea of inviting Hanna Segal? Have you invited other Kleinians since then?

When I heard that Hanna Segal would be coming to a meeting in or around New York sometime around 1970 (my memory for the date is vague here), I induced my boss, Dr Robert Arnstein, at the Yale University Health Service psychotherapy clinic where, on a part-time basis, I then taught and practised psychotherapy, to invite Dr Segal to one of our clinical conferences. She accepted. As I recall, she talked about a case she wrote up and published, that of her brilliant analytic, crisis-like intervention with the old man. That meeting was an exciting occasion.

I was able to meet and talk with Dr Segal and Betty Joseph and enjoy their hospitality when in London in 1975–1976 as the first Freud Memorial Professor at University College, after which, since 1985, my wife (Dr Rita Frankiel) and I have steadily developed a warm friendship with Betty Joseph and the group around her.

In later years, Rita and I were instrumental in bringing contemporary Kleinians other than Segal (Betty Joseph, John Steiner, Michael Feldman, Liz Spillius) to specially organized workshops (cases presented for commentary and discussion) in our home and also our country home, each time capitalizing on the Londoner being in the US. Groups of 25–35 attended most of these workshops. We also organized and ran two ongoing Klein study groups for a couple of years. Responses were varied but it did some good. Additionally, I conducted clinical workshops in San Francisco and later in Cleveland, each time working as best I could along contemporary Kleinian lines and touting the virtues of these analysts, especially Betty Joseph, and soon these study groups were inviting Betty Joseph regularly, perhaps having been influenced by me to do so. And my book on the contemporary Kleinians of London appeared in 1997 and, from what I hear, has been taken up in a number of study groups across the country. Over the past 10–20 years a fair number of senior US analysts have been attending West Lodge conferences and the Melanie Klein Trust meetings and also going to London or communicating by phone to get supervision from the London Kleinians.

JMQ: And now? Are psychoanalytic circles in New York or in North America as a whole still interested in the Kleinian approach?

In recent years, Dr Henry Smith of Boston began to invite the same analysts and also Ron Britton to the two-day clinical workshops he organizes each year at meetings of the American Psychoanalytic Association. These workshops are well attended (double the officially limited size of 25–30) and generally received with interest and appreciation, and showing, each time, the greater readiness of US analysts to think along object-relation lines, so that, even with weak case presentations, the meetings are always exciting.

Our London visitors also speak at major Panels at these meetings. By now, they have also been invited to lecture and do workshops at various Institutes and special conferences in the New York area and elsewhere across the country and continue to do so as interest and use steadily increase. They are now a definite presence here in the East – also in Los Angeles and elsewhere on the West Coast.

This development has been greatly facilitated, I believe, by the growing interest in, and influence of, Winnicott, Loewald, Ferenczi, Kohut's self psychologists, and the so-called Relational School of Analysis, all representing or urging some form of object-relations approach to theory and practice. Kleinian references have had to be included and understood but not centralized. Also, there has been some influx over the years of South American trained analysts who, as far as I can judge, practise a version of Kleinian-Bionian analysis as it is practised in London.

Nevertheless, strictly defined Kleinian analysis remains not widely practised nor endorsed in the US, and some of those who claim to teach it and practise it do not impress me or our London friends as having an adequate and exact grasp of it.

JMQ: What about Segal's influence in North America?

Where is Hanna Segal in all this? Relatively speaking, she has been an infrequent visitor here, though she did make an unforgettable appearance – it was in 1990, I believe – at the Winter Meeting of the American Psychoanalytic Association: she was on a panel with Ed Weinshel, a politically and educationally influential San Francisco analyst, each of them discussing a case presentation by the other; after which they were joined by yet others, including Otto Kernberg, to make up a full Panel discussion. At this meeting, Segal's presentation was impressive; she re-analysed Weinshel's presentation brilliantly and, I think, awed many in the huge audience. Earlier, at an IPA in Rome in 1987 or 1989 as I recall, she, as a discussant, did the same with a case presentation by Anton Kris of Boston, also showing the finest clinical grasp, above all of transference/counter-transference interplay in what seemed to be a confusing presentation, though this time Hanka's was only one of a number of small-group discussions attended by a limited group of international analysts.

Personally, Rita and I can say that Hanka fills the room with her presence (with or without cigar smoke) when she is on the scene and has always been interesting, good-humoured company and – being an avid reader – a great source of significant, non-analytic reading recommendations.

(Interview, September 2006)

Roy Schafer (New York) is a training analyst and supervisor with the American Psychoanalytic Association.

Los Angeles – London: Supervision with Hanna Segal

JMQ: For some years you had supervision sessions with Hanna Segal, partly by phone, partly in London. How did you come to choose her in particular as a supervisor?

Joseph Aguayo: As a graduate analyst of the Psychoanalytic Center of California (PCC) in Los Angeles, I had trained in the only Kleinian institute of its kind in the United States. By this, I mean that only this institute has had training analyst members who themselves had been either trained at the British Psychoanalytical Society or analysed by members of the British Society. Here I'm thinking primarily of Albert Mason, a graduate of the British Society who was analysed by Hanna Segal, and James Grotstein (among others) who was analysed by Wilfred Bion here in Los Angeles. The influence of the first generation of post-Kleinians has been tremendously inspiring to both candidates and members of the PCC. Also, through the institution of the annual Melanie Klein Lecture, we have brought members of the Klein group in London here to Los Angeles for decades now, beginning in the 1960s, when Hanna Segal, Wilfred Bion, Herbert Rosenfeld and Donald Meltzer first came and regularly gave lectures, supervisions and seminars to our group.

I first heard Hanna Segal lecture in 1997 in Los Angeles and was so impressed by her clinical acumen, candour and directness in dealing with clinical material that I sought her out, first to conduct a historical interview with her concerning her involvement with so many other illustrious members of the British Society – Melanie Klein herself, Joan Riviere, D. W. Winnicott and others. After this interview was published in a journal in northern California (Aguayo 1999), my own analyst, Albert Mason, gently broached the issue of my seeking supervision from Hanna Segal. This required quite a bit of working-through since I would have not imagined my work to be good enough to present to Hanna Segal, but with encouragement I finally phoned her, and we began working on a weekly basis beginning in September 2000. We continued meeting by phone on a weekly basis for over five years.

Once a year, when I would go to London on an annual research project involving the Melanie Klein Archives, I would always include visits to Hanna Segal for in-person supervision. I might add that since I am also trained as a historian, I found Hanna Segal's supervision so illuminating that I asked for and received her permission to audio-record our work, which also included many interesting asides about the history of the British Society. So it is no exaggeration to say that I benefited in two very different but complementary ways by having supervision with Hanna Segal.

JMQ: When did you meet her for the first time?

While our work began in September 2000, my first actual in-person clinical meeting with her was on 14 March 2001. Since I recorded all my supervisory sessions with Hanna Segal, the memories of that first meeting are quite vivid – I arrived by taxi in the Queen's Avenue area where she lives and walked in brisk spring weather around the neighbourhood, watching the schoolchildren leave school and then arriving on time for an hour and a half supervision. Sitting in her study amongst all her books, her papers and her cat was quite thrilling, and after a most stimulating discussion I left her home wishing that I could live in London.

JMQ: What brought Segal's psychoanalytic approach to your attention?

What struck me immediately once we began working on a weekly basis was Hanna Segal's capacity to root herself in the patient's internal experience. For a fifty-minute session of supervision, I would generally e-mail two sessions ahead of time and then we would focus on the two most recent sessions over the phone. Hanna Segal would begin by making some summary comments on themes that were either latent for the patient or on interventions/interpretations that I had made, which could be further refined and thought about. The whole process was amazingly efficient, allowing us to go easily through four sessions and thus stay current with the patient's experience.

Of course, Hanna Segal's disinclination to mince words is legendary. One always senses that one is in the presence of someone who knows what she thinks and puts it forward with a directness and brilliance that can be breathtaking. Segal embodies the value of being in contact with one's own psychic reality as it attunes itself to the patient's experience, and then puts it forward as an interpretative hypothesis. I tend to be somewhat obsessive, preoccupied with the patient's early history – in a Bionesque quip, Segal once said of my style that I had a "desire for memory", one which frequently left in the lurch the patient's immediate and spontaneous feelings of the moment. All too true!

Hanna Segal also made constant reference to what good technique, good boundaries and a solid frame were. She commented on my verbosity, word-choice: going on too long in interpretations when a shorter, more compact style would do. And of course, the proof of the pudding lay in watching my professional and personal development – while Hanna Segal remained solidly and consistently dedicated to helping me build my psychoanalytic identity, I was inspired to work harder and become a better analyst. In a time when so many analysts have complained about waning psychoanalytic practices, I have watched my analytic practice grow as a function of this most excellent training.

JMQ: Could you describe the way she works in supervision?

From what I have read and understood about Melanie Klein's method, it seems to me that Hanna Segal works in both the spirit and technique of her analyst. By this, I mean that Segal draws upon concepts like projective and introjective identification to root her supervision in the internal subjective experience of the patient. Segal hovers closely around the patient's experience, most especially with the ebb and flow of the shifting transference reactions as they become manifest in any given analytic hour. Also, very much like Klein, Segal factors in the importance of the patient's early remembered history, be it through conscious recollections or what Klein herself termed "general childhood situations". In short, Segal subscribes to the shaping aspect of the past in the present, but does so in a way that remains actively attuned to the patient's current subjective and emotional experience. Klein herself, in one of her unpublished seminars on technique, talked about how the transference is "a feeler towards early situations", and it is in this sense that Hanna Segal works according to the notion that the analyst must bear some interpretative responsibility for linking the past with the present – and all this is done with great brevity so as to not become stuck in the past.

JMQ: What characterizes her interpretations? Do you have a clinical vignette that could illustrate this?

Brevity and directness. Segal in her many contributions has also elaborated on the importance of the death instinct, but does so in a way that is accessible and extremely helpful in understanding "difficult" patients. Regarding projective identification as often an aggressive, evacuative process, Segal (1992) has discussed the importance of destructiveness in the clinical setting, where she sees this drive as anti-life simply because all pain comes from living, whether it be in the form of thinking, perceiving or feeling. The murdering-off of one's mental or emotional capacities is a process to which Hanna Segal calls attention in her supervisions.

One representative example from a very difficult narcissistic patient I talked to Hanna Segal about for years: after much interpretative work had been done with the patient's tendency to turn up late – or sometimes not at all – for her sessions, the patient had a dream: "I arrived at a murder scene ten minutes before the crime was committed." The irony was that this dream was reported on a day when the patient in fact *did* arrive ten minutes late! Segal commented on what a pre-emptive action arriving late for one's session is. As she said: "The patient disposes of ten minutes of valuable time before her analyst can know what has happened! This enactment is an attack on the analyst's working and perceiving mind because he is prevented from exercising his proper function of analysing and understanding." In short, the patient's murdering-off both of analytic time and of the analyst's mind reflects the annihilation of her own perceiving functions.

JMQ: Could you give some examples of points of convergence and divergence between Kleinian psychoanalysts in Los Angeles and Hanna Segal?

I find many points of convergence between Albert Mason – who was after all analysed by Hanna Segal – and her actual technique. There are many points of convergence: the linking of the past to the present, the ubiquitous nature of infantile phantasy, the ever-hovering attention paid to the patient's internal subjective experience – and the emphasis on destructive, envious attacks.

Contrasting Hanna Segal's technique with that of James Grotstein (who was analysed by Wilfred Bion), I would say that there are many similarities but some notable differences, which are more ones of degree than of kind. For instance, Grotstein (by whom I have also been extensively supervised) roots himself more in the living moment as it emerges in the clinical session, often bringing in the patient's subjective reactions as well as the personal reactions of the analyst himself (i.e. personal feelings, reverie, counter-transference). While Hanna Segal tended to see these more personal feelings and reactions to be within the domain of one's personal analysis, Grotstein tends to actively "play in" these reactions into the actual supervision itself. He is at times rooted in Bion's idea that the patient is actively recruiting the analyst to play one important role or another in the patient's psychic life.

JMQ: What can you tell us of the personal relationship you had with Hanna Segal during supervision?

It's hard to answer such a question simply, because I think Hanna Segal has been so immensely influential in my work. I think of her enduring qualities – her tenacity, rigour and steadfastness in rooting herself in the patient's internal experience are an inspiring model of sticking to it, especially in such a demanding profession as psychoanalysis. And of course, as I have mentioned before, Hanna Segal has been doubly important to my professional growth because of her lucid memories of the many illustrious members of the British Society with whom she had personal contact. When time has allowed, Hanna Segal has been most gracious in providing me with support and encouragement in my historical research into both Klein and the post-Kleinians of the British Society.

Not that this support has been easily garnered – I recall that when I sent her an early version of a paper, which was published eventually in *The International Journal of Psycho-Analysis*, she carried on for half an hour about what a shoddy piece of research it was, but then turned around immediately and took the time to show me how the paper could be improved. And of course she was right – the revised version of the paper was accepted immediately by the Journal.

I cannot finish this brief interview without also saying something about Hanna Segal's sense of humour. In such an arduous field, it is important to laugh – and there have been many instances in which Hanna Segal has made me laugh very much, sometimes to the point of tears. I remember her once telling me that she personally had to make up for my having lacked a rather strict English governess in my upbringing! Although I can be affable, she got onto my thick-headedness with patients rather quickly – and penetrated it many times with her sense of humour. It got to the point where my own wife was thrilled that I was working with Hanna Segal – not because she was such an illustrious psychoanalyst, but because my wife finally had someone who could commiserate with what she herself had long complained about!

(Interview, October 2006)

Joseph Aguayo, who trained initially as a historian, is a psychoanalyst in private practice in Los Angeles; he is a member of the Psychoanalytic Center of California (PCC).

Chapter 10

NUCLEAR TERROR, PSYCHOTIC ANXIETIES AND GROUP PHENOMENA

CAMPAIGNING FOR THE PREVENTION OF NUCLEAR WAR

Attentive to the growing risk that the nuclear arms race represents for the entire planet, Segal has, from the 1980s on, campaigned actively in the anti-nuclear movement which, in Britain as well as in other countries, aims to shake out of their apathy not only the general public but also those in government circles. In that sense, she went back to the political and social vocation that she had given up when, as a young student, she chose to take up medicine then psychoanalysis.

According to Segal, psychoanalysts have a specific contribution to make to the psychological understanding of the causes and dangers of the nuclear arms race. For example, because of the risk of total annihilation they imply, the existence of nuclear weapons triggers anxieties and defence mechanisms that are much more primitive than those evoked by ordinary warfare. These primitive fears are reinforced by psychopathological phenomena involving groups under the influence of their leaders. In 1983, Hanna Segal and Moses Laufer founded an association called Psychoanalysts for the Prevention of Nuclear War (PPNW) in order to heighten the awareness of their colleagues and open up a public debate to fight against the pervasive denial in the face of the sheer madness threatening the whole planet. Her fame as a psychoanalyst greatly increased as a result of her work on this issue. "*From then on, I began to be really well known by the public at large*", said Segal in an interview with the present author in March 2004.

Segal has written several versions of her articles and lectures on this theme. I shall present her main papers in chronological order; in order to avoid too much repetition I have highlighted the elements that correspond to each of the four relevant historical periods.

First period (1945–1990)

From the A-bomb to the fragile equilibrium of the Cold War

"Silence is the real crime"

Segal H. (1987) "Silence is the real crime", *International Review of Psycho-Analysis* 14, 3–12. With Postscript (2002), in C. Covington, P. Williams, J. Arundale and J. Knox (eds.) *Terrorism and War: Unconscious Dynamics of Political Violence*, London: Karnac; also in J. Steiner (ed.) *Psychoanalysis, Literature and War: Papers 1972–1995*, London and New York: Routledge, 1997.

Towards a conceptual model of understanding

Hanna Segal: I wrote "Silence is the real crime" during the time when there were two opposing blocs, but things have changed very much since then. It was a stable paranoid-schizoid organization. "They" were the Devil, and "we" were the Angels. Both were equally omnipotent, hence the absolutely terrible and despicable danger the world found itself in. These two blocs functioned in a completely mirror-image manner. My inclination was, of course, to think of Freud and the "*battle between Eros and Thanatos*", but Klein was necessary too.

At the time of the First World War, psychoanalysts had no conceptual apparatus for formulating any ideas about wars like that. There were texts – I can think of Reich and others – but there were no concepts for really looking at it. To have some sort of basis, I needed, as it were, two legs. One was the conceptualization of the death instinct, and the second was Klein's theory of the paranoid-schizoid position and the transition towards the depressive position – including the whole area of splitting and projective identification, identification with an ideal object, fighting the bad object and projecting all the badness outside. Thanks to those two conceptual tools from Freud and Klein, by the end of the Second World War we did have a conceptual apparatus that helped us to define what was happening between the two blocs in what we then called the Cold War.

(Tape 7, side A, 13 March 2004)

The ever-increasing threat of complete destruction

After the Second World War, the nuclear arms race between the Soviet Union and the United States produced enough bombs to blow up the planet many times over. And all that under the pretext of greater security. Exploding only part of that arsenal would bring about a nuclear winter with, in all probability, no survivors. What are we doing to counter that danger?

Many seem happy with the idea that mutual deterrence will be enough to prevent such a catastrophe. Deterrence, however, implies a constant search for a new equilibrium, so that the nuclear arms race turns into a vicious circle. Therefore, far from being reassuring, the theory of mutual deterrence could actually lead to our own destruction.

Psychoanalysis can shed light on such issues, because it can help us understand why the theory of deterrence could well lead to annihilation. The idea of deterrence implies a wish to be stronger so as to frighten the enemy and block any attempt at aggression. But what would be the reaction of a frightened enemy? That is impossible to predict. In other words, it is because it is based on fear that the nuclear arms race actually increases the risk of instability. "*Preparing for war on both sides promotes the likelihood of a pre-emptive strike out of fear and the equilibrium of a system of mutual deterrence is inherently unstable*" (Segal 1987: 4).

The vicious circle of hatred and fear

Psychoanalysis is very familiar with the vicious circle of hatred and fear: hatred leads to fear and fear to hatred. That said, our clinical experience teaches us also that destructive and self-destructive drives can be modified when individuals can get some insight into their motives and visualize the consequences of their actions on others and on themselves. However, as regards nuclear warfare, powerful defences are raised against any awareness of danger. Denial is the dominant mechanism – denial of the danger and of our own fear. To this is added a particular form of denial and splitting, described by Freud, thanks to which we retain intellectual knowledge of reality but divest it of emotional meaning. That attitude explains why people in their vast majority know of the threat posed by nuclear weapons but do not take any active steps to change the situation. In addition, the fact that manufacturing nuclear weapons is usually kept secret – governments are apprehensive of public opinion – contributes to reinforcing denial of the danger.

Demonizing and despising the enemy

We all tend naturally to disguise our own aggressiveness. We hide it "for security reasons" by having recourse to projective mechanisms that lead to an increase in persecutory feelings: "It's not our fault, it's theirs!" The enemy is presented as the devil. Margaret Thatcher spoke of the Soviet Union as "our hereditary enemy", and Ronald Reagan called it "the evil empire". Similarly, for the Communist world, capitalism was the worst of all evils.

In genocide, another element is added – contempt for the victims, who are presented as subhuman or not even human at all. The corollary of that attitude is that contempt for other people makes us ourselves inhuman.

From a psychoanalytic point of view, this kind of functioning corresponds, in individuals, to the regression from a more developed stage to one which is more primitive. The more developed stage here is what we call the "depressive position" and regression leads back to the "paranoid-schizoid position". The depressive position is characterized by the capacity to recognize one's own aggressive drives, to experience guilt and mourning and to function in reality with the wish to make reparation. Regression to the paranoid-schizoid position is characterized by such mechanisms as denial, splitting and projection.

From individual regression to that of the group

What psychoanalysts have observed in clinical situations with individual patients can also be applied to groups. According to Bion, groups can function in various different ways. The "work-group" has a constructive function because it is reality-oriented and can contain the psychotic phenomena that occur within it. However, in situations of excessive anxiety, a group may behave in a destructive and self-destructive manner which, in an individual, would be called mad. Since this kind of group functions on the basis of a guiding principle shared by all of its members, Bion calls this a "basic assumption" group. Segal gives as a particularly worrying example of this kind of group the born-again Christians, a movement which flourished in the United States during the 1980s. This group actually recommended a pre-emptive nuclear attack on the Soviet Union. Thanks to this Armageddon – God's war – the born-again Christians would cleanse the earth of all evil and pave the way for peace and happiness. It is astonishing that some governments shared these mad ideas, denying the disastrous outcome of nuclear war.

In every group situation, leaders play an important part because they contribute to an overall feeling of safety within the group. In addition, when a group functions in a psychotic way, it tends to throw up leaders who represent that shared psychotic element, as history has so often shown.

The group: for better or for worse

Hanna Segal: The group both generates psychosis and helps to deal with psychosis, because group formation is also based on love, on giving up one's own selfishness and developing concern for the group. We start life as a group, in the initial stages as a baby at the breast. The baby overcomes its ruthlessness with the breast, then the whole family comes into the picture, and the baby's concerns widen. So there is something very positive in group organization which protects us from the combination of fear and hatred. It also sort of socializes us, or socializes our psychosis, which is the dangerous part of ourselves, the part Bion wrote about. In certain situations, it can be a matter of the tail wagging the dog.

For example, so long as a country lies in disputed territory, it's a good thing to have an army because you have to be safe. I have had many discussions with Air Commodore Mackie about how important the feeling of security is socially. It's OK so long as the army serves the whole social organism. Of course, people who join the army must in essence be paranoid and combative – it's one way of keeping them in place, and of organizing the security of the whole group. But it can very easily get out of hand, because the group actually increases psychosis, it doesn't just control it. We know what happens when the army or church take over government. People who know more about this topic are those who actually work with groups.

(Jacqueline Rose interview, 1990)

The threat of total annihilation

One of the consequences of the nuclear arms race is the production of great anxiety and the setting up of massive defences to counteract this. For the first time in history, humanity has the power of total self-annihilation. Beliefs such as Armageddon reveal almost nakedly the death drive. Universal death is seen as universal salvation – the "Nirvana" aspect of the death drive, as described by Freud: *"requiescat in pace"* would be another way of putting it. It follows that the existence of atomic weapons can only awaken a schizophrenic view of the world, one of the characteristics of which is the blurring of the frontier between reality and phantasy. *"Omnipotence has become real, but only omnipotent destruction"* (Segal 1987: 7). We can henceforth, at the press of a button, annihilate the world.

One of the worst consequences of the nuclear danger is that the idea of annihilation of humanity destroys the possibility of what Segal calls symbolic survival. In natural death or even in conventional warfare, men die with the conviction that they will survive symbolically through their children, through their grandchildren, through their work or through the civilization itself of which they are part. That attitude is a sign of maturity, writes Elliot Jaques: *"Coming to terms with the prospect of one's own personal death is a necessary step in maturation and in giving full meaning to life"* (Jaques 1965, quoted in Segal 1987: 7). The prospect of nuclear war makes difficult a growing acceptance of death and symbolic survival, because it produces terror of a different kind. Confronted with the fear of annihilation, our schizoid defences increase and we regress to primitive kinds of relationships that exclude empathy, compassion and concern both for other people and for ourselves.

The loss of "symbolic survival"

JMQ: You have said that one of the things that has changed as regards the nature of terror since the advent of nuclear weapons is the fact that we have lost the possibility of symbolic survival. That's a pretty original idea.

Hanna Segal: Yes, it is, but I'm not the only one to have said that. An American called Robert J. Lifton worked a lot on the idea. The main point is that acceptance of death is needed for life to be meaningful, otherwise we live in cloud cuckoo land. If we can't accept our death, we can't really face any other reality. In a way – strangely enough – the death instinct is full of destruction yet death is not viewed as the normal end of life; it is seen as an effect of the death instinct. And then either we go to Heaven – if we're on the right side – [. . .] or, if you're on the wrong side, well, you're destined for Hell. So that there is really a continuation – there is no true acceptance of the finality of things, i.e. that there is neither Hell nor Heaven – it all just comes to an end!

JMQ: Would you agree that Western civilization is more than ever under the impact of the conflict between life and death?

The death instinct is present everywhere. It invades everything now. You know what Euripides said: "Whom the Gods would destroy, they first make mad." Nowadays, we have an anti-mind civilization. It goes also with sexual perversions. Normal sex is perverted – it's no more part of the life instinct of forming a couple, creating a family – all sorts of distortions are now possible. All of this is an attack on the mind and on human relationships.

(Tape 7, side A, 13 March 2004)

"Nukespeak" – when language itself becomes meaningless

In all wars, there is a distortion of language, the aim of which is to cover up the absurdity of the destructiveness of what is being carried out. The idea is to remove any aggressiveness from warlike impulses so as to make them more acceptable. For example, if we take the term "nuclear deterrence", we can see how, over the years, it has completely changed its meaning. Initially, possessing an atom bomb was meant to discourage any attack from another country which did not have the atom bomb. But once the potential enemy also had the atom bomb, there was a kind of equilibrium, so that each would deter the other. What if more and more countries began stockpiling nuclear weapons? More recently, the idea of deterrence has changed again, when some people began to speak of a "rational nuclear war" and of "flexible response" – another attractive phrase invented to cover the change from a defensive posture to the aggressive use of strategic nuclear weapons.

The same is true of the expression "Star Wars", which conjures up the picture of a war in space that would not affect our planet in any way.

The fragmenting of responsibility

Given that there are no clearly defined areas of accountability as regards nuclear weapons, responsibilities are fragmented – a mental phenomenon typical of schizophrenia. For example, it is impossible to hold any one government accountable for the proliferation of nuclear weapons, given that developing programmes of this nature extends over several decades, during which governments come and go – no one government, therefore, can be held responsible. In addition, the military–industrial complex increasingly acquires its own dynamic, beyond the control of governments, whether in a capitalist or in a totalitarian system. All these factors contribute to the fragmentation of responsibilities not only as regards the development of this kind of weapon but also with respect to the increasing number of command centres – the number of army commanders authorized to press the nuclear button is increasing, and they are deployed in many different locations. The danger of nuclear warfare has increased in recent years because of the risk of proliferation: an ever greater number of countries or groups may well come into possession of such weapons.

Mechanization and dehumanization

The growth of technology gradually leads to depersonalization and dehumanization. Pressing a button is enough to annihilate parts of the world that we have never seen. From a psychoanalytic perspective, this too has to do with mechanisms such as denial and splitting. Further, counter-attack response is being delegated more and more to highly sensitive machines – for example, the nuclear early-warning system – so that the danger of an unstoppable nuclear exchange can only increase. Having recourse to machines with no human control generates in each of us feelings of increasing terror and helplessness. We protect ourselves against such anxiety by denial and projection: we say that there is nothing we can do about it – denial – and that the real responsibility lies with the government or with the military – projection.

Is the situation hopeless?

According to Segal, we should nevertheless remain hopeful. In individual analyses, we learn that when drives and defences are taken over by the death instinct, hopeless situations are the result. But we learn also that destructive and self-destructive tendencies can be reversed, so that more constructive tendencies can come to the fore. In normal development, the life drive (Eros) can integrate the death drive and turn it into useful life-promoting aggressiveness. It is in situations of acute anxiety that the vicious circle between the death drive and the defences against it precludes any such movement towards integration.

In 1930, Freud was already envisaging the possibility that different groups might exterminate one another until there was no-one left. He argued that the fateful question was whether and to what extent the development of civilization would allow the human species to master the conflicts linked to the need for living together. These conflicts, he wrote, are closely bound up with the aggressive and self-destructive drives that are part of every human being (Freud 1930a [1929]).

What role can psychoanalysts play?

Firstly, we must look into ourselves without turning a blind eye: even though we are psycho-analysts, we are in this respect like other human beings; we have the same destructive and self-destructive drives, we use the same defences and we have the same desires. We have to keep ourselves informed of the facts not only of external reality, but also of internal psychic reality: "*We must face our fears and mobilize our forces against destruction*" (Segal 1987: 10–11).

Secondly, we have a specific contribution to make. Thanks to our clinical work, we are familiar with mechanisms such as denial, splitting and magic omnipotent thinking. We should therefore be able to contribute something to the overcoming of apathy and self-deception in ourselves and in others. "*We who believe in the power of words and in the therapeutic effect of verbalizing truth must not be silent*" (1985: 11).

Second period (1990–1991)
From the collapse of the Soviet Union to the Gulf War
The search for a new enemy

Segal, H. (1997c) "From Hiroshima to the Gulf war and after: socio-political expressions of ambivalence", in J. Steiner (ed.) *Psychoanalysis, Literature and War. Papers 1972–1995*, London and New York: Routledge (pp. 157–168). This chapter contains material from two articles: Segal, H. (1992) "The achievement of ambivalence", *Common Knowledge*, 1: 92–104 and Segal, H. (1995) "Hiroshima, the Gulf War and after", in A. Elliott and S. Frosch (eds.) *Psychoanalysis in Contexts: Paths between Theories and Modern Cultures*, London: Routledge.

Segal, H. (2002b) "Not learning from experience: Hiroshima, the Gulf War and 11 September", *International Psychoanalysis*, 11(1): 33–35.

Missed opportunities

Hanna Segal: Then came *perestroïka* and we wrote a lot about it – about the missed opportunity, because *perestroïka* was the time when we realized that this fantasy world, the Cold War, had really fallen apart – there was no enemy any more. That could have been used in very perceptive ways. Instead of which, we took it as a triumph of our superior power – I saw it as a kind of violent negative therapeutic reaction. There was a bit of getting together on mutual projects, and I – no, I'll say "we", because we discussed it a lot even though I did most of the conceptualization – we put forward several ideas. If we did stop this split then we would have to face up to our own unemployment, our own guilt about unjust wars, for instance Vietnam, our own guilt about colonization, and our own internal problems. That's what happened in the other war – Galtieri and Thatcher (the Falklands War): they both felt completely threatened as regards their power. Thatcher had the lowest ever rating of an incumbent Prime Minister, yet the moment the war started she won the election. We went into all that in our discussions, and of course we predicted the Gulf War. One judges the validity of any scientific theory very much on its power of prediction. We said: "Look, if we don't change our attitude to *perestroïka*, on either side we are bound to have another war." We needed another enemy – which then became the Asians. Of course economic factors came into it too, unfortunately for the oil-rich countries. Iraq's disaster is that it has so much oil.

Then came the second phase. We wrote papers. Again, I say "we" because there are many unpublished papers – Geoffrey Baruch wrote a lot about the manic defences in this situation: we employ powerful manic defences against the depressive position. That was when we predicted the Gulf War – except we never thought it would be Saddam Hussein because he was the darling of both sides in his opposition to Iran. He was a friend until he massively gassed the Kurds – and we were the ones who supplied him with the wherewithal to do so. In my view, we lost the Gulf War, but that was completely denied.

Now the situation really has changed – there are no longer two blocs. It's the bloc of the American/British and even European imperialism – *we've* got the power, now, *and* we have GOD on our side! All of them are religious fanatics. God is on the side of the big battalions. But there is a tremendous rebellion against that; I really don't think the Islamic world was anywhere near united enough, rich enough, to represent a threat. The threat was to global capitalism.

You see, what are the real rogue countries? Not those that have a horrible record like Saddam Hussein, because we still have among our allies some equally awful people. I think that the worst rogue states with weapons of mass destruction are America and its little vassal, Great Britain. These are the rogue states. If you define a rogue state as one which threatens world peace with bloodthirsty dictatorship, one where nothing is banned, one where they give themselves the right to use, pre-emptively, nuclear weapons – what state could be more of a rogue than those two?

JMQ: Was the group Psychoanalysts for the Prevention of Nuclear War active at that time?

Well, it was like this. The group was extremely active until *perestroïka*, and then people said, "That's it! Now we've got peace, so forget about it." As a result, the membership has dwindled completely.

(Tape 7, side A, 13 March 2004)

Saddam Hussein: the new enemy who fitted the bill

Sensing that in the immediate aftermath of the disappearance of the Soviet threat a new danger was looming for the Western world, the different groups that were campaigning against the danger of nuclear weapons published repeated warnings in the media: if we do not have a change of mentality and refuse to take the new political and military situation into account, we will soon start looking for a new enemy.

Unfortunately, these warnings went unheeded. *Perestroïka* did not last very long and the Western powers could not agree on nuclear disarmament. Quite the contrary, in fact, they embarked on a search for a new enemy in order to justify their arsenal and its constant modernization. Saddam Hussein fitted the bill admirably, because the Iran–Iraq war had just ended and Saddam himself was looking for a new enemy.

Segal quotes Einstein who said that with the advent of atomic power, everything had changed except our way of thinking. In a way, she says, he was of course right – our way of thinking has certainly not changed for the better.

Psychoanalysis and conflicts within wider society

There is quite a widespread opinion according to which psychoanalysts are authoritative only when they talk about their clinical work and individual psychology. That is not Segal's opinion; she believes that psychoanalysis has to do with the human mind in all its dimensions – hence, she argues, it is quite legitimate to explore the political and social aspects of the mind. In particular, psychoanalysis has a significant contribution to make to the study of conflicts between constructive and destructive impulses in individuals; her experience in this domain enables her to shed light on the part played by the destructive forces that are prevalent in social and political life.

The nature of ambivalence

In her 1997 paper, Segal emphasizes above all the conflict involving ambivalence between love and hate, which is one manifestation of the conflict between the life and death drives. She goes back to what she had written in 1987 about the transition that takes place not only within individuals but also in group behaviour. That explains why a group can function in a highly developed way – the "work-group" – or in a primitive and psychotic manner, as in basic assumption groups. Here, however, Segal goes even further in her study of group functioning. She explores in detail the role of love and hate in the transition from the paranoid-schizoid to the depressive position, and discusses ambivalence and its vicissitudes.

Segal observes that, for Melanie Klein, the conflict between love impulses and their destructive counterparts is experienced from the very beginning of life in relation to objects, and more particularly to the mother's breast. There is an immediate splitting between negative experiences, which are attributed to the hated object, and positive experiences, which are attributed to the good object. This early phase is closely bound up with ambivalence between feelings of love and hate, hence its designation "paranoid-schizoid position" because of the split that separates idealized experiences from persecutory ones.

When projection decreases and a more realistic image of self and object is built up, the infant becomes aware of his or her ambivalence; mother is perceived as a whole object, in other words as a person who both satisfies and frustrates, one who is both loved and hated. This phase is called the depressive position, because awareness of ambivalence brings with it the threat of losing the object and the depressive feelings associated with that. This is a fundamental turning point in emotional life: "*Guilt replaces persecution, and this is of great importance because persecution has no resolution: hatred brings persecution and persecution brings hatred*" (Segal 1997c: 159). However, when ambivalence is consciously acknowledged, aggressiveness is felt to be damaging the object that is also needed and desired. This new situation brings in its wake not more hatred but a mobilization of love as well as the wish to repair and restore the object. At this level, aggressiveness is not absent but it becomes proportional to what causes it, as do the guilt feelings that are attached to it. This process constitutes the foundation for constructive sublimation. It must be said, however, that awareness of ambivalence, guilt feelings and the fear of losing the object are experienced as extremely distressful.

In other words, the depressive position leads to a truly fundamental re-orientation towards reality, internal as well as external. We begin to take responsibility for our own impulses, and this is a crucial stage in development. On the other hand, any flight from ambivalence brings about a regression to primitive mechanisms typical of the paranoid-schizoid position – denial, splitting, projection, fragmentation. Again, observations from our clinical work with individual patients can be applied also to the manner in which groups function.

Group behaviour

Whether we like it or not, we belong to a great variety of groups. We choose some of them, while our very birth ties us to others such as social class, country of origin and religion.

What has psychoanalysis done to develop our knowledge of the way in which groups function? In *Group Psychology and the Analysis of the Ego*, Freud (1921c) says that group functioning is governed by the libido and that its aim is to reach sufficient harmony so that it can accomplish its task. This constructive process, however, may be distorted by destructive impulses arising from the death drive. Although Freud was concerned about the danger that the world was facing given the rise of Nazism, as he showed particularly in his correspondence with Einstein, Segal says that she is surprised by the fact that in the 1930s so few psychoanalysts publicly expressed concern over the increasing risk of war and destruction. After the Second World War, however, things changed, and several psychoanalytic papers about the war and the rise of the Nazis have been published.

From the 1940s on, psychoanalysts began working directly with groups, and this furthered our understanding of the phenomena which occur in such a context. Generally speaking, we tend to project into the group parts of ourselves that we find difficult to cope with individually; since these are usually the most disturbed – i.e. psychotic – parts, we tend to project them first into the group. In normal circumstances, when the overall atmosphere is constructive, realistic functioning within the group has the upper hand, so that these psychotic aspects are kept firmly under control. Groups, however, do tend to behave in a way that would be considered mad if any normal individual did the same thing. For example, most groups have a grandiose and paranoid self-image, and they are capable of giving themselves over to outbursts of destructive aggressiveness that no single individual would ever contemplate.

Bion (1961) gave a new fillip to the psychoanalytic understanding of how groups function. He argued that our psychotic aspects merge with the group identity, to such an extent that we do not feel ourselves to be mad because our opinions are acceptable to the group as a whole.

A large group – a state or a nation, for example – may function overall in that manner, or it may delegate such functions to subgroups such as the Army or the Church. When a group becomes too powerful – as with fascist, communist or nationalist groups – basic assumption group mentality becomes more and more widespread, so that it begins to function in a destructive manner.

Political groups are even more dangerous

The prevalence of psychotic processes over constructive work makes political groups particularly dangerous, whether they are based on nationalism or on some specific ideology. The reason is that the aim of their work as a group is less well-defined. When a group which has a specific and well-defined aim – like a research group in a scientific laboratory, for example – allows itself to be drawn towards psychotic assumptions, it quickly becomes obvious that it cannot carry out its work properly. This is not the case with political groups, which are easily dominated by feelings of superiority and guided by the firm belief that they have a messianic mission to accomplish. To these various factors one must add the pursuit of power, a tendency that is particularly active in political groups; this tendency is based on primitive drive-related aims.

In fact, politics is always involved in every sizeable grouping. "*It is an unrealistic ideal to think that one can have an organization or a society without politics*" (Segal 1997c: 163). In political groups, there are more tensions that are likely to lead to destruction as a result of rivalry and the pursuit of power. When the group functions properly, these tensions are resolved and its members work towards the common goal, as in a properly functioning family in which love and kindness can contain and transform violence and hate. The following maxim does not apply to political groups: "*Too much politicking will not be tolerated because it will disrupt the work*" (1997c: 163). After all, the only task a political group has is to be in politics. In addition, such a group tends to choose as its leader someone who conforms to its general orientation – in other words, to the same pathological megalomania that permeates the group. That is why "*there is a dangerous interaction between a disturbed group and a disturbed leader, increasing each other's pathology*" (1997c: 163).

The role of guilt feelings in the origins of war

Psychoanalysis shows us also the role of guilt feelings not only in the mental life of individuals but also in the behaviour of groups and nations. In addition to the feelings of guilt linked to a nuclear-oriented mentality, it is the case that wars are often started as a defence against feelings of guilt arising from previous wars, as the psychoanalyst Franco Fornari has shown (1966). For example, in the United States, feelings of guilt linked to the Vietnam war went unacknowledged for a long period of time, both as regards the damage done to the enemy and with respect to the humiliation and setback which that war meant for the United States itself. These unacknowledged feelings of guilt were no doubt one of the factors that made the Gulf War inevitable, in order to dispel the depression that followed on from the war in Vietnam.

When she wrote her paper in 1997, Segal noted that the Gulf War had already been forgotten, as though it were ancient history.

> *There is a universal denial of what we have done and what the consequences are. The countless victims, the devastation of the whole area and the continuing human and ecological disaster is ignored. The guilt remains unacknowledged and the dangers of such a stance remain with us. Those who do not remember their history are bound to repeat it, but facing the reality of history exposes us to what is most unbearable. This is particularly difficult in groups where the task is one of admitting that we made a mistake of vast proportions and have to take responsibility for the consequences. But unless we do that, our manic and schizoid defences will make us blind to these realities and lead us to further disasters.* (1997c: 166–167)

Third period (1991–2001)
From the Gulf War to 11 September 2001
"Those who don't remember their history are condemned to repeat it"

Segal, H. (2002b), "Not learning from experience: Hiroshima, the Gulf War and 11 September", *International Psychoanalysis*, **11**(1): 33–35.

An extraordinary impact

Why did the terrorist attacks of 11 September 2001 have such a major impact? Segal asks herself the question, thinking of other crimes against humanity that have caused innumerable victims – in Rwanda, for example, and the former Yugoslavia. According to Segal, the trauma of a terrorist attack has an additional factor: "*the crushing realization that there is somebody out there who actually hates you to the point of annihilation and the bewilderment that that causes*" (2002b: 33). We may recall that one of President Bush's first reactions was similar to that of anyone caught up in the shock of a trauma: "Why us? We are good people." Segal argues that the attacks on the Twin Towers and on the Pentagon had a specific symbolic impact because it awakened the most primitive fears – the suicide bombers had challenged the military, financial and technological omnipotence of the United States. "*I, with my little knife, can puncture your high-flying balloons and annihilate you*" (ibid.).

Segal warns us: "*Those who don't remember their history are condemned to repeat it*" (ibid.).[1] The September 11th attacks reminded her of the Gulf War, which took place some ten years before. "*When I listen to Bin Laden and Bush exchanging boasts and threats, I am reminded of similar exchanges between Bush Senior and Saddam Hussein*" (ibid.). The United States seem to have forgotten that the Arab fundamentalists they had used to carry out their own dirty work – they called them "*our* sons of bitches" – were the same people who turned against them. How can we even *imagine* that the massive bombing of Afghanistan in retaliation for September 11th is the best way to a new world of freedom, peace and democracy?

Understanding history in the light of psychoanalysis

It is not just a matter of remembering history but of understanding it. To grasp the chaos and horror of the period after 11 September 2001, we have to understand something of its roots. According to Segal, the advent of nuclear weapons brought about a change in our mentality, as she showed in one of her earlier articles: "*The threat of nuclear annihilation profoundly changed the nature of our collective anxieties, turning the normal fear of death and understandable aggression into the terror of actual total annihilation*" (2002b: 33). Going back to her earlier ideas, Segal shows that psychoanalysis helps us to have a better understanding not only of psychosis but also of group phenomena. She had already argued that the Cold War, for example, with its confrontation between the Soviet bloc and the West, was based on typical schizoid mechanisms such as denial, splitting and projection. That attitude soon led to dehumanization, fragmentation and the distortion of language and communication. In other words, faced with the threat of nuclear annihilation, a deep-rooted psychotic process took over and determined both group thinking and our own reactions.

The fragile equilibrium of the Cold War

During the Cold War, the "basic assumption" of the group was that war had become impossible because the two opposing blocks were too afraid of mutual annihilation. Not only was the nuclear threat always present, but also the arms race increased fear and hatred – the very psychological factors that can lead to war. To that effect was added that of war by proxy. The two great powers could avoid a direct confrontation by attacking each other indirectly through their support of factions engaged in regional conflicts and acts of terrorism. That, says Segal, led to even more fragmentation and to the very anxiety that provided a cradle for terrorism.

Looking for a new enemy

With *perestroïka*, the equilibrium that had existed during the Cold War between the Soviet bloc and the US-led West collapsed. "*We could now recognize, if only briefly, that our belief in an evil powerful enemy was in fact delusional*" (2002b: 34). It was an all-too-short time of hope, a possibility of changing attitudes – but it did not last. NATO went in search of a new enemy to justify its continued military power. So it transpired that, despite the disappearance of the supposed Soviet threat, Western countries could not even conceive of nuclear disarmament. Quite the contrary, indeed – nuclear weapons continued to be fine-tuned, just as though nothing had happened.

Manic defences and triumphalism

In the 1990s, we in the West witnessed a reaction typical of the one we see in clinical practice with some patients – when they start to get better, they feel depressed because they are faced with the reality and the confusion that are brought about by their illness. "*We are familiar with those moments of hope, clinically, when a paranoid patient begins to give up his delusions, or when an addict begins to give up the drug and get better*" (2002b: 34). Instead of continuing to improve, such patients relapse into illness. This is what, in psychoanalysis, we call a negative therapeutic reaction. Formidable manic defences can be mobilized against this depressive pain, with a revival of megalomania and in its wake a return of paranoia. According to Segal, the same kind of phenomenon occurred when the Soviet empire collapsed: when we stopped believing in the "evil empire" we had to turn to our internal problems – unemployment, economic decline and industrial disputes. The West then turned to triumphalism, so as to forget the problems that we had to face: *perestroïka* was felt to be the triumph of our superiority. Our nuclear mentality had not changed – we had to find a new enemy – this time, one that we could really crush.

The Gulf War: a pyrrhic victory

During *perestroïka*, Segal and her colleagues had publicly issued warnings about the danger of finding a new enemy if there was no change in our nuclear mentality. Events were soon to prove them right: the Gulf War began. "*Apparently we won, but that pyrrhic victory was soon forgotten and a formidable denial set in. [. . .] The power of such monumental denial is not only destructive but self-destructive, it destroys our memory, our capacity for realistic perception and all that part of us capable of insight, love, compassion and reparation. And we do not learn from experience*" (2002b: 34).

Delusions of omnipotence

After the Gulf War, some of Segal's colleagues who were opposed to nuclear weapons wrote papers on the increasing danger of another war and were alarmed at a change of attitude: triumphalism turned into a more *explicit* megalomania. That change was perfectly summarized in a statement by General Powell: in his opinion, technology had become so sophisticated that the United States could crush any enemy, no matter where, simply by dropping bombs from on high, without the lives of any American soldiers being put at risk. According to Segal, that myth of invincibility was shattered on 11 September 2001.

From that point of view, the terrorist attacks of September 11th were highly symbolic. Segal says that we have been precipitated into a world of confusion and psychotic terror – we no longer know who are our friends and who are our enemies. Old enemies like Soviet Russia are now our friends, and old friends have become enemies – Chechnya, for example. The same confusion and fragmentation can be seen in the Arab world. "*This is the most primitive terror in our personal development – not ordinary death, but some vision of personal disintegration imbued with hostility. And the situation is made much worse when God comes into the equation*" (2002b: 35).

What next?

Segal's article was published in 2002, a few months before the invasion of Iraq. In her view, the war in Afghanistan and the invasion of Iraq must henceforth be added to the list of pyrrhic victories, thus confirming the hollowness of the "crusade against terrorism". Segal says that we are at a crossroads; the choice lies between remembering the lessons of the Gulf War and blindly repeating our disastrous mistakes. The belief that we can obtain freedom and democracy by using force and destructiveness is just as illusory as other fundamentalist beliefs. "*The real battle is between insanity based on mutual projections and sanity based on truth*" (2002b: 35).

Fourth period (2001 and after)

The consequences of the September 11th attacks

Pessimism and/ or optimism?

Segal, H. (2003b) "From Hiroshima to 11th September and after", *Psychodynamic Practice*, **9**: 257–265.

A demotivating effect on militants

JMQ: And after 11 September 2001?

Hanna Segal: Well, after 11 September 2001, Bin Laden achieved his aim – because his aim was disorganization and polarization. And of course he did achieve that. For Bush it was a present from heaven because for two years he was planning a war against Iraq and Iran and other places – the "rogue states", as he and Blair called them – and that gave him the most marvellous opportunity of all.

He grasped it immediately. One of the things that always accompanies this kind of thing is telling lies – it's part of the schizoid mechanism. You tell lies, you tell stories, you invent things. It's quite clear that Saddam Hussein had no weapons of mass destruction and that he had no link with Bin Laden at all. He had nothing to do with the fanatic Islamist thing and was never into terrorism of that kind. His terrorism was genocide and things like that. Even if he had wanted to invade the world, he had a ruined country with no weapons left. So there was all this mythology playing on fear, creating a monster. Obviously Bush and Blair were aware of it – the security services told them that any attack on Iraq would increase the threat of terrorism. But they didn't care about that, they had their excuse for invading another country, for colonizing it and grabbing its oil resources. Bin Laden was delighted that they invaded Iraq. Terror only produces more terror.

I think that psychoanalysts, as always, are there to expose lies and the underlying motives. Here we, the scientists, the economists and Marxists can go together. "That Iraq was a threat to world peace is a lie – that Saddam was the source of terrorism is a lie. The true motivation was this and that – and would you go along with that?" That's the kind of thing we can say; people know we tell the truth. People may be ambivalent, but they're not basically bad, as it were. When they're confronted with a question such as: "Are you in favour of destroying millions of people in order to get cheap oil?", they'd say no; but it's all too easy to arouse fear because it touches on the unconscious, on identification, on the wish for revenge . . . So, you see, all these group processes are so important, because groups are so much more savage than individuals are.

JMQ: A psychotic functioning?

. . . A psychotic functioning with the sanction of the group, or of God in religious groups.

To return to what you were asking about the PPNW [Psychoanalysts for the Prevention of Nuclear War]: it was very sad in a way, because when *perestroïka* came along our organization just disappeared. "Things are OK now" – a complete denial.

JMQ: Is PPNW still ongoing?

Not quite to the same degree. I think now it's more dispersed. There's nothing we can do in the present situation. Well, no, that's not quite true, even in America. Recently, I was reading Chomsky's essays – he is usually so sharp, and pretty pessimistic as a rule. Well, he has just said that he's not pessimistic, because now Americans are so much more aware that there is another world, and there are more protests now than there ever were during the war in Vietnam. It's the same here. I mean, when the war started we thought that the protest movement would be very small, you know, simply because the war had started – but almost two million people took to the streets. However, as I said, the PPNW has never been revived.

(Tape 8, side A, 13 March 2004)

The authoritative opinion of one of the forefathers of the atom bomb

In this paper, Segal adds some new elements to what we knew of her ideas. She quotes the opinions of famous scientists and politicians who have reached conclusions similar to those of Segal herself:

the threat that the nuclear arms race poses to the whole world has not diminished – in fact, it is more important now than it ever has been.

Segal says she was pleased with the statement made by Professor Joseph Rotblat (2003), a nuclear physicist and sometime laureate of the Nobel Peace Prize. The opinion of a scientist working in the "core" sciences usually carries more weight with the general public than that of psychoanalysts. In a conference held in January 2003, Rotblat observed that the situation which followed the September 11th attacks did not appear out of the blue – the seeds were sown at the very beginning of the nuclear age.

Rotblat, as Segal points out, knows what he is talking about. He was one of the pioneers in the field of nuclear technology, one of the first to carry out research into the atom bomb with James Chadwick in Liverpool in November 1939, two months after the start of the Second World War. At that time, he agreed to collaborate on the project in the United Kingdom and later on the Manhattan Project in the United States, because he thought then that only by possessing the bomb could a Nazi victory be prevented. He soon realized that in fact it was not being developed in order to deter Hitler, but with the intention of dominating the world after the end of the war. In the years that followed, Rotblat realized the fallacy of the nuclear deterrent concept as it was drawn up during the Cold War. Rotblat draws the conclusion that, in his view, the threat posed by the arms race has never been greater than it is today. He is thus in agreement with Einstein, who stated that our way of looking at the world changed completely with the arrival of nuclear weapons. That view is shared by Hanna Segal.

Segal goes on to summarize what she had already stated in her earlier published work (see above). She quotes the opinions of politicians and diplomats who have come to realize the threat posed by the proliferation of nuclear weapons. She refers, for example, to statements made in 1982 by Robert McNamara, former US Secretary of Defence. When he took a second look at the nuclear policy adopted by the United States from the 1960s on, he acknowledged that the threat his country posed to the Soviet Union had quite clearly led the Soviet Union to go on fine-tuning their own arsenal of nuclear weapons. The US ambassador George Kennan was shocked to discover that, despite the disappearance of the supposed Soviet threat, Western countries did not at any time contemplate nuclear disarmament. Quite the contrary: ongoing fine-tuning of this kind of weapon has become an addiction, to use Kennan's own words, with the pretext – altogether fallacious – of having to modernize them.

Counting on the fraternity of human beings

Even though the threat posed by nuclear weapons is as great now as it was at the end of the Cold War, Segal observes that activists campaigning against nuclear weapons are becoming increasingly demotivated. Most organizations have seen a decrease in the number of activists and a gradual decline in attendance at their meetings. There was, of course, a great sigh of relief in the 1990s, with the wish to believe that everything would be much better from then on. At the same time, however, the denial of any potential nuclear threat simply increased.

In the face of this loss of interest, we have to unite our energies and intellectual capacities to take a stand against such a folly. Segal concludes her talk with a reference to the French Revolution and its ideals of liberty, equality and fraternity. At present, liberty and equality are locked in conflict. On the one hand, unrestrained liberty leads to chaos and to the exploitation and destruction of other people; on the other, unrestrained equality leads to the loss of individual liberty, to the dehumanization of the world and to dragging everyone down to the lowest common denominator. "*But the uniting factor is fraternity. Where love and mutual support and goodwill are the main factors then liberty and equality can enter a fruitful dialogue and be reconciled. [. . .] We have strength in fraternity*" (Segal 2003: 265).

Should psychoanalysts take a political stance?

Avoid imposing our own opinions on our patients

Jacqueline Rose: Analysts seem to be very cautious about participating in public debate – I presume for clinical reasons; but that may produce a sense that the analytic community is cut off from the outside world. Can you say something about what you see as the appropriate relationship, or limits to the relationship, between psychoanalysis and the public domain?

Hanna Segal: Psychoanalysis and politics is a very tricky issue. I understand the caution of my colleagues because the first duty of any psychoanalyst is, as far as possible, not to impose his or her own opinions, however strongly held they may be, on patients. One has to be aware of one's points of view. In some ways I find it is almost easier to analyse people from another culture because you don't unconsciously collude with cultural patterns which happen also to be your own. So I don't blame my colleagues for saying just don't get mixed up in any of this.

On the other hand, I think psychoanalysis can have an enormous influence in an indirect way – by throwing light on certain phenomena. That's why the work of those in the Tavistock Institute of Human Relations, or Bion's work on groups, which to me is fundamental, are all so important. Our influence has to be very indirect, but anything that draws people's attention to certain phenomena, or creates awareness and integrity, eventually percolates. For instance, in England after the war primary school education, both nursery and elementary, was probably the best in the world. Those were the days! I'm sure that a large part of that was due to the influence of Susan Isaacs at the Institutes of Education, as well as to the gradual percolating of her ideas.

Sometimes it is absolutely necessary to take a stand

There are certain situations in which an attitude of absolute non-engagement may lead to living in an ivory tower. In Argentina, the so-called more classical analysts, and that includes the Kleinians, were only concerned with what was going on in their consulting rooms – yet all the time, outside, people were disappearing and being destroyed. Psychoanalysis ought to have taken a stand. There are basic issues of human rights that go beyond politics where, in my view, psychoanalysis has to make its position clear. It has to do also with what you analyse – I just do not believe that you can analyse someone properly if thousands of people are disappearing and being tortured without any of this coming into the material, apparently. It would mean for me that there was something wrong with the analysis – the whole point surely is that, if you take up the patient's denial of internal and external realities, he or she can thereupon become more aware of what's going on in the outside world.

JR: In his book The Repression of Psychoanalysis: Otto Fenichel and the Political Freudians, *Russell Jacoby discusses the split between, on the one hand, the culturalists in America, with their stress on family and politics, who discarded the classical concepts of psychoanalysis, and, on the other, the classical Freudians, who held on to those insights but who tended not to engage with political or cultural issues. Is this a pattern?*

Reich was of course central to that. It is very difficult to integrate the two aspects without causing confusion – they are different tools. What Marie Langer, whom I knew very well, and Emilio Rodrigué, whom I supervised as a student, were doing was "psychoanalysis in the service of the revolution". I don't think psychoanalysis can be in the service of any ideology, whether it be a religion or a political movement, because psychoanalysis aims at the discovery of psychic truths. On the other hand, as I say, there are issues, such as Nazism, on which it is impossible not to take a stand. As individuals, many analysts – Muriel Gardiner, for example, who was an underground courier – did an enormous amount, but in those days analysts didn't really have the conceptual weapons to make an analytical statement about what was going on. Today, our knowledge of group mechanisms gives us a conceptual weapon for saying: "Look here, in this group phenomenon, such and such is happening, take a good look at it."

Analysing the patient's political opinions

On the question of the couch and outside the couch. At a psychoanalytic symposium I attended in Boston, the Americans were asking why it is that patients never bring up issues about nuclear warfare or weapons in their sessions. I suggested that it may be because of the way you analyse, because if you analyse just at the Oedipal level and don't go into the paranoias and terrors of death, then patients are much less likely to bring these political realities into their analysis. One analyst at the symposium, Dr Jacobs, added that, in the past, whenever a patient started talking about political issues, he (Dr Jacobs) would more or less say that that was not what the patient was on the couch for. Whereas today, if a patient says "I saw such and such a programme, but that's not what I'm here for", Dr Jacobs would say: "Why don't you want to talk about the political programme you saw?" So they're moving in that direction. For me, of course, the great decision was whether or not to go public – because it does exert an undue influence on patients when they hear me outside the consulting room expressing my views.

JR: You mean that if you go public on a political issue it affects your patients, because they might identify with you or react against you?

It's better if they react against you than identify with you.

JR: Better psychically but not politically in this case.

No, really, better even politically, because you can analyse the reaction and then you know that if they do come to the same point of view, then it is their own. The worst thing that can happen is that they become enthusiastic simply because you are. But I do want to say that Moses Laufer, who, by the way, is a classical Freudian, and myself, as the co-founders of Psycho-analysts for the Prevention of Nuclear War, thought that the issue was so important that the risk of taking a public stand had to be accepted.

There are limits to the analyst's counter-transference

JR: You say that the analyst must not impose her or his political convictions on the patient and that, in the analytical setting, the analyst must be politically neutral, so I am always very interested in those moments where that seems particularly difficult to sustain. In your inaugural lecture to the Freud Memorial Chair at University College, London, you described a patient who equated wealth with godliness and considered poverty to be a result of fecklessness; that patient gradually came to recognize the unconscious greed behind these attitudes and how crippling they were. It seemed that this was getting very close to saying that a certain form of Conservatism rests on unresolved greed and persecutory anxiety.

My husband was Chairman of the St John's Wood Labour Party, and he read them a paper on envy as a determinant of socialist convictions . . . Well, they didn't like that at all! You see, it cuts both ways. Whatever the political opinion of your patient, it has to be analysed. Mind you, I think I probably would not be able to analyse an out-and-out fascist, because I would feel unable to deal with my counter-transference. A very good friend of mine, the French analyst Jean Kestemberg, had an ex-SS guard in consultation who was troubled by the complications that his sadism was producing in his marriage, but who otherwise wasn't at all concerned about his past; Jean just didn't take that patient on. He told him quite simply: "Look, I don't think I am the right analyst for you." I don't know to whom Jean sent him, but he felt he just could not cope with that. But otherwise my sort of left-wing patients are as much under scrutiny as my right-wing people. My own left-wing tendency came under a lot of scrutiny in my own analysis.

(Jacqueline Rose interview, 1990)

A delicate relationship with the British Psychoanalytical Society

JMQ: Since 1985, you have been Secretary of Psychoanalysts for the Prevention of Nuclear War (PPNW), created in 1983 after the British Psychoanalytical Society (BPAS) decided not to affiliate en bloc to a "political" organization. What kind of relationship was there between the British Society and the group of its members who were campaigning against nuclear weapons?

Geoffrey F. Baruch: I think that the relationship between PPNW and the British Psycho-analytical Society was similar in character to Bion's observation of how the big group can delegate (and thus get rid of) unwanted functions and problems to the small group. The relationship was harmonious, up to a point. PPNW was allowed to use the administration and the building of the Society as if PPNW was part of the Society, like one of its committees, for instance the Applied Section in Psychoanalysis. But Ron Britton, who was very involved with PPNW, questioned whether this "cosy" relationship weakened the PPNW's capacity to act as a pressure group. The relationship allowed the rest of the British Psychoanalytical Society to create an illusion of safety in the feeling that "something is being done". Also, the possibility of debate among psychoanalysts who did not share the views of colleagues who were members of PPNW was stifled by the marginalization of the whole nuclear issue. Indeed, behind the respect and tolerance shown to PPNW by the British Society those analysts involved could be thought of as the "nominated" activists who were looked upon as childish or adolescent, overanxious and even cranky in their concern about nuclear weapons. And there is no doubt that we responded by taking on the role of being the "enlightened". In this way a peace movement ghetto is created. So long as we stayed in this position we were tolerated. However, when we didn't play by the rules we were seen as threatening. I recollect that when the Gulf War started, under the auspices of PPNW, I hired for a meeting the Ernest Jones Room, in the premises of the Institute of Psychoanalysis in London, without having obtained permission from the executive of the British Psychoanalytical Society (BPAS). I was "told off" for not seeking permission since there was a worry that the charitable status of the Society might be compromised if it appeared as though the Society and PPNW were the same organization holding a political activity. From then on we were very careful to ensure the independence of PPNW from the BPAS. I have to say that the position of the BPAS was no different from that of other professional organizations, for example the British Medical Association, in keeping anti-nuclear war organizations separate from their main bodies.

JMQ: It is really exceptional that so many psychoanalysts – a third of the BPAS membership – militate for such a "political" cause. What was the atmosphere like in the early years of PPNW?

The early years of PPNW saw a great deal of constructive and creative activity. Workshops and a number of open meetings were set up to discuss various aspects of the nuclear issue. What was interesting in that time is the dialogue that took place between psychoanalysts involved with quite eminent people from other organizations. These meetings were very well attended. A PPNW Bulletin was regularly published, as was one for the international psycho-analytic community.

By 1986 a feeling of disappointment began to creep into those involved in PPNW. There was a feeling of not having made an impact on our colleagues. Membership of PPNW had risen only a little above the original 132 out of a BPAS membership of 400. The workshops had faded and there were only a dozen or so people who were working actively, some complaining of feeling overburdened and unsupported. I remember speaking with Hanna Segal about the development of PPNW and the wider psychoanalytic community and wondering whether she was disappointed but in reply she said things had turned out much as she had anticipated.

The break-up of the Soviet Union in the 1990s hastened a growing apathy about the nuclear issue everywhere, including among analysts still involved in PPNW. Nevertheless, there was a small but active group of analysts whose commitment helped sustain PPNW. Despite this apathy a number of papers were written at this time which presented new psy-choanalytic thinking about the risks of nuclear war in the post Cold War period. What is striking about them is a convergence of views, because they all concerned different aspects of the manic defence, although the papers were written independently. In a paper I wrote in 1992, I linked the use of triumph over the object as a denial of valuing and caring for the object with some features of the international situation. For example, our inability to face depressive concerns and guilt on the one hand and the excitement aroused by the weakness of Russia on the other hand created a state of triumphalism among some leaders in the West. Russia became the convenient focus on to which the weaknesses of our own societies, our sense of inferiority and our guilt for failing to attend to our own social, economic and environmental problems, could be projected. And if not Russia, then a new enemy, such as Iraq, had to be found. This process of seeking enemies revives the paranoia that fuelled the Cold War. It shows how entrenched the need to have nuclear weapons is and how difficult it is to give them up when we seek and "create" enemies in the Third World, some possibly armed with nuclear weapons. Jane Temperley (1992), a colleague in PPNW, was also impressed by the manic excitement engendered by the end of the Cold War and the Gulf War. She thought that behind this excitement lay omnipotent destructiveness.

JMQ: Is PPNW still active today?

No. But I would say it still has an existence although we don't meet any more. Segal has given papers and has been involved in panels at conferences convened following recent international crises, after 9/11 and the invasion of Iraq, which have provided an opportunity to show powerfully that the same processes underlie these crises. Hence the danger from a nuclear conflagration is as much present today as in the 1980s before the end of the Cold War. In 2003 before the invasion of Iraq there was a proposal to march at the very big demonstration in London under the banner of PPNW. There was a lot of correspondence by email, but it didn't happen, it didn't materialize. That was really the last time the old group came alive, but not quite. My guess is that if there were a crisis, which would much more directly involve nuclear weapons, the group would come alive. In other words, given the "right" crisis I believe the group would reawaken.

(Interview, October 2006)

Geoffrey F. Baruch (London) is a member of the British Psychoanalytical Society.

NOTES

1 HANNA SEGAL: A PSYCHOANALYTIC AUTOBIOGRAPHY

1. A Swiss federal councillor, at that time Head of the Ministry for Internal Affairs (author's note).

2 PSYCHOANALYSIS AND THE AESTHETIC EXPERIENCE

1. An allusion to the subterranean cavity upon which Jocelin was attempting to build the spire. (Footnote by Hanna Segal in the *International Review of Psycho-Analysis*.)

3 THE PSYCHOANALYTIC TREATMENT OF PSYCHOTIC PATIENTS

1. For reasons of confidentiality, clinical illustrations give only sufficient background material for understanding the issues involved.

4 FROM SYMBOLIC EQUATION TO SYMBOLIC REPRESENTATION

1. In German *"symbolische Gleichung: Penis = Kind"* (*G.W.* **14**: 27; *S.E.* **19**: 256). This occurs also in "The Dissolution of the Oedipus Complex" (Freud 1924d; *G.W.* **13**: 401; *S.E.* **19**: 179).
2. See Birksted-Breen, D. (1996).

5 THE FUNDAMENTAL CONFLICT BETWEEN THE LIFE AND DEATH DRIVES

1. Quinodoz, J. M. (2001 [2002]).

10 NUCLEAR TERROR, PSYCHOTIC ANXIETIES AND GROUP PHENOMENA

1. Cf. "Those who cannot remember the past are condemned to repeat it" (Santayana 1905: 284).

BIBLIOGRAPHY

(References to Freud's published work follow the model adopted in *The Standard Edition of the Complete Psychological Works of Sigmund Freud* (hereinafter referred to as *S.E.*) in which entries are numbered by means of a distinguishing letter in lower case – see Editor's Note in *S.E.* **24**: 45.)

Abraham, K. (1911) "Giovanni Segantini. A psycho-analytic study", *Psychoanalytic Quarterly*, **6**: 453–512, (1937); also in *Clinical Papers and Essays by Karl Abraham* (1955), London: Hogarth Press, pp. 210–261.
—— (1912) "Notes on the psycho-analytical investigation and treatment of manic-depressive insanity and allied conditions", in *Selected Papers of Karl Abraham* (1927), London: Hogarth Press, pp. 137–156.
—— (1919) "The applicability of psychoanalytic treatment to patients at an advanced age", in *Selected Papers of Karl Abraham* (1927), London: Hogarth Press, pp. 312–317.
Aguayo, J. (1999) "An interview with Dr. Hanna Segal", *Fort da*, **5**(1): 50–58.
Alanen, Y. (1975) "The psychotherapeutic care of schizophrenic patients in a community psychiatric setting", in M. Lader (ed.) *Studies of Schizophrenia*, Ashton, Kent: Headley Brothers.
Amati-Mehler, J., Argentieri, S. and Canestri, J. (1994) *La Babel de l'inconscient. Langue maternelle, langue étrangère et psychanalyse* [*The Babel of the Unconscious. Mother tongue, foreign language and psychoanalysis*], Paris: Presses Universitaires de France.
Balint, M. (1968) *The Basic Fault. Therapeutic Aspects of Regression*, London: Tavistock.
Baruch, G. (1992) "Do we really need International Psychoanalysts Against Nuclear Weapons?", *Psychoanalysts for the Prevention of Nuclear War Newsletter*, pp. 2–5.
—— (1998) "The nuclear arms race revisited", paper presented at the Hanna Segal Day, 30 January 1999.
Bell, D. (ed.) (1997) *Reason and Passion. A Celebration of the Work of Hanna Segal*, London and New York: Karnac Books.
—— (1999) *Psychoanalysis and Culture. A Kleinian Approach*, London and New York: Karnac Books.
Berberian, M. (2003) "Communal rebuilding after destruction: The World Trade Center Children's Mural Project", *Psychoanalytic Social Work*, **10**: 27–41.
Bion, W. R. (1958) "On hallucination", *International Journal of Psycho-Analysis*, **39**: 341–349.
—— (1961) *Experiences in Groups*, London: Tavistock.
—— (1963) *Elements of Psycho-Analysis*, London: Heinemann; reprinted Maresfield Library (1984).
—— (1967) *Second Thoughts*, London: Heinemann; reprinted London: Karnac Books (1984), New York: Jason Aronson.
Birksted-Breen, D. (1996) "Phallus, penis and mental space", *International Journal of Psycho-Analysis*, **77**: 649–657.
Bridge, M. (1992) Book review: *Psychic Experience and Problems of Technique* by Harold Stewart (Routledge, 1992), *British Journal of Psychotherapy*, **3**: 91–93.
Britton, R. (1989) "The missing link: Parental sexuality in the Oedipus complex", in J. Steiner (ed.) *The Oedipus Complex Today*, London: Karnac Books.
—— (1992) "The Oedipus situation and the depressive position", in R. Anderson (ed.) *Clinical Lectures on Klein and Bion*, London: Routledge (New Library of Psychoanalysis).
Canestri, J. (2006) *Psychoanalysis: from Practice to Theory*, London: Karnac Books.
Chadwick, M. (1929) "Notes upon the fear of death", *International Journal of Psycho-Analysis*, **10**: 321–334.
Diatkine, R. and Simon, J. (1973) *La Psychanalyse Précoce. Le Processus psychanalytique chez l'Enfant* [Early psychoanalysis. The psychoanalytic process in children], Paris: Presses Universitaires de France.
Ellonen-Jéquier, M. (1985) "Psychanalyse d'enfants: Signification et dynamique de l'agi des parents" [Child psycho-analysis: significance and dynamic aspects of parental enactments], *Psychanalyse 1985*, Neuchâtel: A La Baconnière.

Ferenczi, S. (1913) "Stages in the development of the sense of reality", in *First Contributions to Psychoanalysis*, London: Hogarth Press (1952), pp. 123–239.

Fornari, F. (1966) *Psicanalisi della guerra*, trans. (1974) A. Pfeifer, *The Psychoanalysis of War*, Garden City, NY: Anchor Press.

Freud, S. (1895d) [with Breuer, J.] *Studies on Hysteria, G.W.* **1**: 77–312; *S.E.* **2**: 1–309.

—— (1900a) *The Interpretation of Dreams, G.W.* **2–3**; *S.E.* **4–5**.

—— (1905a) "On Psychotherapy", *G.W.* **5**: 13–26; *S.E.* **7**: 255–268.

—— (1910c) *Leonardo da Vinci and a Memory of his Childhood, G.W.* **8**: 128–211; *S.E.* **11**: 57–137.

—— (1911c) "Psycho-Analytic Notes on an Autobiographical Account of a Case of Paranoia (Dementia Paranoides)", *G.W.* **8**: 240–316; *S.E.* **12**: 3–82.

—— (1914b) "The Moses of Michelangelo", *G.W.* **10**: 172–201; *S.E.* **13**: 211–238.

—— (1914c) "On Narcissism: An Introduction", *G.W.* **10**: 138–170; *S.E.* **14**: 73–102.

—— (1915e) "The Unconscious", *G.W.* **10**: 264–303; *S.E.* **14**: 166–215.

—— (1917e [1915]) "Mourning and Melancholia", *G.W.* **10**: 428–46; *S.E.* **14**: 239–260.

—— (1919h) "The Uncanny", *G.W.* **12**: 229–268; *S.E.* **17**: 219–256.

—— (1920g) *Beyond the Pleasure Principle, G.W.* **13**: 3–69; *S.E.* **18**: 1–64.

—— (1921c) *Group Psychology and the Analysis of the Ego, G.W.* **13**: 73–161; *S.E.* **18**: 65–143.

—— (1923b) *The Ego and the Id, G.W.* **13**: 237–289; *S.E.* **19**: 1–59.

—— (1924c) "The Economic Problem of Masochism", *G.W.* **13**: 371–383; *S.E.* **19**: 155–170.

—— (1924d) "The Dissolution of the Oedipus Complex", *G.W.* **13**: 395–402; *S.E.* **19**: 173–179.

—— (1925j) "Some Psychical Consequences of the Anatomical Distinction between the Sexes", *G.W.* **14**: 19–30; *S.E.* **19**: 241–258.

—— (1930a [1929]) *Civilization and its Discontents, G.W.* **14**: 421–506; *S.E.* **21**: 57–145.

—— (1940a [1938]) *An Outline of Psycho-Analysis, G.W.* **17**: 63–138; *S.E.* **23**: 141–207.

Glover, E. (1933) *War, Sadism and Pacifism: Three Essays*, London: George Allen & Unwin Ltd.

Golding, W. (1964) *The Spire*, London: Faber & Faber.

Green, A. (1986) "Pulsion de mort, narcissisme négatif, fonction désobjectalisante" [Death drive, negative narcissism, de-objectalizing function], in *La pulsion de mort, Premier Symposium de la Fédération Européenne de Psychanalyse (Marseille, 1984)* [The death drive, first Symposium of the European Psycho-Analytical Federation, Marseilles, 1984], Paris: Presses Universitaires de France.

Grosskurth, P. (1988) *Melanie Klein: Her World and Her Work*, New York: Jason Aronson.

Haynal, A. (1987) *The Technique at Issue: Controversies in Psychoanalysis from Freud and Ferenczi to Michael Bálint*; trans. E. Holder (1988), London: Karnac Books.

Isaacs, S. (1948) "The nature and function of phantasy", *International Journal of Psycho-Analysis*, **29**: 73–97.

Jacoby R. (1993) *The Repression of Psychoanalysis: Otto Fenichel and the Political Freudians*, New York: Basic Books.

Jones, E. (1916) "The theory of symbolism", in *Papers on Psycho-Analysis* (1918), 2nd edn, London: Baillière, Tindall and Cox.

Junkers, G. (ed.) (2006) *Is It Too Late?: Key Papers on Psychoanalysis and Ageing*, London: Karnac Books.

King, P. (1980) "The life cycle as indicated by the nature of the transference in the psychoanalysis of the middle-aged and the elderly", *International Journal of Psycho-Analysis*, **61**: 153–160.

Klein, M. (1923a) "Infant analysis", in *Contributions to Psychoanalysis 1921–1945*, London: Hogarth, 1948, pp. 87–116.

—— (1923b) "The role of the school in the libidinal development of the child", in Klein, M. (1975) *Love, Guilt and Reparation and Other Works. The Writings of Melanie Klein, vol. I*, London: The Hogarth Press (reprinted London: Karnac, 1992).

—— (1929) "Infantile anxiety situations reflected in a work of art and in the creative impulse", in *Contributions to Psychoanalysis 1921–1945*, London: The Hogarth Press, 1948, pp. 227–235; also in *Love, Guilt and Reparation and Other Works. The Writings of Melanie Klein, vol. I*. London: The Hogarth Press (reprinted London: Karnac, 1992).

—— (1930) "The importance of symbol-formation in the development of the ego", in *Contributions to Psychoanalysis 1921–1945*, London: The Hogarth Press, 1948, pp. 236–250; also in *Love, Guilt and Reparation and Other Works. The Writings of Melanie Klein, vol. I*. London: The Hogarth Press (reprinted London: Karnac, 1992).

—— (1932) *The Psychoanalysis of Children*, London: The Hogarth Press.

—— (1946) "Notes on some schizoid mechanisms", in J. Riviere (ed.) *Developments in Psychoanalysis*, London: The Hogarth Press; also in *Envy and Gratitude and Other Works, 1946–1963. The Writings of Melanie Klein, vol. III*, London: The Hogarth Press (reprinted London: Karnac, 1993).

—— (1950) "On the criteria for the termination of a psycho-analysis", *International Journal of Psycho-Analysis*, **31**: 78–80; also in *Envy and Gratitude and Other Works, 1946–-1963. The Writings of Melanie Klein, vol. III*, London: The Hogarth Press (reprinted London: Karnac, 1993).

—— (1955) "On identification", in *Envy and Gratitude and Other Works, 1946–1963. The Writings of Melanie Klein, vol. III*, London: The Hogarth Press (reprinted London: Karnac, 1993).

—— (1955–1960) Letters to Marcelle Spira.

Lagache, D. (1953) "Some aspects of transference", *International Journal of Psycho-Analysis*, **34**: 1–10.

Laplanche, J. (1986) "La pulsion de mort dans la théorie de la pulsion sexuelle" [The death drive in the theory of the sexual drive], in *La pulsion de mort, Premier Symposium de la Fédération Européenne de Psychanalyse (Marseille, 1984)* [The death drive, first Symposium of the European Psycho-Analytical Federation, Marseilles, 1984], Paris: Presses Universitaires de France.

Little, M. (1990) *Psychotic Anxieties and Containment: A Personal Record of an Analysis with Winnicott*, Northvale, NJ: Jason Aronson.

London, J. (1909) *Martin Eden*, Harmondsworth: Penguin Books.

Maldonado, J. L. (2006) "Vicissitudes in adult life resulting from traumatic experiences in adolescence", *International Journal of Psycho-Analysis*, **87**: 1239–1257.

Manzano, J. and Palacio-Espasa, F. (2006) *La dimension narcissique de la personnalité* [The narcissistic dimension of the personality], Paris: Presses Universitaires de France.

Milton, J. (1667) *Paradise Lost and Paradise Regained*, The Signet Classic Poetry Series (2001), New York: New American Library.

Palacio-Espasa, F. (2003) *Dépression de vie, dépression de mort* [Life depression, death depression], Toulouse: Eres.

Proust, M. (1913–1927) *A la recherche du temps perdu* [Remembrance of things past/In search of lost time], Paris: Gallimard.

Quinodoz, D. (1997) *Emotional Vertigo. Between Anxiety and Pleasure*, trans. A. Pomerans (2003), London and New York: Routledge.

—— (2002) *Words That Touch. A Psychoanalyst Learns to Speak*, trans. Ph. Slotkin (2003), London: Karnac Books.

Quinodoz, J. M. (1991) *The Taming of Solitude*, trans. Ph. Slotkin (1993), London and New York: Routledge.

—— (2001) *Dreams That Turn Over a Page*, trans. Ph. Slotkin (2002), London and New York: Routledge.

—— (2004) *Reading Freud. A Chronological Exploration of Freud's Writings*, trans. D. Alcorn (2005), London and New York: Routledge.

Rilke, R. M. (1922) *Duino's Elegies*, Berkeley: University of California Press (1961).

Rizzolatti G., Fogassi F. and Gallese V. (2001) "Neurophysiological mechanisms underlying the understanding and imitation of action", *Nature Reviews/Neuroscience*, **2**: 661–670.

Rocha-Leite Haudenschild, T. (1997) "Retaking the first steps towards symbolisation. A 6-year-old emerges from adhesive identification", *International Journal of Psycho-Analysis*, **78**: 733–753.

Rose, J. (1990) "Hanna Segal interviewed by Jacqueline Rose", *Women: A Cultural Review*, Summer, **1**(2): 198–214.

Rosenfeld, H. (1964) "The psychopathology of narcissism", in Rosenfeld, H. (1965) *Psychotic States: A Psychoanalytical Approach*, London: Hogarth Press; New York: International Universities Press (reprinted London: Karnac, 1982).

Rotblat, J. (2003) Guardian/RUSI Conference on "Nuclear Policy and Proliferation", London, 8 January 2003, *The Guardian*.

Rushdie, S. (1991) *Haroun and the Sea of Stories*, Harmondsworth: Penguin.

Sandler, A. M. (2002) "Institutional responses to boundary violations: The case of Masud Khan", *International Journal of Psycho-Analysis*, **85**: 27–44.

Santayana, G. (1905) *The Life of Reason. Reason in Common Sense*, New York: Scribner.

Schafer, R. (ed.) (1957) *The Contemporary Kleinians of London*, Madison, CT: International Universities Press.

—— (1968) *Aspects of Internalization*, New York: International Universities Press.

Segal, H. (1950) "Some aspects of the analysis of a schizophrenic", *International Journal of Psycho-Analysis*, **31**: 268–278; reprinted (1981) in *The Work of Hanna Segal*, New York and London: Jason Aronson, pp. 101–120.

—— (1952) "A psycho-analytical approach to aesthetics", *International Journal of Psycho-Analysis*, **33**: 196–207; reprinted (1981) in *The Work of Hanna Segal*, New York and London: Jason Aronson, pp. 185–206.

—— (1954) "A note on schizoid mechanisms underlying phobia formation", *International Journal of Psycho-Analysis*, **35**: 238–241; reprinted (1981) in *The Work of Hanna Segal*, New York and London: Jason Aronson, pp. 137–143.

—— (1956) "Depression in the schizophrenic", *International Journal of Psycho-Analysis*, **37**: 339–343; reprinted (1981) in *The Work of Hanna Segal*, New York and London: Jason Aronson, pp. 121–129.

—— (1957) "Notes on symbol formation", *International Journal of Psycho-Analysis*, **39**: 391–397; reprinted (1981) in *The Work of Hanna Segal*, New York and London: Jason Aronson, pp. 49–65.

—— (1958) "Fear of death: Notes on the analysis of an old man", *International Journal of Psycho-Analysis*, **39**, 178–181; reprinted (1981) in *The Work of Hanna Segal*, New York and London: Jason Aronson, pp. 173–182.

—— (1964) *Introduction to the Work of Melanie Klein*, London: William Heinemann Ltd.

—— (1967a) "Melanie Klein's technique", in B. B. Wolmann (ed.) *Psycho-analytic Techniques*, New York: Basic Books; reprinted (1981) in *The Work of Hanna Segal*, New York and London: Jason Aronson, pp. 3–24.

—— (1967b) "Melanie Klein's technique of child analysis", in B. B. Wolmann (ed.) *Psycho-analytic Techniques*,

New York: Basic Books; reprinted (1981) in *The Work of Hanna Segal*, New York and London: Jason Aronson, pp. 25–37.

—— (1974) "Delusion and artistic creativity: some reflexions on reading *The Spire* by William Golding", *International Review of Psycho-Analysis*, **1**: 135–141; reprinted (1981) in *The Work of Hanna Segal*, New York and London: Jason Aronson, pp. 207–216.

—— (1975) "A psychoanalytic approach to the treatment of schizophrenia", in M. H. Lader (ed.) *Studies of Schizophrenia*, Ashford, Kent: Headley Brothers; reprinted (1981) as "A psychoanalytic approach to the treatment of psychoses", in *The Work of Hanna Segal*, New York and London: Jason Aronson, pp. 131–136.

—— (1978) "On symbolism", *International Journal of Psycho-Analysis*, **55**: 515–519; reprinted (1997) in J. Steiner (ed.) *Psychoanalysis, Literature and War. Papers 1972–1995*, London and New York: Routledge.

—— (1979a) *Klein*, Glasgow: Fontana/Collins.

—— (1979b) "The play technique", in *Klein*, Glasgow: Fontana/Collins, pp. 35–44.

—— (1979c) "Psychoanalysis of children", in *Klein*, Glasgow: Fontana/Collins, pp. 45–62.

—— (1979d) "The 'Controversial Discussions' ", in *Klein*, Glasgow: Fontana/Collins, pp. 91–111.

—— (1981) *The Work of Hanna Segal*, New York and London: Jason Aronson.

—— (1981a) "The function of dreams", in *The Work of Hanna Segal*. New York and London: Jason Aronson, pp. 89–97; also in J. S. Grotstein (ed.) *Do I Dare Disturb the Universe?*, Beverly Hills, CA: Caesura Press.

—— (1981b) "Manic reparation", in *The Work of Hanna Segal*, New York and London: Jason Aronson, pp. 147–158.

—— (1987) "Silence is the real crime", *International Review of Psycho-Analysis*, **14**: 3–12. With Postscript (2002) in C. Covington, P. Williams, J. Arundale and J. Knox (eds.) *Terrorism and War: Unconscious Dynamics of Political Violence*, London: Karnac Books; also in J. Steiner (ed.) *Psychoanalysis, Literature and War. Papers 1972–1995*, London and New York: Routledge (1997).

—— (1988) "Sweating it out", *Psychoanalytic Study of the Child*, **43**: 167.

—— (1991) *Dream, Phantasy and Art*, London and New York: Routledge.

—— (1992) "The achievement of ambivalence", *Common Knowledge*, **1**: 92–104.

—— (1993) "On the clinical usefulness of the concept of the death instinct", *International Journal of Psycho-Analysis*, **74**: 55–61; reprinted (1997) in J. Steiner (ed.) *Psychoanalysis, Literature and War: Papers 1972–1995*, London and New York: Routledge.

—— (1994) "Salman Rushdie and the *Sea of Stories*", *International Journal of Psycho-Analysis*, **75**: 611–618; reprinted (1997) in J. Steiner (ed.) *Psychoanalysis, Literature and War: Papers 1972–1995*, London: Routledge.

—— (1995) "Hiroshima, the Gulf War, and after", in A. Elliot and S. Frosch (eds.) *Psychoanalysis in Contexts: Paths Between Theory and Modern Culture*, London: Routledge.

—— (1997a) "The uses and abuses of the counter-transference", in J. Steiner (ed.) *Psychoanalysis, Literature and War. Papers 1972–1995*, London and New York: Routledge, pp. 111–119.

—— (1997b) *Psychoanalysis, Literature and War: Papers 1972–1995*, J. Steiner (ed.), London: Routledge.

—— (1997c) "From Hiroshima to the Gulf War and after: Socio-political expressions of ambivalence", in J. Steiner (ed.) *Psychoanalysis, Literature and War. Papers 1972–1995*, London and New York: Routledge.

—— (2000a) "The Oedipus complex and symbolization" (unpublished paper).

—— (2000b) "The story of Adam and Eve and that of Lucifer", in *Yesterday, Today and Tomorrow*, N. Abel-Hirsh (ed.), London: Routledge (2007).

—— (2001) "L'interprétation des rêves cent après", trans. F. Drossart [The Interpretation of dreams – one hundred years on], *Journal de la psychanalyse de l'enfant*, Vol. 28.

—— (2002a) "Not learning from experience: Psychotic process in large groups", UCL Conference, London, December 2001.

—— (2002b) "Not learning from experience: Hiroshima, the Gulf War and 11 September", *International Psychoanalysis*, **11**(1): 33–35.

—— (2003a) *Le rêve et le moi* [Dreams and the ego], in A. Nakov *et al. Le rêve dans la pratique psychanalytique* [Dreams in psychoanalytic practice], Paris: Dunod.

—— (2003b) "From Hiroshima to 11th September and after", *Psychodynamic Practice*, **9**: 257–265.

—— (2004) "Motivation: The artist and psychoanalysis", verbatim transcription of seminar held at the Royal Festival Hall, 21 September 2004.

—— (2007) *Yesterday, Today and Tomorrow*, N. Abel-Hirsch (ed.), London and New York: Routledge.

Spillius, E. (2007) "Melanie Klein revisited: her unpublished thoughts on technique", in *Encounters with Melanie Klein: Selected Papers of Elizabeth Spillius*, London and New York: Routledge.

Steiner, J. (1997) "Introduction", in Segal H. (1997) *Psychoanalysis, Literature and War: Papers 1972–1995*, J. Steiner (ed.), London: Routledge.

Steiner, R. (2007) "Index, icon, symbol? Can Peirce's descriptive classification be of any use to psychoanalysis?", in G. Ambrosio, S. Argentieri and J. Canestri (eds.) *Language, Symbolization, Psychosis*, London: Karnac Books.

Stern, D. (2006) Personal communication (quoted by J. Manzano).

Stewart, H. (1989) "Technique at the basic fault/regression", *International Journal of Psycho-Analysis*. **70**: 221–230.

—— (1992) *Psychic Experience and Problems of Technique*, London and New York: Routledge.

Stokes, A. (1965) *The Invitation in Art*, London: Routledge.

Temperley, J. (1992) "Whither the psychoanalytic perspective on the nuclear danger?", *Psychoanalysts for the Prevention of Nuclear War Newsletter*, pp. 8–12.

Widlöcher, D. (2003) " 'Ut pictura . . . psychanalytica'. Le psychanalyste entre l'historien et l'amateur [The psychoanalyst between historian and aficionado]", *Revue Française de Psychanalyse*, **67**: 603–616.

Wollheim, R. (1998) "Emotion and the malformation of emotion", in D. Bell (ed.) *Psychoanalysis and Culture: a Kleinian Perspective*, London: Tavistock/Duckworth (Tavistock Clinic Series); reprinted (2004) London: Karnac Books.

NAME INDEX

SUBJECT INDEX

acting-out/acting-in, 16, 58, 60, 95, 106, 110, 112, 116, 117, 121, 122, 133

aesthetic experience, 21–41; aesthetic values, 22; beauty and ugliness, 31–2, 37–8, 41; excellence in art, 31; impact of, 24; and inhibition of creativity, 21, 22, 25, 28–9, 44; and insight, 22, 24–5; integration, 37; and mental health, 33; philosophy of, 33; role of the death drive, 32; Segal's influence, 33–5; and sublimation, 30; and symbol formation, 29–30, 72; *see also* art, creativity

aesthetic pleasure, of the artist's public, 30–1; *see also* aesthetic experience

aggressiveness, aggression: and artistic creation, 23, 38; and the death drive, 82, 84; and nuclear terror, 143, 145–6, 149, 151; repressed in dreams, 157; in sadism, 16; and symbol-formation, 70; towards the mother, 101; towards the sexual parental couple, 33; turned against external objects, 101

alpha-elements, beta-elements 45, 50, 64, 74, 119,

ambition, 14, 126

ambivalence, 27, 70, 80, 88, 100, 101, 102, 110, 127; in groups, 148–9

American Psychoanalytic Association, the, 138–9

analysis, Segal's analysis with Melanie Klein, 12–13, 94–5; *see also* psychoanalysis

Anna Freud Centre, the, 136

anti-Semitism, 4

anxiety, annihilation, 83, 84; castration, 47, 49, 62, 118; depressive, 6, 27–39, 42, 51, 52, 72, 101–3, 105, 127; separation, 16, 20, 30, 71; unconscious, about death, 125, 128, 129

Argentina, 19, 87, 134, 155

art, 21–41; artisan, the artist as, 24, 38; artistic creativity, 21, 22–4, 25, 26, 29, 32–3, 36–9; beauty and ugliness, 31–2, 37–8, 41; and the body, 39–40; and communication, 33, 39, 40–1; and the death drive, 32; and delusion, 32–3; excellence in, 31; Freud's view of, 36–7; and reparation, 27, 30, 34, 37–9, 40; *see also* aesthetic experience, creativity

artist, failure of creativity in, 28; importance of the body, 39–40

attacks against linking, 49, 64

autism, autistic, 56–7, 61, 63, 68

autobiography (Hanna Segal's psychoanalytic autobiography), 1–20

"balance", 104

"basic fault" (Balint), 15–17

beauty, beautiful, 23, 31–2, 35, 37–8, 41

body, the, and artistic creativity, 39–40

British Psychoanalytical Society (BPAS), 1, 2, 14, 15, 17, 21, 34, 35, 131, 135, 136, 139, 141, 156–8

California, 115, 134, 139

catatonic, 57–8, 87

Catholicism, 4, 6, 7

Champel, 6

Chelsea, 10

child analysis, 18, 20, 91, 109–15; specific issues in, 109–10; *see also* technique

childhood experiences, 1, 3, 6, 27, 58, 95–6, 101, 127, 133, 140

Cleveland, Ohio, 138

communication, in art, 33, 39, 40–1; dreams and, 117, 121; in psychosis, 54–5, 58; role of symbols in, 72

compulsion to repeat, 81, 85–6, 87, 112

concrete, 23, 42, 44, 47, 55–6, 62, 63–4, 65, 68, 69, 71–2, 73, 74, 87, 94, 121; *see also* symbol formation

condensation, in psychosis, 59–60; in dreams, 118

conflict between life and death drives, 78–89, 148; in dreams, 117, 120; *see also* life drive, death drive

construction, 40, 76; *see also* reconstruction

containment, 25, 43–4, 56, 66, 74–5, 76, 88, 99, 114, 121, 150

"Controversial Discussions", the, 13, 109

counter-transference, 14, 45, 50, 57–8, 59, 60, 68, 83, 104–5, 107, 138; and political opinions, 156; with older patients, 130; in group supervision, 57–8, 131

creativity, creation, 21–41, 63, 80; artistic, 21, 35, 37, 38, 120; and the body, 39–40; creating a new world, 27, 37, 92; creative impulse, 21, 27, 28, 29, 34, 35, 37, 38, 92; creative process, 22, 26, 27, 28, 63; difference between creativity and delusion, 33; equivalent of procreation, 29; and psychotic delusion, 32–3, 43; and working-through the depressive position, 29, 35, 37, 102; *see also* art, aesthetic experience, reparation

dance, 21, 39–40, 65